PUBLIC THEOLOGY

PUBLIC THEOLOGY

INDIAN CONCERNS, PERSPECTIVES, AND THEMES

Gnana Patrick

FORTRESS PRESS
MINNEAPOLIS

PUBLIC THEOLOGY
Indian Concerns, Perspectives, and Themes

Copyright © 2020 Fortress Press. All rights reserved. Except for brief quotations in critical articles or reviews, no part of this book may be reproduced in any manner without prior written permission from the publisher. Email copyright@fortresspress.com or write to Permissions, Fortress Press, PO Box 1209, Minneapolis, MN 55440-1209.

Cover image: © iStock 2019; The Blue City Stock Photo by manjik
Cover design: Emily Drake

Paperback ISBN: 978-1-5064-4917-3
eBook ISBN: 978-1-5064-4918-0

Dedicated to

the community of learners

(students and teachers)

at the University of Madras

AUTHOR

Gnana Patrick, PhD, Professor and Head of the Department of Christian Studies, University of Madras, holds a doctorate in Christian Studies. He was awarded a post-doctoral fellowship in 2004 to do a research on Asian religions and cultures in Hong Kong Chung Che College. In the year 2013, he was awarded the Fulbright–Nehru Visiting Lecturer Fellowship and taught a course on *Public Religion: Learning from Indian and American Experiences* at the Harvard Divinity School. He co-edited a volume with Professor Elisabeth Schussler Fiorenza under the title *Negotiating Border–Theological Explorations in the Global Era (2008)*. Other publications that he has authored include *Religion and Subaltern Agency* (2003); *Wings of Faith–Public Theologies in India (2013)*; *Oral Traditions and Theology (1996)*; and *Resonances (Tamil), Indian Christianity and Its Public Role (edited, 2019)*. He has penned 86 research articles, published in various peer reviewed journals. He served as the Chief-editor of *Indian Journal of Christian Studies* from 2012 to 2016. He was also the recipient of the Best Researcher Award by the University of Madras for the year 2017–18.

CONTENTS

Preface xi
1. Relating Political Theologies to the Indian Context 1
2. Thinking of Public Theology in India 15
3. An Indian Public Theology of Mission 31
4. Faith and Culture: A Christian *Poiesis* 53
5. Nurturing Transcendence: Church and Civil Society 69
6. Religious Pluralism and Democracy 85
7. Subalternity and Religion in India 103
8. Ambedkar's Philosophy of Religion as a Political Theology 123
9. Biblical Hermeneutics: A Subaltern Perspective 135
10. A Subaltern Public Theology of the Holy Spirit 149
11. Encounter of End-Time Beliefs as It Occurred
    in Pandita Ramabai 165
12. Conversation on *Dharma* 175
Glossary 187
Bibliography 189
Index 203

PREFACE

Eyebrows are being raised today when one speaks about public theology in the Indian context. Reasons for the scepticism could be many. Public theology, as it is being discussed in the international arena, seems to go with certain features which are specific to North American–European contexts, the birthplaces of this theology. First of all, the reality of secularisation which privatised the faith (Christian faith) obtains rather thickly in these continents, and there is some appropriateness when someone is concerned about the "naked public sphere" in these contexts. Second, the phenomenon of resurgence of religion, as being observed by social theorists, corresponds well to these contexts, and it is perceived to be very fitting to speak about the reality of post-secularity, public religion, and so on here. Third, the political framework appropriate for speaking about public theology which is none other than democracy itself which, though varying from liberal to post-liberal types, with all its institutions, has grown for centuries together in the West, makes it realistic to speak about public theologies there. Fourth, the most important of all is the prevalence of Christianity as the religion of the majority, in spite of the fast changing scenario, makes it viable to speak about a Christian theological approach to the public sphere and public life.

The question then could be, "How does India fare with regard to these realities?" If not faring well, "What is the relevance of speaking about public theology here?"—could be the question implied. It is indeed true that some of these features are qualitatively different, some quantitatively so, and some others do not match at all with the Indian reality. For better or worse, a process of secularisation has not occurred in the Indian context to the point of privatising religion so as to speak of a "naked public sphere"; one cannot speak of a "resurgence of religion" here, because it never disappeared from the private or public life of Indians; the political framework, though being claimed as the world's largest democracy, lacks substance; and, above all, Indian Christianity is a miniscule minority religion, that is, religion of about 2.34 percent of Indians only.

However, this incongruence does not make an effort to relate public theology to the Indian context irrelevant. What gives the fundamental validity for an Indian public theology is the fact that religion, as it is the case in North America and Europe, finds itself being related to the political process and the policies affecting public life today. What is the nature of this involvement, what are the types of impact it makes, what could be the positive roles different religious traditions play, and so on are questions not merely for students of sociology of religion, political theory, cultural studies, and psychology, but also for theologians who wish to initiate a positive response to the emergent context. Even if from a miniscule minority, a Christian theologian can indeed think of a public theological response to concerns of democracy, public sphere, civil society, and public life. Biblically speaking, it is the minority—a prophetic minority, which has exercised the deepest impact in the history of the biblical people. Serving as an effective catalyst goes beyond any numerical strength.

Moreover, Indian Christianity is one that has been creatively responding to the ever-emerging newer contexts, however inadequate or circumstantial the responses may be. It has been responding to the demand for indigenisation and inculturation with methods of adaptations, to the question of religious pluralism in an Indian-specific way, to the issue of social discrimination with contextual theologies, to the concern of nationalism with participation in nation-building, to problems of poverty and hunger with social welfare schemes and relief measures, to the question of human/civil rights violations with conscientisation, mobilisation, social movements, and so on. It is therefore fitting that Indian Christianity responds to the contemporary reality of religion in the public sphere with its own public theology.

Indian Christian concerns, perspectives, and themes, in our contemporary global world, are characteristically different not only from those of earlier Indian contexts, but also from those of other countries or regions of the globe. Indian Christianity, while in earlier contexts, existed less self-consciously and engaged with the Indian reality with more spontaneity, today it meets a situation wherein it becomes conscious of its history, culture, minority status, and identity, even while expressing concerns as regards its future. The kind of majoritarian cultural politics with which it is being challenged is unprecedented. How does it understand itself, relate with others, engage with public issues, and construct an Indian democratic nation are the important challenges today.

Although that being the case with the wider reality, Indian Christianity is being examined today by the wider public on its own credentials as well. Its public image as a religion, proclaiming the values of equality and justice, is increasingly being examined today in the public. "Can it free itself from the casteist forces dominating its inner world?" is an important question Indian Christianity has to address itself to, not in the comfort of its

Preface

private space, but in the heat of the public arena today. It needs to take up the challenge of being accountable to itself and to others.

It is against such challenges that this volume makes an effort to reflect on public theology in the Indian context. It is presented in two parts with twelve essays. The first part consists of essays which deal with generic concerns, themes, and perspectives related to public theology, but of course as they obtain in the Indian context. Relating the broader genre of Christian political theology to the Indian context, exploring the relevance here of a public theology, reflecting on Christian mission in the light of public theology, and thinking of Indian public theology in relation to culture, civil society, and democracy are the attempts presented in the first part of the volume. And the other part consists of essays which treat public theology in relation to subaltern religions and their dynamics. The specific contribution of this volume could be said to be lying with this proposal for Indian Christianity to engage the public from the vantage point of the subaltern people of India. It would mean envisioning a public conversation from the socio-cultural locus of the subalterns. Though both the parts deal with the Indian context, the former one could be said to provide the width, while the latter gives the depth of commitment for public theology in India.

The first essay relates the genre of political theology to Indian Christian theology, with the help of Daniel Bell, Jr. Going by the strands of political theology proper, liberation theology, public theology, and the "emergent tradition", as identified by him, the essay tries to find the correlates in the Indian context. In addition to demonstrating the correlates, what is intended in the first essay is to situate the reflection upon public theology in the historical trajectory of Christian political theology. The second essay dwells upon the global context of emergence of such kindred realities like public religion, public philosophy, and so on, before speaking about public theology proper and its concerns in India. It identifies constructing a substantive participatory democracy being the central one, with which it aims at transforming the Indian society with the ideals of equity, social justice, liberty, and protection of the environment.

The third essay reflects on a public theology of mission. Underlining the method of participating in public conversations as a relevant one for a public theology of mission, the essay points out to the site and location of Christian public theology in India and reflects on some salient issues it faces today. The fourth essay envisions the relationship between culture and Christian faith as one of Christian *poiesis*, a form of practical cultural imaginary, rather than a theoretical normative criterion. The fifth one takes the reflection on public theology to its sphere of involvement, the civil society, and points out how the church can act as a sign and defender of transcendence in the wider society. And the sixth one takes up a philosophical theological enquiry into the reality of religious pluralism and its place in a democratic polity. These essays of the first part, thus, deal with the basic components which a public theology in the Indian context has to grapple with.

The second part goes into the Indian-specific location and concerns of public theology; it names the subaltern location as the preferred one. The first essay of the second part unpacks the theme of subaltern as it emerged in the recent subaltern studies, and relates it to religion by arguing for a *sui generis* approach to the study of subaltern religion, without reducing it to any sociological or psychological datum. It gives also a phenomenological account of the way the subaltern self in India has expressed its agency through the religious idiom. The second essay, following up on the first, explores as to how Ambedkar, in his account of philosophy of religion, gives a relevant scheme for the evaluation of religion, in terms of its value for fostering the transforming ideals of justice, equality, and liberty to nourish the democratic polity of this country. The essay argues that Ambedkar's evaluatory scheme is relevant to be applied to different religions as they participate in the public sphere today. The third essay undertakes to present a subaltern perspective to biblical hermeneutics to inspire those doing public theology from subaltern locations. It points to the relevant methods of reading the Bible, and goes on to point out some important sites of hermeneutical encounters. The fourth essay goes further to do a subaltern public theology of the Holy Spirit. It surmises that such a theology would look for the activities of the Spirit in opening the public spaces to subaltern selves. The fifth essay follows up by presenting an encounter of end-time beliefs as they occurred in a subaltern person. Such encounters, the essay contends, need to become free occurrences in our public space today. And the final essay presents the historical contours of the famous Indian doctrine of *dharma*, and shows what could be new in a public conversation on *dharma*.

This volume is a very modest attempt at relating Christian public theology to the Indian context. It lays out some of the basic concerns, perspectives, and themes which would be considered in such a theology. It is only a beginning, and the efforts at doing public theology in India has to go a long way, taking up the relevant themes and issues for its exploration and reflection. It is a call also for other religious traditions to participate in public conversations with their own public theologies. It would enrich the Indian public, and its democratic polity, if only different religions can involve in such an endeavour to mutually enrich one another. Needless to say that such a parliament of public theologies will go a long way in weakening the violent closures that get generated at the meeting points between different religions, and between religions and statecraft. I am sure this will also serve as a wellspring of transcendence for the entire humanity.

I wish to acknowledge the good role played by Mr. Will Bergkamp, Vice President, Fortress Press, and Dr. Jesudas Athyal, Acquiring Editor, South Asian Theology, Fortress Press, in contacting me and giving me this opportunity to work with them. I am appreciative and thankful of the opportunities provided by the University of Madras, and its authorities, to pursue researches in its departments. I remain thankful to Prof. Felix Wilfred who, with his vast experience and knowledge, introduced the theme of public theology to the Indian context and continues to pursue his reflections. Thanks to my colleague at the Department of Christian Studies, Dr. James Ponniah, for his cordiality and collaboration, to Ms. Majella Fernando for administering the office well, to Mr. Vinayaga Murthy for assisting us tirelessly, to Ms. Priyanka for the computer assistance, to Mr. Parthiban, the production contact, and to all the research scholars and students of the Department for continuing to inspire me with their learning.

I take this opportunity to specially thank Prof. Elisabeth Schüssler Fiorenza (Harvard University), Prof. Felix Wilfred (Emeritus Professor, University of Madras), Prof. Wesley Ariaraja (Emeritus Professor, Drew University), Prof. Susan Abraham (Pacific School of Religion), Dr. Jacob Parapally (Editor, *Journal of Indian Theology*), and Dr. P. T. Mathew (Executive Assistant, Kerala Jesuit Province) for going through the manuscript within a very short time and giving perceptive endorsements for the book. I am grateful to them. Their observations point not merely to the relevance of the volume but also to the need of further explorations in this area of public theology in the Indian context.

1

RELATING POLITICAL THEOLOGIES TO THE INDIAN CONTEXT

Political theology, Christian political theology to be specific, endeavours to relate the theological vision (or language) of Christian faith with the political process, understanding politics to be the involvement of human beings to deliberate for a collective life—be it an undifferentiated simple community (clan, tribe, village-level polities, etc), or a civil society, a nation, or a State as understood in the modern political parlance. This relationship manifests the deeper aspirations of Christians to live in communities, participate in collective thinking and acting, envision a future (through a philosophy, a theology, an ideology, etc), converse with others, receive criticisms with radical openness,[1] and journey together for realising the ideals of common good.

Different political theologies, down through the centuries, have imagined the relationship differently and, with their unique perspectives, have given substance and orientations to the practice of Christian political theology in history. Beginning with the exclusionary position of having no relationship at all with the "this-worldly" politics (though this position too had an indirect political impact), Christianity had gone on to establish a Christendom with a church-centric political theology that treated the "worldly power" as its handmaiden, and later, during the modern period, had given birth to the State which was imagined initially in a Christian way[2] and then, in the context of the "wars of religions", gave way to a "secular" State which followed the principle of separation of the church and

---

[1] As Peter Scott and William T. Cavanaugh would have it, "The task of political theology might then be to expose the ways in which theological discourse reproduces inequalities of class, gender, or race, and to reconstruct theology so that it serves the cause of justice". William T. Cavanaugh and Peter Scott, "Introduction", in *The Blackwell Companion to Political Theology*, ed. Peter Scott and William T. Cavanaugh (New York: Blackwell, 2004), 2.

[2] The way Calvin went about establishing a Christian polity is a case in point. Harro Höpel, *The Christian Polity of John Calvin* (Cambridge: Cambridge University Press, 1982).

the State, and has now come down to the contemporary era wherein the relationship has become much variegated and contextually nuanced.[3] Though it would do well to survey the entire history of Christian political theology,[4] considering the focus of this essay, I go by the classification given by Daniel M. Bell, Jr.,[5] a political theologian who identifies the different strands in the new political theologies, and I try to relate them to the Indian context.

Bell identifies three dominant strands in the new political theologies of the twentieth and twenty-first centuries, as (1) political theology proper, (2) liberation theology and (3) public theology, and goes on to add a fourth one which he calls the emergent tradition of the post-liberal type. By political theology proper, he means the tradition initiated in the 1960s by theologians such as Johann Baptist Metz, Jürgen Moltmann, and Dorothee Solle who proposed a political commitment of the church against the privatisation of Christianity obtaining in the then European secular context; by liberation theology, he means the well-known theological movement initiated by theologians such as Hugo Assmann, Leonardo Boff, and Gustavo Guttierrez, who spoke of the socio-political commitment of the church to transform the world on behalf of the poor; by public theology, he means the strand that emerged in the North-American context with initiatives from Catholic and Protestant theologians such as John Courtney Murray, Richard John Neuhaus, David Tracy, Martin E. Marty, Max Stackhouse, Ronald Thiemann and so on who spoke of the relevance of Christianity for public life and public sphere; and, by the emergent post-liberal tradition, he means the tradition initiated by theologians such as Stanley Hauerwas, John Milbank, Oliver O'Donnovan, and others, who, drawing inspiration from the works of post-liberal theologians such as George Lindbeck and

---

[3] The two major types of relationship that have come to provide the framework for the contemporary debate are: (1) the revisionary type, the one that postulates two positions between the Christian faith and the secular world, and attempts to relate the former to the latter in an ongoing manner, revising, in the process, the understanding not merely of the relationship itself, but also the two realities, in the light of one another (What David Tracy and Schubert Ogdon have done are good examples); (2) the post-liberal type, which does not recognise a "secular" world independent of Christian faith and pursues the actualisation of the Christian faith, in which process the secular world emerges (John Milbank, Stanley Hauverwas, and others).

[4] For readings in Christian political theology, Johann Baptist Metz, *Faith in History and Society—Toward a Practical Fundamental Theology*, trans. David Smith (New York: The Seabury Press, 1980); Metz, *A Passion for God—The Mystical-Political Dimension of Christianity*, trans. J. Matthew Ashley (New York: Paulist Press, 1998); William T Cavanaugh and Peter Scott, eds., *The Blackwell Companion to Political Theology* (New York: Blackwell, 2004); Raymond Plant, *Politics, Theology and History* (Cambridge: Cambridge University Press, 2001); Glenn Tinder, *The Political Meaning of Christianity—The Prophetic Stance—An Interpretation* (San Francisco: Harper, 1991).

[5] Daniel M. Bell, Jr., "State and Civil Society", in *The Blackwell Companion to Political Theology*, ed. Peter Scott and William T. Cavanaugh (New York: Blackwell, 2004).

Hans Frei, have come to speak of the true politics of the church, freed from political captivity by the modern secular reason.

I take Bell's classification as useful to reflect on political theology in the Indian context as well.

Political Theologies Proper

The political theology proper, according to Bell, emerged in a context dominated by political and cultural elements which privatised the church, making it a middle-class phenomenon. The then powerful existentialist philosophy, against the backdrop of the forceful current of secularisation, had effectively associated Christian faith with the personal decision of the individual. The salience of private religion, sustained by an extreme variant of secularity intoned by the French Revolution, was so dominant that the mainline churches failed to respond adequately to such historical emergence of evils such as the Nazi holocaust, and failed to critically challenge the bourgeois Christianity that was being nurtured by a personalist orientation to Christian faith. The Catholic Church, for its part, from its anti-modernist stance, continued to restrict the participation of the church in worldly/secular matters. Thus, both the mainstream Christian traditions had, in effect, come to restrain their believers from active participation in societal political processes, leaving the public to the vagaries of unethical power-hungry forces.

Johann Baptist Metz took on this situation with his proposal of a political theology, by which he meant an intention to deprivatise theology to play a critical role at the societal-political level, and more positively, to publicly hold, in the sense of a practical fundamental theology, the eschatological hope of the Christian faith. In his own words, "The deprivatising of theology is the primary critical task of political theology[6] and the *positive task* of political theology is … to determine anew the relation between religion and society, between Church and societal 'publicness' between eschatological faith and societal life".[7] Such a relationship would cure the privatising element of the existentialist personalism, and relate the here and now to the eschatological future characterised by the promises of justice and peace. Life, in a primordial sense, is one of relationships, and it gets constituted relentlessly in the sites of relationships. Existence for him, as paraphrased by J. Mathew Ashley, "needs to be complemented, corrected, or even subsumed by a *political account* (italics mine) that stresses more radically the ways we are constitutively related to one another, not just in 'I–thou' relationships of personal encounter with the other, but in

---

[6] John Baptist Metz, *Theology of the World*, trans. William Glen-Doepel (New York: Herder and Herder, 1969), 110.
[7] Metz, *Theology of the World*, 111.

and through ambivalent historical traditions and conflict-ridden social institutions (now on a global scale)".[8] These "historical traditions and conflict-ridden social institutions" connect the individuals to the "lives and experiences of other persons, both present and past".[9] A political theology would relate these with the "dangerous memory of the cross" as well as the eschatological hope as manifest in Jesus Christ.

Jürgen Moltmann, inspired by Metz, came up with his own version of the theology. For him, politics was the art of imagination of the real, and political theology was "anticipating the Christian eschatological hope through an imagination of the real present", or making the Christian hope present here and now. Sharing the concern of Metz on the privatisation of Christianity that legitimised a bourgeois culture of individualism, Moltmann wanted Christian theology to play a critical role in the church as well as among the wider public to inspire a new moral consciousness. He called his political theology a public theology—"a public, critical, and prophetic complaint to God—public, critical, and prophetic hope in God",[10] of which he further said: "It gets involved in the public affairs of society. It thinks about what is of general concern in the light of hope in Christ for the kingdom of God. It becomes political in the name of the poor and the marginalised in a given society."[11] For him, public political theology had more to say on the kinds of contradictions of modernity—between modernity and sub-modernity such as the contradiction inherent in the division between the rich and the poor, than on issues of religious pluralism alone.

It is in place to remember that these political theologies had emerged out of the Christian commitment at the practical level. For example, one could think of the Left Catholicism that had emerged during the first quarter of the twentieth century in western Europe. Drawing inspiration from the social teachings of the Catholic Church, the Catholic Action groups began to speak of social action and social change. The initiative of Joseph Cardijn to impart awareness to workers on their conditions and rights was intoning a new orientation to Christian commitment. Or one could think of Walter Rauschenbusch's movement of the Social Gospel, which

---

[8] J. Mathew Ashley, "Johann Baptist Metz", in *Blackwell Companion to Political Theology*, ed. Peter Scott and William T. Cavanaugh (New York: Blackwell, 2004), 254.
[9] Ashley, "Johann Baptist Metz", 254.
[10] Jurgen Moltmann, *God for a Secular Society—The Public Relevance of Theology*, trans. Margaret Kohl (London: SCM Press, 1999), 5.
[11] Moltmann, *God for a Secular Society*, 1.

proclaimed that "we have a social gospel!", and called for commitment to the unfolding of the "Reign of God" on earth.[12]

Did India have a political theology proper? During its very long tradition of rather creative theologising, it was during the second part of the twentieth century that the Indian Christian thought was beginning to engage with the socio-economic and political realities of the wider society. As far as Catholic theology was concerned, it may well be surmised that it was due to the progressive orientation of the Second Vatican Council to open the church towards the world. A new ecclesial consciousness, giving importance to laity in the church and promoting their secular social involvement to transform the world was on the theological horizon. Among the Protestant Indian theologians, we could see a change-over from theologising on the basis of the sanskritic religio-philosophical traditions to thinking theologically about historical societal transformations.[13] The works of M.M. Thomas, for example, began to show a new direction in Indian Christian theology to think of "salvation as humanisation", and of the Christian contribution to the sensitisation about human dignity and rights. The process of secularisation, for Thomas, meant God's providence that was "creating in Asia the basic conditions of greater human dignity, enhanced human creativity, and mature human living".[14] He said: "The process of secularization which is already at work in the world and the secular patterns of understanding human existence which have already emerged, are themselves the product of the ferment of the Gospel working in traditional societies."[15] He believed that "The gospel of salvation must work itself out also in the realm of history and politics, and in the campaign to provide conditions where men (sic) can live as real men (sic)",[16] because, the core of Christian faith, according to him, is "the message that

---

[12] In this context, we need be aware also of the "absolutist political theologies" proffered by persons like Carl Schmitt, for whom, church should exercise political power like a sovereign, after the model of "constitutional dictatorship". Since we are dealing with a "new political theology", as Johann Baptist Metz had intoned, we are leaving Schmitt's political theology behind to look for a relevant political theology, situated within the democratic political paradigm.

[13] Robin Boyd, *Introduction to Indian Christian Theology* (Delhi: ISPCK, 1994 [1969]). Several studies have pointed out today that the corpus of theological writing known as the "Indian Christian Theology" had taken to the sanskritic traditions as its partner in theology, to the neglect of the traditions existing among marginal and subaltern people. It may then be pointed out that this corpus, though not having a political theological component, went with a politics of theology, a cultural politics to be specific, in allying with the traditions of the dominant. It was certainly due to the Indian Christian orientation of the time, mirroring that of the Western Christian theology, to inculturate the Christian faith in the Indian soil with the help of the textual religio-philosophical traditions of India.

[14] Boyd, *Indian Christian Theology*, 318.

[15] Boyd, *Indian Christian Theology*, 320.

[16] Boyd, *Indian Christian Theology*, 318.

God has acted in a unique way in a secular historic event, namely the incarnation, life, death and resurrection of Jesus Christ, to inaugurate the kingdom".[17]

Growing more in awareness of the Christian commitment for societal transformation, Indian Christianity got readily involved in programmes of nation-building, by undertaking projects to alleviate poverty and to stand in good stead with the poor and the marginalised in times of famine and natural calamities. *Caritas India*, for example, with its vision of a "welfare society", took initiatives for the development of the poor.

We see, thus, certain aspects of political theology developing in the Indian context as well. However, a point clearly visible here is a difference emerging between the perspectives of European political theology and the incipient political concerns of Indian theology: while the former was thinking theologically to free itself from the overweening secular polity which had privatised Christianity, Indian theology was thinking of constructing a secular polity as part of the Christian commitment. Secularisation, far from being a privatisation of religion, was considered a process to free the public political space from the control of unmeaning and obscurantist feudal powers. It was an inchoate political theology, orienting the church towards the secular temporal world and its practical concerns.

Liberation Theologies

Latin American liberation theology added its specific attributes and dynamism to the development of political theology. Having been inspired by the project of *aggiornamento* of the Vatican II, and getting its initial impetus from the Medellin Conference (1968) of the Latin American Bishops, the theology unfolded in the liberative praxis of Latin American Catholics, especially of the Base Christian Communities, and got articulated by theologians such as Hugo Assmann, Gustavo Gutierrez, Leonardo Boff, and others.

A Theology of Liberation, the pioneering work by Gustavo Gutierrez, envisioned an integral liberation from sin which involved political, psychological, and anthropological liberation. With the theological statement that God, the universal divine being, took side with the poor in history so as to reconcile the world to God's self, liberation theologians reflected upon how human sin made a rupture in communication among human beings and with God; the rupture, according to them, got objectified in social and political structures, and reigned against God. It was God who took the initiative in grace to redeem this humanity by calling for repentance through the incarnate God, Jesus Christ, and it was thereby incumbent upon human beings to collaborate with the divine initiative and bring

---

[17] As cited by Boyd, *Indian Christian Theology*, 320.

forth total liberation for humanity. In this collaborative praxis, human beings had to draw strength from the word of God, read through a hermeneutical circle between action and reflection, which was to be aided by an analytical mediation of social sciences. The theology of liberation, thus unfolding, took a momentum in the acts of resistance to dictatorial political powers, sacrificing several lives in the course of action.

The theology came in for criticism from certain theological sections and for strictures from the Catholic hierarchy. The core criticism was that it tended to be reductive, giving in to social sciences, especially to the Marxian social analysis. And the criticism was responded to by Gutierrez with a refutation of the accusation of reductionism, and with an affirmation of the divine grace as the origin and development of action for liberation.

Coming to the Indian context, Indian theologians developed Indian-specific liberation theology, drawing inspiration from the teachings of Vatican II and from the Latin American Liberation theology. They charted a different course, by identifying Indian realities of poverty on the one hand and the rich religiosity on the other as the framework for liberation theology in India and Asia as well.[18] In doing so, they were much concerned about the question of Christianity's relationship with other religions, and were sensitised by the emerging grassroots activism among the faith-based NGOs working on different aspects of the project of liberation. And, the social analysis being disseminated by the political Left movements and the emerging human rights discourse in the wider public provided the ambience for Indian liberation theology to take shape.

One of the pioneers to reflect about it in India was Sebastian Kappen, with his publications under the titles: *Jesus and Freedom* (1977), *Jesus and Cultural Revolution: An Asian Perspective* (1983), *Liberation Theology and Marxism* (1986), and so on. He proposed a foundational theology which would bring together the experiences of the Divine as found in various traditions for social transformation. An important theological event in this regard was the seminar organised with the initiative of D. S. Amalorpavadoss on "The Indian Church in the Struggle for a New Society",[19] and the subsequent volume edited with the same title, which brought about a good theological debate on the ministry of the church in terms of its commitment for socio-political transformation. Activist Christian scholars such as Stan Lourdusamy worked with people's movements, which in solidarity with the Left movement, worked towards the

---

[18] Aloysius Pieris, *The Genesis of an Asian Theology of Liberation—An Autobiographical Excursus on the Art of Theologizing in Asia* (Gonawala-Kelaniya, Sri Lanka: Tulania Research Centre, 2013).

[19] D. S. Amalorpavadass, *The Indian Church in the Struggle for a New Society* (Bangalore: National, Biblical, Catechetical and Liturgical Centre, 1981).

dawning of socialism in India.[20] Another theologian to note was Samuel Rayan, who, with his involvement in the All India Catholic University Federation (AICUF), produced very inspiring theological writings which relate liberation to the works of the Holy Spirit.[21] Michael Amaladoss related liberation theology to dialogue of cultures and religions,[22] and Felix Wilfred[23] explored the inter-disciplinary terrain of social sciences and ecclesiology to speak of Indian and Asian liberation theology. Social analysts such as John Derosche, Walter Fernandes and others, and institutes such as the Indian Social Institute, contributed significantly to the development of Indian-specific liberation theology. The Indian Theological Association served a good cause in taking forward liberation theology in the Indian context. The themes reflected in their annual conventions contributed much to shape up the Indian Christian liberation perspective.[24]

The concept of third world theology gained increasing significance in the discourse on Indian/Asian liberation theology, and the Ecumenical Association of Third World Theologians (EATWOT) contributed meaningfully to advance liberation theology in the Indian and Asian soil. Other Asian theologians such as Aloysius Pieris, Tissa Balasuriya, Kosuke Koyama, and C. S. Song made their contributions felt at the Indian level as well.

The articulations of these scholar-theologians, along with those of the activist theologians, who were involved in the struggles of the poor, shaped up the Indian liberation theology. An important activist to note

---

[20] Stan Lourdusamy, *People's Liberation—Characteristics of Parties, Movements and People's Struggles in India* (Bangalore: Indian Social Institute, 1985).

[21] Samuel Rayan, S.J., *Jesus—The Relevance of His Person and Message for Our Times*, Selected Writings of Samuel Rayan, S.J., vol. I, ed. Kurien Kunnumpuram, S.J. (Mumbai: The Bombay Saint Paul Society, 2011); Rayan, *In Spirit and Truth—Indian Christian Reflections on Spirituality and Worship*, Selected Writings of Samuel Rayan, S.J., vol. II, ed. Kurien Kunnumpuram, S.J. (Mumbai: The Bombay Saint Paul Society, 2012); Rayan, *Nature, Woman and the Church—Indian Christian Reflections on Ecology, Feminism and Ecclesiology*, Collected Writings of Samuel Rayan, S.J., vol. I, ed. Kurien Kunnumpuram, S.J. (New Delhi: ISPCK, 2013); Id., *Doing Theology—Indian Christian Reflections on Theologizing in India Today*, Collected Writings of Samuel Rayan, S.J., vol. II, ed. Kurien Kunnumpuram, S.J. (New Delhi: ISPCK, 2013).

[22] Michael Amaladoss, *Life in Freedom: Liberation Theologies in Asia* (Maryknoll: Orbis Books, 1997); Amaladoss, *Making Harmony—Living in a Pluralist World* (IDCR & ISPCK, 2003); Amaladoss, *The Asian Jesus* (IDCR & ISPCK, 2005).

[23] Felix Wilfred, *From the Dusty Soil—Contextual Interpretation of Christianity* (Chennai: Department of Christian Studies, University of Madras, 1995); Wilfred, *On the Banks of Ganges—Doing Contextual Theology* (New Delhi: ISPCK, 2002); Wilfred, *Asian Dreams and Christian Hope—At the Dawn of the Millennium* (New Delhi: ISPCK, 2003); Wilfred, *Margins—Site of Asian Theologies* (New Delhi: ISPCK, 2008); Wilfred, *Dalit Empowerment* (New Delhi: ISPCK, 2007); Wilfred, *Christians for a Better India* (New Delhi: ISPCK, 2014).

[24] One may find the annual statements of ITA at http://www.itanet.in/ITA%20Statements2017.html.

was Fr. Thomas Kocherry who was involved heart and soul with the struggles of the fisherfolk for their rights and dignity and for the protection of the fast-depleting marine resources. There were other activist priests who, being inspired by the project of conscientisation as proposed by Paulo Freire, involved themselves in conscientising the Christians about the structural sins of the society, and played an effective role in mobilising the people for public demonstrations and solidarity with social-political movements working for the liberation of the poor and oppressed. Locally rooted Christian collectives, based on aspects of political theology, worked in solidarity with secular social movements and political forces for the cause of liberation from structural oppression. It may be noted that these activities came to be recognised in the secular media as forming the Christian Left in India.

In the subsequent phase, liberation theology in India gave birth to a stream of contextual theologies, the most significant being Dalit theology. The preferential option for the poor, as put forth by the Latin American liberation theology, needed to be qualified to say "preferential option for the subaltern poor" in the Indian context. The experience of poverty in India goes inextricably with social marginality and subordination. Centuries of social exclusion, premised upon the perceived ritual impurity, attendant with the denial of social, political, and cultural power had made the subaltern class of people poor. It was but natural then that Indian liberation theology, aiming at integral social transformation, led to the emergence of the subaltern Dalit theology. Distinguishing it from liberation theology, Arvind Nirmal, one of the pioneers of Dalit theology, said:

> I felt that liberation motifs in India were of a different nature, the Indian situation was different and that we had to search for liberation motifs that were authentically Indian. The Latin American Liberation Theology in its early stages at least used Marxist analysis of socio-economic realities—the haves and the have-nots. The socio-economic realities in India, however, are of a different nature and the traditional doctrinaire Marxist analysis of these realities is inadequate in India. It neglects the caste factor which adds to the complexity of Indian socio-economic realities.[25]

Acknowledging the presence of caste oppression and evoking the commitment for its abolition are indispensable for the evolution of an Indian liberation theology. This theology, since it is rooted in the historical consciousness of the pathos of the most oppressed people, the Dalits, can meaningfully be called as Dalit theology, which, according to Nirmal is synonymous with Christian theology in the Indian context (being a Christian in the sense of a person holding on to a hope of redemption

---

[25] Arvind Nirmal, "Towards a Christian Dalit Theology", in *A Reader in Dalit Theology*, eds. Arvind Nirmal and V. Devasahayam (Madras: Gurukul Lutheran Theological College & Research Institute), 56.

against the present-day suffering means being a suffering Dalit). It identifies the suffering of the Dalits with that of the son of Man, the Christ, and hopes for a liberation wrought by the Holy Spirit as it occurred to the "dry bones" when the Spirit blew over them (Ezek 37: 1-14).

Dalit theology made its impact felt within the walls of Indian Christianity. Dalit Christian movements emerged to address the problems of discrimination within the churches, and they led to certain, however limited though, democratisation of the inner spheres of the churches and sensitisation of the Christian community to recognise the legitimate demands of the Dalit Christians for sharing of power within the churches. In addition, the Indian Christian community, along with the Dalit Christians, began to demand from the Indian government the benefits of affirmative action offered in the Indian Constitution to the Dalits. The struggle goes on until this day.

Indian Christian contextual theology found its expressions also in such variants as Indian Christian feminist theology, ecumenical theology, tribal theology, eco-theology, and so on. In all of them, the Indian-specific schemes of hierarchy, purity-pollution, social exclusion, and marginalisation are being interrogated, and an egalitarian, holistic, universal, inclusive, and empowering scheme of relationship, premised upon the values of the Reign of God are proclaimed.

These variants of liberation theology, however hopeful they were to impact upon the wider political and civil sphere, remained yet to be intra-textual theologies, motivating the Christian mind to act. Though its relevance continues to be acknowledged in different forms, its vitality has weakened, due to, among others, the reason that the contemporary global world faces a general weakening of social movements and collective efforts for social transformation, and that religious identity consciousness, along with the consciousness of a thick plurality of religions, is superseding the social consciousness and concern for structural transformation. It is time for the emergence of new political theologies.

PUBLIC THEOLOGY

The third strand of political theology, as suggested by Daniel Bell, is public theology and theology of public life that have re-emerged during the last two and a half decades or so. They are concerned with the relevance of theology, Christian theology in our case, for the wider public (public sphere and public life) today; or, to put it differently, they are concerned with the publicness of Christian theology, and the nature of the public role Christianity is called upon to play in our global world. The salient issues implied in discussing the publicness of Christian theology are the place of religion and religious plurality in the functioning of the secular State and civil society, and the role religions, along with different initiatives (movements, ideologies, and philosophies), can play for realising the ideals of common good (social justice, gender justice, economic equity, eco-justice, etc). They can be spelt out into simple questions such as, "What is the role of theology/religion in the public sphere today?"; "What is the relationship between religion and public reason?"; "How do religions interact with modern secular states and civil society within a democratic political framework?"; "How does religious plurality function in relation to public life or issues of common good?"; and so on.

Public theologians such as Jürgen Moltmann, Marty E. Marty, Duncan Forrester, Ronald Thiemann, Richard John Neuhaus, and others propose a positive role for religion/theology in the public sphere and public life, but within a constitutional democratic framework. Christianity, according to them, needs to be active in the public sphere to contribute to nurturing the public sphere with the faith-dimension of transcendence and moral sensitivity for common good. Their proposal has evoked different responses from liberal secularists. Richard Rorty, a hardcore secularist, considers religion as a conversation stopper in the public sphere, and argues, therefore, for confining religion strictly to the private sphere. John Rawls and Jürgen Habermas are more nuanced in their approaches. They do acknowledge the role of religion in the public sphere especially for the moral regeneration of humanity, but they find religions, as "incommensurable comprehensive doctrines" posing a challenge for interactions in the public sphere. Thinking of the possibility of arriving at an "overlapping consensus" between the "comprehensive doctrines", they propose a liberal method of translating them into secular neutral language to make them intelligible to others. There are others who object to this proposal saying that the comprehensive doctrines, which are generally rendered in the language of mythos, lose their potential while getting translated; and instead, they propose the practice of *conversations*, wherein every comprehensive doctrine is called upon to present itself as itself and allows for appreciation and criticism from others.

Relating public theology to the Indian context is something of a new attempt and is challenging, but filled with promises and potential; and that will be attempted in the next chapter of this volume on Indian Public Theology.

THE EMERGENT TRADITION

Bell speaks about the emergent tradition, pointing out to the post-liberal theological tradition as evidenced in the emergent theologies, such as the Radical Orthodoxy as proposed by John Milbank, Stanley Hauerwas, Graham Ward, Catherine Pickstock, and others. They find the effort of

Christian public theology to relate itself to secular democratic institutions of State and civil society as meaningless and unwarranted, because State, civil society and liberal democracy are products of the secular reason and are ultimately only the derivatives of Christian theology and not independent autonomous true publics in themselves; these modern institutions and ideologies have failed today; moreover, these secular modern institutions, according to them, have held Christian theology or any religion in their captivity (euphemism for secularism holding religion in a private sphere) for long to the detriment of the wellbeing of the general public. Milbank holds that "once there was no secular" and he calls for going back to the pre-modern moment which presented a real picture of the true public world; accordingly the church was the true public, and we should be able to construct that public today as well. Drawing upon the Augustinian call to treat the church as the *City of God* in this temporal world, Radical Orthodoxy is calling upon the Church to become the true public in this world.

Relating this emergent tradition of the Radical Orthodoxy to the Indian context is perhaps too early an effort; however, certain observations may not be irrelevant. Though not drawing upon the Radical Orthodoxy, there are some perspectives of mission present among some sections of Christianity in India, who go about constructing the church as the true public, treating other publics as parts of an evil empire. For them, Indian liberal democracy is relevant only to the extent it provides an opportunity to construct their public; otherwise, neither the liberal democracy nor its secular reason have any value. This perhaps is not a meaningful way of approaching the Indian public—a space that consists of innumerable vital publics (different religions, communities, gender, and other NGOs, social movements, subaltern political parties, etc).

Throwing out the secular reason (which the Religious Right in India is trying to do) and its associates of State, civil society, and so on, are detrimental to the Indian public, and to the subaltern people who still invest a great hope in the democratic institutions in India. A radical political theology in the Indian context should take the lead from theologies such as those of M.M. Thomas, Sebastian Kappen, and Felix Wilfred, who have found elements of salvation in secularisation, and have found values in the secular democratic institutions in the Indian context. It is indeed time to challenge the liberal and neoliberal democracy, which is indifferent to questions of poverty, social, and gender discriminations. Persons such as Ambedkar who, though he had worked wholeheartedly to construct a liberal democratic government, got dismayed with it when it came to be controlled by the elites of India, and looked for alternatives, including religious ones, to bring about a real transformation in India, are our forerunners in the search for radical democracy. In solidarity with such seekers, an Indian Christian political theology should endeavour, though agonistically, to build up a radical democracy for India. In this context, politics need not be understood only as that practice leading to the partaking of parliamentary bureaucratic and legal power, but also of constructing and deconstructing the symbolic-cultural power from the lifeworlds of the subaltern people of India.

By Way of Concluding

It is heartening to see that aspects of Christian political theology have been present or initiated in the Indian context. Indian Christian theology, especially during the second half of the twentieth century, engaged with the socio-economic and political realities of India, even while endeavouring to relate with different religions and cultures. Indian liberation theologies and contextual theologies are the best evidences. The contemporary context is rather challenging, because the erstwhile political theologies are waning due to various factors brought in by forces of globalisation. There are also promises in this global era. Constructing a radical democracy that integrates the role of religion, which however does not give in to anti-democratic forces but keeps atop the concerns of the subaltern and marginalised sections of the people is the best way of doing a relevant Christian political theology in India today. It would be a subaltern public theology undertaken in collaboration with the subaltern religio-cultural and ideological traditions of India.

2

THINKING OF PUBLIC THEOLOGY IN INDIA

Religion in the Contemporary World

Our world is witnessing today what is called in the Western context a resurgence of religion, by which is meant a revival or comeback from an estrangement. The modern world, by privileging secularity, seemed to have turned either hostile or indifferent to religion. Theories of modern disciplines like sociology, psychology, or anthropology considered religion to be either opium of the people, or an illusion/obsessive neurosis, or a primitive stage in human evolution. Sociologists of religion spoke of the process of secularisation, attendant with modernisation, industrialisation, and urbanisation, and predicted that as these forces develop, religion would fade away from human civilisation. But, contrary to these predictions, religious practices and beliefs have increased manifold; religion has come back from the so-called exile imposed upon it by modernity; it has resurged from the sheaths of secular consciousness accrued upon it through the modern age.

From our own day-to-day experience too, we can ascertain the fact that the religious fervour is all around us today: constructing or renovating of church/temple/mosque buildings are being undertaken on a large scale; festivities and other religious observances are increasing in numbers; media presentation of religious activities are thick; religious pilgrimages are increasing in numbers; and so on. People are ready to spend more today than ever on religious observances.

Advanced communication technologies are significantly aiding the practice of religion. The cyberspace is providing facilities for virtual practice of religion: Those who study religion in the cyberspace speak of "religion-online" and "online-religion", where the former stands for the availability of religious resources on the net and the latter for the very practice of religion through the net. That people undertake even virtual pilgrimages through the net is a typical example of the latter variety.

It is worth considering that even the economic corporate houses practice religion in their campuses. CEOs of corporate houses not merely function like "high priests" with their own authority, but also propagate spiritual practices among the workers. They have regular religious or quasi-religious exercises conducted within the workplaces. Yoga, for example, is becoming a global corporate spiritual exercise in order to increase the skills of the workers and to free them from job-related stresses.

This increasing observance of religion is being taken note of and discussed within the disciplines of the social sciences as well. Social theory, for example, is gripped with the reality of the resurgence of religion. Those who had held on to anti-religious secular thought that religion would fade away as the secular modern rational thought progressed, have changed their positions. Peter Berger, for example, who was one of the well-known secularisation theorists, has, for some time now, spoken about the emergence of "de-secularisation".[1] Along with him, there are others who speak about the coming of a "post-secular" society today, which approaches religion with more openness. Jürgen Habermas, John Rawls, and other social contract theorists, who earlier could not find any place for religion for the public life or in the public sphere, had become more open to the role of religion for the moral regeneration of the public sphere. Gianny Vattimo, the well-known Italian post-modern thinker, identifies the post-secular society with the resurgence of the positivity of religion from centuries of its imprisonment by the secularist thought.[2]

An empirical study by Pippa Norris and Ronald Inglehart, conducted across 70 countries, concludes that our contemporary global world is generally turning to be religious (going by the practice of religion among the majority), while some zones (in Europe and North America) remain secular.[3] Grace Davie, a well-known sociologist from UK, while confirming the resurgence of religious belief, surmises however that the kind of religious belief found in the Western context is one that believes without belonging, as different from the traditional type of belonging without believing.[4] Peter Beyer brings in yet another insight which holds that religion today is more performative, in terms of other social sub-systems like politics, economics, and so on, rather than being functional, that is, leading people

---

[1] Peter L. Berger, ed., *The Desecularization of the World—The Resurgent Religion and World Politics* (Washington DC: Ethical and Public Policy Centre, 1999).

[2] While these social scientists speak then about the emergence of post-secularity today, there are others who think of the contemporary world as one capable of both the secular as well as the religious thinking. Charles Taylor, for instance, speaks about the emergence of the "buffering self", which, having developed an "immanent frame" of the secular framework of thinking, can engage with religious as well as secular thinking non-problematically.

[3] Pippa Norris and Ronald Inglehart, *Sacred and Secular—Religion and Politics Worldwide* (Cambridge: Cambridge University Press, 2004).

[4] Grace Davie, "Believing without Belonging—Is this the Future of Religion in Britain?" *Social Compass*, 37, no. 4 (1990): 455–469.

to otherworldly salvation, liberation, and so on.[5] Whatever be its nature, religion has undeniably come to exist in its own right, within the modern ethos.

Indian or Asian situation may not correspond to the Western context of post-secularity. First of all, the forces of secularisation have not developed here as they have done in the Western context, and therefore one cannot speak strictly about a post-secular context here; second, whatever level or kind of secularity that has happened here has been so unique to the Indian/Asian context that religion has neither been estranged nor alienated from the general consciousness of the people even at this moment of advancing modernity. Therefore, one cannot say that there is a religious *resurgence* in the Indian/Asian context. However, we may well speak of a process of vitalisation of religion happening in the Indian and Asian contexts today. Religious practices have seen a manifold increase[6] and religious beliefs inform the lives of wider sections of people. Public manifestations of religion, like festivals, pilgrimages, ceremonies, construction of sacred buildings, media representations, and so on, are evidences to the inexorable growth. The way religion goes virtual, as "religion online" and "online religion", increases the practices of religion. Virtual religion has become an undeniable resource for individual and collective living. It would, therefore, be appropriate to speak of religious vitalisation, if not religious resurgence in Indian/Asian contexts.

Public Religion

Against the background of religious resurgence or revitalisation, scholars of religion speak of the emergence of public religion.[7] Jose Casanova, in his *Public Religion in the Modern World*,[8] published in 1994, spoke of the emergence of *public religion* in the Western context. He thought of it as a reality involved in the processes of the public sphere, consequent upon what he called the de-privatisation of religion. His thesis found support from those who had begun to re-think the theory of secularisation and to speak about de-secularisation,[9] return of the religious,[10] post-secularity,

---

[5] Peter Beyer, *Religion and Globalisation* (Canada: University of Ottawa, 1994).
[6] Pradeep K. Chhibber, *Religious Practice and Democracy in India* (Cambridge: Cambridge University Press, 2016).
[7] Jose Casanova, *Public Religion in the Modern World* (Chicago: The University of Chicago Press, 1994).
[8] Casanova, *Public Religion in the Modern World*.
[9] Berger, *The Desecularization of the World*.
[10] Gianni Vattimo, "The Trace of the Trace", in *Religion*, ed. Jacques Derrida and Gianni Vattimo, trans. David Webb et al. (Stanford: Stanford University Press, 1998); Gianni Vattimo and Rene Girard, eds. *Christianity, Truth, and Weakening of Faith—A Dialogue* (New York: Columbia University Press, 2006).

and so on.¹¹ Reflecting upon the experience of religion in the European-American context, he opined that religion went public in the 1980s when it contributed to political changes in Iran, Poland, Latin America, and North America. According to him, these events portended a process of de-privatisation, whereby religion came out of the private sphere assigned to it by Western modernity. Along the same lines, Peter L. Berger spoke about a process of de-secularisation whereby religion held on to its vitality in the public realm falsifying the secularisation thesis.¹² Charles Taylor, acknowledging the reality of public religion, spoke about it as not something that supersedes, but that lives on in the very midst of the secular age.¹³ More and more of literature on public religion, adapting to different contexts, keep emerging.¹⁴ Casanova today furthers his theory by applying it to the global context. Stating it to be an indisputably global social fact, he points out three arenas where religion becomes public: sites related to modern State, political society, and civil society.¹⁵ While his earlier understanding dealt with public religion in relation to the civil sphere, his recent views relate it to the State and political society.

Public sphere and public life have come to be the sites of public religion. Public sphere, broadly speaking, stands for any sphere that contributes to public decision-making at any level; it may stand for civil spheres, political spheres, spheres of governance, and so on. However, in its strict sense, as used by theoreticians like Jürgen Habermas, it stands for that intermediary space between the wider civil society and the specific political society (political parties, parliaments, assemblies, etc)—a space characterised by active debates contributing to the emergence of representatives who would make decisions on behalf of wider sections of people in a democratic statecraft. Habermas would mention three types of public spheres: (1) public spheres in the political domain (a domain which is proximate and yet different from the State, preparing individuals for statecraft), (2) public spheres in the world of letters (discussions and debates in the domain of

---

[11] Charles Taylor, *A Secular Age* (Cambridge: Belknap Press of Harvard University Press, 2007); Jürgen Habermas has come to open himself up to the possibility of religion playing a positive role in the public sphere (when translated into intelligible language) for the moral regeneration of humanity—Jürgen Habermas and Joseph Ratzinger, *Dialectics of Secularization—On Reason and Religion* (San Francisco: Ignatius Press, 2006); Thus, we see an array of viewpoints on the resurgence of religion in our secular/post-secular era, and its role in the public sphere.

[12] Berger, ed., *The Desecularization of the World*.

[13] Charles Taylor, *A Secular Age* (Cambridge: Belknap Press of Harvard University Press, 2007).

[14] John Micklethwait and Adrian Wooldridge, *God is Back—How the Global Rise of Faith is Changing the World* (London: Penguin Books, 2009).

[15] Jose Casanova, "Rethinking Public Religions", in *Rethinking Religion and World Affairs*, eds. Timothy Samuel Shah, Alfred Stepan, and Monica Duffy Toft (Oxford: Oxford University Press, 2012).

literatures, academia, press, clubs, and so on, which, with its relative independence, debates upon the State as well as the courts), and (3) public spheres in the town in coffee houses, salons, table societies, and so on, which cultivate the general population for creating public opinion to participate in public reason. Religion has come to play an active role in these public spheres today. It informs also the spaces of public life, as found in the civil society, bureaucracy, and statecraft. All these bear witness to the fact that religion has gone public in an undeniable manner.

Religion has gone public in the Indian context as well. Indian civil sphere is being enriched with increasingly growing religious initiatives, even while being faced with acute problems on account of religion. The democratic political system—with its activities of mobilisation, electioneering, and representative politics—is increasingly taking to religion in a conspicuous manner. The state mechanism, in its parliament, judiciary, and bureaucracy, is grappling with religious issues more frequently.

Needless to say that this public religion has gone with positive and negative experiences! As the world experiences a high quantum of mobility (migratory—actual and virtual), as very high scores of crossing of borders occur, and as an increasingly wider section of humanity partakes of life-affirming opportunities (social, cultural, political, economic, etc), religion, with its positivity of transcendence, journeys with humanity in an empowering way; it serves as a resourceful agent to organise life in common, for solidarity, justice, charity, common good, acts of altruism, and so on; it has become a meaningful medium and resource to imagine a selfhood, construct an identity, and fashion creative skills; it has rendered various sites of public sphere participatory by drawing in more and more of people for collective projects. On the other hand, occasions of instrumentalising religion have also proliferated: narrow political ends are sought to be achieved with the misuse of religion; gruesome violence is inflicted in the name of religion; exploitative economic aggrandisement takes place through the utilisation of religion; oppressive and hegemonic identities seek to make a comeback or stabilise themselves under the garb of religion; more than anything else, religion is instrumentalised to induce closures in consciousness by way of freezing the signs in terms of commercialising (commodifying), fundamentalist, communal, and ethnocentric projects. Positive experiences on the one hand, and the negative ones on the other, seem to inform the resurgent public religion today.

Public as a Philosophical Category

In order to appreciate the significance of public religion, it would do well to understand the category of the *public* from a philosophical perspective as well. Hannah Arendt's philosophical reflections are relevant here.

Arendt speaks of two closely related dimensions of the term public: First, "Everything that appears in public can be seen and heard by everybody and has the widest possible publicity".[16] Appearance and publicity, for her, mean those dynamic aspects which wean realities out of the private realm and give them the *relevance* with which they can be tolerated (in a positive sense) and sustained in a transcendental manner, as something that comes to us and goes beyond us into earthly immortality. They constitute a relevance, which cuts across the charm of projected appearance and publicity, and withhold a permanence reckoned in terms of the common good. Second, "The term public signifies the world itself, in so far as it is common to all of us and distinguished from our privately owned place in it".[17] Arendt distinguishes the public-likeness of a private world from the radical public, by pointing out to the fact that most often, private worlds of charm or passion can be extended into the public, reproduced endlessly in the public domain, thereby obtaining a public-like character. Contrary to this manner of privatising the public by publicising the private, living in the public means acknowledging that "a world of things is between those who have it in common, as a table is located between those who sit around it".[18] It is a world that relates one to the other, and yet separates each other in a wholesome way. "The public realm, as the common world, gathers us together and yet prevents our falling over each other, so to speak."[19] Arendt brings together sameness (identity) and difference as hallmark attributes of the public. In her words,

> Being seen and being heard by others derive their significance from the fact that everybody sees and hears from a different position. This is the meaning of public life, compared to which even the richest and most satisfying family life can offer only the prolongation or multiplication of one's own position with its attending aspects and perspectives. The subjectivity of privacy can be prolonged and multiplied in a family, it can even become so strong that its weight is felt in the public realm; but this family world can never replace the reality rising out of the sum total of aspects presented by one object to a multitude of spectators. Only where things can be seen by many in a variety of aspects without changing their identity, so that those who are gathered around them know they see sameness in utter diversity, can worldly reality truly and reliably appear.[20]

Arendt goes on to reflect upon the viability of a common world as that which emerges only in a public, and survives across time in a public. As she puts it, "Such a common world can survive the coming and going of the generations only to the extent that it appears in public. It is the

---

[16] Peter Baehr, ed., *The Portable Hannah Arendt* (New York: Penguin Books, 2000), 199.
[17] Baehr, *The Portable Hannah Arendt*, 201.
[18] Baehr, *The Portable Hannah Arendt*, 201.
[19] Baehr, *The Portable Hannah Arendt*, 201.
[20] Baehr, *The Portable Hannah Arendt*, 204.

publicity of the public realm which can absorb and make shine through the centuries whatever men may want to save from the ruin of time".[21] This common world is sustained through a common bond between individuals, created by a transcendental or metaphysical value, belief, or ideology, which constitute individuals into a community of people. "Without this transcendence into a potentially earthly immortality, no politics, strictly speaking, no common world and no public realm, is possible."[22]

Thus, Arendt's philosophy of the public underscores the dynamics of appearance and publicity, identity and difference, and, unity and separation as indispensable elements for constituting a public, a common world for humanity. This public emerges in a significant manner in a democratic polity, wherein individuals sit around a table of parliament, protecting one another's different identity, even while striving towards the sameness or the common bond of humanity.

PUBLIC THEOLOGY

Public theology, impregnated with such a philosophy of the public, emerges in the context of the public religion today. Public theologies[23] are the creative wings of public religion, with a force of value-oriented conviction based on transcendental frames for commitment in the public sphere. They come with the possibility for transforming the public into a site of peace and harmony, nurtured with values of freedom, justice, equality, dignity, fulfilment of basic necessities, and healthy identity negotiations! It is this promise which inspires us to explore the potentials of public theologies today.

Public theologies seek to build upon the existing political, liberation, and contextual theologies, as pointed out in the previous chapter. While these theologies are also public in an important sense, the wider public, the public where *multiple others* are present remains still an external reality to the pursuit of political theologies.[24] For example, a Dalit theology in the

---

[21] Baehr, *The Portable Hannah Arendt*, 202.
[22] Baehr, *The Portable Hannah Arendt*, 202.
[23] I consciously address them in the plural, as John de Gruchy does in the South African context, because they can only be so in the multiple configurations of public spheres to which they respond or in which they are involved. John W. De Gruchy, "From Political to Public Theologies: The Role of Theology in Public Life in South Africa", in *Public Theology for the 21st Century—Essays in Honour of Duncan Forrester*, eds., William F. Storrar and Andrew Morton (London: T & T Clark, 2004), 45-64. However, when it refers to the generic notion, it is rendered in the singular.
[24] A very common question is, "What is different in public theology from liberation-contextual theologies?" "What liberation theology spoke of in terms of socio-political and economic liberation, public theology seems to repeat, and so, what is the difference between the two?" My answer, very succinctly, would be that which constitutes our global world makes the difference. Liberation theology and its variants of contextual

Indian context motivates the Christian public to interrogate the inhuman hierarchy of caste; but it does not embark, as a conscious theological endeavour, upon the responsibility of motivating the wider public, constituted by religious and non-religious others, to interrogate the reality of caste. Public theology, on the other hand, takes up the challenge of interrogating the public realities through a theological vision—a vision constituted in solidarity with religious and secular others. It envisions a characteristically different public engagement wherein the whole public becomes a theological category. In its constitution, the incommensurably different comprehensive doctrines[25] (religions, ethical doctrines, humanist ideologies, etc.) are brought together in an interactive engagement. Every religious tradition, with its own heritage and resources, is called upon to propose a vision of the public, even while each tradition is motivated to be engaged with others to envision a common public.

Public theology treats politics, the site where public decisions are made, as its important arena of involvement. It theologises publicly on public dimensions of human living like the nature of the State, democracy, economics, market, society, civil society, bureaucracy, public policies, public institutions, public issues, cultural institutions, and public life. By so doing, it embarks upon a highly challenging path which involves in

> theologies emerged in a context prior to the advancement of the global world, and their audiences were typically the Christians; but today, we want every religious or secular community to make liberation their ideal, and therefore the need of proposing a public liberation–contextual theology. Another associated question is, does public theology not emerge from the erstwhile political theology, which was named by Latin American liberation theologians as the bourgeois theology of the rich? Again, my short answer would be, politics is not any more the domain of the bourgeois, and people's politics needs to be revolutionised in an important way today. A public theology, as undertaken from the Indian context will be at once contextual and public, and therefore, we could pursue a subaltern public theology. Another question that comes from philosophically oriented people is: Is it not an aspect of the post-modern trend today? Perhaps, it needs a longer answer: Public theology is both post-modern and modern in its philosophical underpinnings. It does not get satisfied with the post-modern understanding of reality as fragments, though it does, along with the post-modernists, question the eternal validity of universal meta-narratives. It envisions bringing about an interactive, inter-subjective universality between the *fragments* so as to be able to hold a public opinion in a global world. In addition, it believes in the need of a transcendental referent for our public life, be it in its political, economic, social, cultural, and familial aspects. Yet another important question could be, "Can public theology proposed by Christians in India, a minority population, be really public?", "Does it not suit countries which are predominantly Christian?" My answer would be: countries are increasingly becoming multi-religious, and no country can assume power over the public due to the salience of one particular religion; in the Indian context too, we are acutely becoming aware of the multi-religiosity of our country, and it is precisely in such a context that public theology, which is inter-religious and ecumenical, becomes meaningful and necessary.

[25] It is a phrase from John Rawls to stand for the religio-ethical doctrines which give a comprehensive explanation of reality.

politics without however seeking to establish itself at the level of a constitutionally democratic State.[26]

Its modus operandi is *conversation* on public policies and means to achieve common good. It means that we begin to reflect upon public issues from the perspective of faith, and that we consider Christianity, with all its denominational variants together ("communion of communion") as a public church in relation to other religions, ideologies, and statecraft.

Public Theology in the Indian Context

Though the concerns of public theology are basically common between the continental and the Indian variants, they seem to approach these concerns from different standpoints. The political theology proper that arose in Europe was aimed at de-privatising the Christian faith so as to intervene and contribute to a political process to heal such negativities as Nazism, Facism and world wars. The context of its emergence was a public life thickened with secularity, carrying the legacies of the French Revolution and the birth of hardcore secularism, denying any role for religion in the public sphere. The public theology of the North American context emerged from a context of a different rendering of secularity wherein religion was practised as fervently as protecting the wall of separation between the State and religion. What was of crucial importance for the public theology of North America was the question of plurality of religions, and its relationship to the public sphere and the State. Thus, the context of emergence of public theology, in spite of their common concerns, varied significantly even in the Euro-American context.

Public theology in India needs to proceed from a different standpoint, considering the history of the relationship between the State and religion in India. One of the central concerns here is to contribute to the development of a substantive democratic State with a discursive public sphere and an interactive civil society. The institutions of democracy in India are yet to grow in quality and strength to address questions of eradication of poverty and social discrimination, equity, social justice, human rights, community rights of minorities, sustainable development, and inter-religious amity.

Aloysius Pieris identifies the realities of poverty on the one hand, and deep religiosity, on the other, as the twin realities which provide the form and content of public and political theology in Asia. It has to hold together, he says, "The two baptisms of Jesus: first at the 'Jordan of Asian religiosity'

---

[26] It is in place to quote Charles Davis, who, speaking about theology and political society says: "Political society expresses its faith in the transcendent by its refusal to establish an official religion." Charles Davis, *Theology and Political Society* (New York: Cambridge University Press, 1980), 20.

... and second on the 'Calvary of Asian poverty'"[27]that Christ "does not compete with the founders of other religions but cross-fertilises Asian religiosity with the politics of poverty as no other teacher has done".[28] As Pieris surmises, the concerns of inter-religious relationship and the commitment for the eradication of poverty do present themselves to be the salient concerns of public theology in India and Asia. Felix Wilfred gives further emphasis to Pieris's reflections, by identifying four major areas of concerns for Asian public theology: (1) defence of freedom against State despotism of various kinds and grades, (2) defence of the poor from the tyranny of the market, (3) creation of harmony and non-exclusive communities, and (4) protecting the environment.[29] Observing that Christianity in Asia is generally "isolated from the public life of society", Wilfred calls for an active involvement in the enhancement of "public reason" to address matters of public concern. Sebastian Kim, another contributor to public theology in global and Asian contexts, speaks about the public role Christian theology, and Christian Scripture as a public book, can play to address issues of common good, to work for economic justice, to inspire interactive pluralism between religions, and to nurture the church to grow to be a public body. What we find highlighted by these theologians as important concerns of public theology in the Asian/Indian context are not so much the reflexive questions of whether theology can or need to play a public role as the concerns of common good to which public theology has to respond to.

In this context, it is not so much the concerns of taking on a privatising secularity as in Europe and a condition of religious plurality as in North America, but the question of strengthening a democratic state, with its discursive public and civil spheres, which obtains priority for political and public theology in India today. A substantively participatory democracy is of theological value because of peoples' hopes and aspirations attendant upon such a political vision for India. When a constitutional democracy was established in India, the hopes especially of the subaltern people of India were raised: they began to imagine a political community which would ensure economic equity, social equality, civil liberties, human rights, and dignity to all sections of people. Dr. Ambedkar, the chief architect of the Constitution, integrated these transforming hopes in the democratic instrument. The secular Constitution came as an instrument of hope that opened up an agenda for social justice (the affirmative action), embodying the general will for retributive justice to the subalterns. In this context, there was no negative understanding of the role of religion in the

---

[27] Aloysius Pieris, "Political Theologies in Asia", *Blackwell Companion to Political Theology*, eds., Peter Scott and William T. Cavanaugh (New York: Blackwell, 2004), 260.,
[28] Pieris, "Political Theologies in Asia", 261.
[29] Felix Wilfred, *Asian Public Theology—Critical Concerns in Challenging Times* (New Delhi: ISPCK, 2010), xii–xiv.

public sphere.[30] The focus was on *opening the public* to everyone. That the Constitution provided for the right of the State to intervene and open up the temples for the subalterns is a case in point. Thus, the Constitution and the general ethos of the subalterns stood for a secularity that brought radical opening of the public, implying action for social justice. A subaltern public theology would then premise itself upon this hope of an *emancipatory secularity* that keeps opening the public, opening up the spaces of freedom and opportunities.

This, however, brings in the question of the relationship of religion to the democratic State in India. "Can this principle of secularism guide the relationship of religion to the Indian state?", "If yes, what is the nature and content of this secularism?"—are relevant questions here. It needs to be straightaway clarified that what we are concerned about here is political secularism, that is, secularism as a principle to guide political decisions, and not creation of a secular culture or ethos as prevalent in Western societies. Donald E. Smith, one of the early commentators on the matter, opined that India's success as a secular State depended upon how it performed in terms of freedom of religion (freedom to believe, practise, propagate, and so on, including associational practice of religion), citizenship (entitlements for equality and equity), and separation of State and religion (mutual non-interference). He assessed that India stood a fair chance of emerging to be a secular State. His yardsticks, however controversial and programmatic though, are not irrelevant today, especially when one wishes India to work towards realising the egalitarian values. Independent India, in its initial stages, was indeed guided by these inner components of Indian secularism, even while facing serious challenges in terms of the emerging communal forces, including the trauma of Partition. However, the emergence of the majoritarian communal political force during the post-independent phase of Indian history, seeking to delegitimise the vision of secularism enshrined in the Constitution as pseudo-secularism, has brought in serious challenges to the secular democratic State of India. This force, as it has become a ruling dispensation today, seeks not only to dominate the political arena but also to hegemonise the religio-cultural consciousness of the people of India with such intents as manufacturing consent, constructing a Hindu identity to be presented to the global arena, retaining the ascriptive social hierarchy by strengthening the cultures attendant upon it, and so on. Its voice is growing louder, resulting in silencing of minority voices, stifling of civil liberties attendant upon one's citizenship, shrinking of the democratic space of debate and dissent,[31] and

---

[30] It is revealing to see Ambedkar, the architect of the Indian Constitution, taking recourse to conversion to Buddhism in order to ameliorate the conditions of the subalterns.

[31] Romila Thapar, *The Public Intellectuals in India* (New Delhi: Aleph Book Company, 2015).

relegating ultimately the transforming hopes of the subaltern people to the backyard of politics.

Alternatives to this dominant force are growing feebler today. The Left movement, with its doctrinaire understanding of secularism, is growing thinner at the national level. The centrist forces too are dissipating. It is at this juncture that we are being challenged to reflect on a political theology that can contribute to the strengthening of the Indian democratic State and its attendant public and civil spheres.

The interpretation of Indian secularism as principled distance by Rajeev Bhargava is a rather good insight. He makes an argument that this secularism is different from the Western *laicite* and wall of separation varieties, and best suited for situations of deep religious diversities as in India.[32] Though Bhargava's proposal is relevant, one is left with a question whether the principled distance will be able to keep a *principled* distance under the weight of majoritarian political force and hegemony.

We need an effective secular principle which neither establishes any religion in any manner at the level of the State, nor gets closed up against the contributions of religions. Indian secularism would be tested by the success it achieves in terms of realising the transformative goals of the Constitutional State. The relationship of religion to the State and the public sphere too, therefore, needs to be tested on the touchstone of these transforming goals. As Donald E. Smith envisaged, the touchstone of secular democracy was the relative autonomous functioning of citizenship, religion, and State, freed from mutual interference and domination. This triad is the cornerstone of a substantive democracy, which would ensure the realisation of the transformative goals. Citizenship stands for the duties and rights, including the entitlements to freedom from multiple wants; freedom of religion stands for the rights of an individual for choice of religion; and, the State, politically separated from religion, stands for the common good a community is pursuing politically.

We Christians need a public theology which contributes to the nurturance of these three triads in India. The form and content of citizenship draw their vitality from the Christian theological anthropology of "created in the image and likeness of God", which is, as the contemporary critique has brought home, less anthropocentric and more theocentric to network with the entire creation in constructing the form and content of citizenship. Freedom of religion is the source of transcendence for a humanity that is being choked by immanentist impulses today. Religions need to

---

[32] Rajeev Bhargava, "How Should States Deal with Deep Religious Diversity?—Can anything be learned from the Indian Model of Secularism?" in *Rethinking Religion and World Affairs*, eds. Timothy Samuel Shah, Alfred Stepan and Monica Duffy Toft (Oxford: Oxford University Press, 2012), 73–114.

play an active role in the civil sphere to help humanity imbue the spirit of transcendence and transpersonal relationships of sacrifice, dedication, and mutuality. Civil society is the sphere where different religions can come together in an ambience of freedom to work for common good. The strength of religious plurality lies in its ability to be in relationship with others. A secular State provides the space where people as citizens can relate to one another but on a transcendental basis, journeying towards ever greater realisations of common good. While a theory of social contract, as proposed by liberal politics, undergirds the emergence of the modern State, it is the need of the hour to nourish the State with transcendental dimensions, lest it becomes an instrument of human creed and power-mongering. A transcendental nourishment of the State, even in the Indian context wherein religiosity is already high among the people, is of crucial importance.

Church as a Public Body

Church in India has been, openly or latently, doing a form of political theology for a long period in history. Its notable phases began with the sixteenth century, when Catholic missionaries introduced the printed literature to Indian society and, strengthened the practices of debates which Indian litterateurs were used to having in exclusionary circles.[33] Debates on religious issues, increasingly growing by the production of classical literature (religious and secular), began to nurture a discursive practice of argumentation in the public. During the nineteenth century, when the Protestant missionaries and colonial officials showed interest in printing Oriental as well as English literatures, the discursive practice further grew in the Indian public. The significant contribution of the Protestant missionaries, and later the colonial dispensation, made to introduce modern mass education provided the essential component of the discursive practices. The church was present in these debates, albeit in a latent and indirect manner.

In spite of these significant contributions to the public sphere, the Indian church (consisting of various churches) today remains rather isolated from the wider Indian public. This is due to several reasons: first, it still carries the tag of being Western, because of its missionary inception and apparent patronage in different ways; second, its cultural identity is marked out significantly from other cultural communities in India; third, its political identity of being a minority community, both imposed and assimilated, isolates it invisibly, and; fourth, its social identity, constituted primarily by the subaltern people of India, works as a subtext for social exclusion. These and other reasons have kept the Indian church estranged

---

[33] Amartya Sen proposes the theory that Indians are known for their argumentative behaviour. Amartya Sen, *The Argumentative Indian—Writings on Indian Culture, History and Identity* (London: Penguin Books, 2005).

from the wider public, in spite of the fact that its contributions have been undeniable.

The church in India needs to become a *public body* today, by overcoming these hurdles. It needs to become public not so much to project itself and its activities as to bear witness to its faith in a transcendent God, whose revelation the community called the church experienced in the words, deeds, death, and resurrection of Jesus Christ, the incarnate God. It was in Jesus Christ that this community began to experience the encounter of history and mystery of transcendence in a transforming manner. A call for transformation of relationships, embodying mutuality, creativity, and peace, was the core of this encounter. This transforming experience needs to continue through history and church as a community needs to be a catalyst in this. In so doing, the church finds the liberal democratic institutions of the State and civil society, however fragile and failing though, the most solicitous, and brings itself in participatory solidarity with these institutions to mediate the experience of transforming relationships.

Inasmuch as these institutions are public, the church body itself is a public. It cultivates the character of publicness within its own body as much as in the wider society. It makes itself a public body, by imbibing the spirit and practice of democracy, doing away with unmeaning hierarchies; it makes itself a public sphere, wherein a public reasoning can take place among the believers; and it makes itself a civil society wherein the spirit of participatory democracy among the community of equals can be cultivated.

It should become public also in the sense of becoming more interactive in the wider public. There are several ways in which it can become publicly interactive. A very unassuming but firmly witnessing way is to bear witness to the Christian values whenever or wherever we hold public offices. Christian subjects, in their embodied personhood, can be the best witness to the transforming values. Another way of becoming public is interacting in conversational publics with the Christian vision of events and issues. Needless to point out the fact that the Christian voice does not emerge significantly in media publics, at least not proportionate to the education that it has received. Yet another important way, challenging though, is becoming accountable to the wider public in matters public. Churches have the highest level of human resources, individually and collectively; but, what is the output of the church to the wider society? Can we have an auditing of human resources? Similarly, can we institute mechanisms for social auditing, opening ourselves for external examination as to how inclusive and open our communal relationships are? This is not an argument to enflame the communal consciousness; but only to see that the Indian church becomes truly public, effectively interacting in the public, without burying its head in deep furrows of self-pity and defeatism.

By Way of Concluding

Public theology was born in the West against the forces of privatisation of religion, rendering the public vulnerable to greed, instrumentalism, power-hunger, prowess of exploitation, and so on, and it emerged as a viability of religious plurality, existing within a democratic polity. It took on the reality of secularity critically, and sought to go beyond its dictates. But the reality is different in India, rather, in the Asian context. Political theologies here have been endeavouring to construct a meaningful secularity, seen as the attribute of the very salvation that Christian faith is speaking about, to actualise the transforming ideals of liberty, equality, justice, and civil liberties in human societies. Going along with this lead, Indian public theology would endeavour to strengthen the rudiments of political secularism so as to make it capable of achieving the transforming goals, especially opening the public spaces to the subaltern people of India. It would imagine a public that secures the individual identities of different others, even while fostering a common bond between them.

3

AN INDIAN PUBLIC THEOLOGY OF MISSION

"Journeying with the Spirit"

The mission command of Jesus, as presented by the evangelists, is to "proclaim the good news to the whole creation" (Mark 16: 15) and "make disciples of all nations" (Matt 28:19) by announcing "repentance and forgiveness of sins" (Luke 24:47). It was an invitation to believe in the arrival of the Reigning of God with its ultimate freedom for the whole of creation. It was a call which emerged, not just at the end of Jesus's mission, but through the life, death, and resurrection of Jesus, and was given out unto the eschatological times; and that took root in history as an event of mission.

Early Christians gave meaning to this mission through a life of sharing and sacrifice. By witnessing to their faith in Jesus even through martyrdom, they gave unfathomable depth to the event of mission. Paul, with his reflections and missionary activities, constructed a theological horizon to this event. Good News, in his theological vision, stood for redemption from human sinfulness through the justifying faith (Rom 1:17), resulting in the freedom of the children of God (Rom 8: 21; Gal 5:1).

The Patristic era added its own semantic layer to the mission command. The church became the embodiment of mission. Augustine of Hippo portrayed the church as analogous to Noah's ark to take humanity on board from the deluge of sinfulness that continuously engulfed them. Doctrines developed through a critical process of approval and disapproval, after which the church, along with its structures and creed, became the visible reality to be created everywhere by Christian mission. The long period until the birth of the Reformation had lived with this ecclesia-centric vision of mission, taken in a very broad sense.

The Reformation era shifted the site of mission from the church to the believer, the human person. Experiencing directly the divine revelation through the help of the Scriptures, the believer had to decide for or against God, in order to avail the eternal life destined for the children of God.

Bondage of the will, suffered due to the depravity of human nature, had to be overcome with the aid of divine grace, approached through faith alone. Consequent upon this realisation, the event of mission came to centre round the act of proclamation, the evangelical act mediating the promise of salvation to the believer. Reading, understanding, and preaching the word of God became a desideratum for the event of mission during the Reformation era.

It may be said that our global world shifts the site of mission to the wider public. Public is the space where different others, even incommensurably different others meet, converse, and have their living and being. This is a space that is constituted by plurality of religions, ethical doctrines, cultural traditions, scientific disciplines, and ideologies besides social, cultural, economic, and political activities and systems. In this space, the church and the believer are certainly the visible agents of mission, but they do it inter-subjectively, listening to the voices heard from different others.

The meaning of becoming effective agents of mission in the public is joining in with the Spirit of God at the public sphere. Rowan Williams said it well on Christian mission as "finding out where the Holy Spirit is at work and joining in". The well-known *Missio Dei* mission paradigm exhorted us that mission is the church joining in with the initiative of the Triune God—the Father sending the Son and the Spirit to redeem and reconcile the creation with God's own self. From within this Trinitarian mission paradigm, today, going by the signs of the time, we are called upon to join in with the Spirit of God who discloses God's self to us. As the Spirit of God blows where she wills (John 3:8), by going beyond boundaries, we too need to cross the boundaries to join in with the Spirit of God. Public is that space beyond boundaries, and public theology is the light with which we search for the Spirit of God in that space.

The early Christian and the patristic eras presented mission as a command to continue to actualise the self-communication/revelation of God that occurred in Jesus Christ. Preserving the fullness of this revelation and passing it on effectively to successive generations became a major concern for mission. The Reformation era presented mission as proclaiming the self-communication of God here and now to the believer. Rather than remembering a past, actualising a present (here and now) gifted by God became the major concern of the Reforming mission. Continuing along these orientations upon the past and the present, our mission today has an eschatological orientation, and it is the Spirit of God, who leads us towards this future. One remembers the prediction of the mystic Joachim of Fiore (1135–1202) that the future is going to be an era of the Holy Spirit.

Opening the Public by the Spirit of God

The Spirit of God opens the public transformatively so that every form of life (nature, humans, and life other than humans), especially that which gets subjugated through the manipulations of the dominant, *participates in the public conversation* and experiences the creative, redemptive, and accompanying presence of the Spirit of God. The public is the meeting point of different individuals and collective/institutional others, to mediate life and freedom. Meeting points, unfortunately, are infected today with the sinfulness of the created reality, as evident in its intransigence and closure towards the future and towards different others. Social, psychological, cultural, political, and economic factors which initiate and maintain such closures are forms of exclusions, accumulations, deprivations, and discriminations. At the root of these closures are the historical mutations of the evil spirit, the embodiment of fear and insecurity in the face of the other.

The Spirit of the living God initiates us into the public, by gracefully opening the public for us. She opens the shutters—social, cultural, religious, political, and economic—which exclude the marginalised from the public. She, with her prophetic promptings, interrogates the hegemonic closures imposed on the public on the one hand, and, with her indwelling presence, enables (empowers) us to partake of the public, on the other. She gifts her indwelling presence in a public through multiple mediations, the religio-cultural traditions of the subaltern people being an important one at that.

This presence of the Spirit of God initiates a radical openness not merely to eternity, but to the future of the historical time as well. As Jürgen Moltmann put it, "This presence of the Spirit is the presence of future glory, which fulfils the times; it is not the presence of eternity, which obliterates time altogether... snatch people out of time but makes them open for time's future".[1] History, sometimes, has tempted or is tempting us to be pinned down to the past and selfishly glued to the immediate present. The Enlightenment modernity has contributed its share to the human experience of being lost in the immediate present. That, of all the millennia when human beings have lived on this earth, the past three-four modern centuries have contributed to the vandalising of the eco-system is a case in point. The instrumental rationality, when pushed to an extreme, spreads the sinful spirit of narrow immediacy. The Spirit of God motivates us to open ourselves, our consciousness in particular to the future.

---

[1] Jürgen Moltmann, *The Trinity and the Kingdom—The Doctrine of God* (Minneapolis: Fortress Press, 1993 [1981]), 124–125.

The opening, again, is a radical motivation to emerge out of self-centredness to go out to meet with the multiple strange others in the public. This horizontal opening towards historical others is a dynamic act which keeps overcoming multiple barriers on the way. The contemporary world presents us with the hurdles of fundamentalism based on religio-cultural and social identities. It is, then, the Spirit of God who expands our hearts and structures, and enables us to open the public from these fundamentalisms. Moses experienced this Spirit of God when he refused, on a complaint from Joshua, to stop Eldad and Medad from prophesying, saying, "Would that all the people of the Lord were prophets! Would that the Lord might bestow his spirit on them all!" (Num 11: 27-29). The well-known Pneumatological text of Joel 2: 28-29, speaking about pouring out the spirit on all flesh—sons, daughters, young, old, male, and female, gives a universal outreach to the realm of the Spirit and it resonates well with the open public. This openness is a singular gift of the Spirit of God specially meant for public life. Jesus, upon being anointed by the Holy Spirit, initiated a proclamation to open the public to the poor, captives, blind, and the oppressed (Luke 4: 16-19). Paul, led by the Spirit, mediated the offer of salvation to the Gentiles, and stoutly defended it. These openings of the Spirit of God continue in history today in and through individuals, organisations, movements, and ideologies which struggle to open the public for all the creation of God.

THE CONTEXT OF THE PUBLIC THEOLOGY OF MISSION

It sounds rather odd to propose a public theology of mission for the Indian church, when majoritarian politics seems to engulf the Indian public, relegating minority religious traditions to defensive, indifferent, and relatively silent positions! Against such a background, the Indian church going public with its mission would seem to go against the mood present generally among minority religious communities to silently suffer the domination; or, it would seem practically imprudent to go public, when the public is dominated by a majority. It is at this juncture that I propose the relevance, meaningfulness, and even the vibrancy of public mission with a public theology of mission.

Public theology's new context of emergence is the public world that we are witnessing today. The global world goes public in more than one way: there is no more a private world which is not impacted or brought into conversation with others; there is a steady crossing of boundaries between religious, cultural, social, political, and economic worlds; the advancing communication technologies are making most of the private matters public through social media; and, most important of all, the public—the base of the human population, is beginning to participate in the hitherto esoteric and specialised domains of knowledge and wisdom, which is witnessed to in the emergence of disciplines like public sociology, public philosophy, public theology, and practical theology. Public world, therefore, is the increasing pool of common life, progressively shared by the base-section of the human population.

The varied features of the public world comes to hinge upon two fundamental processes of the contemporary world: one, the ubiquitous experience of radical pluralism in all aspects of human living like religion, ethics, aesthetics, culture, and so on, including medicine, economics, and politics. There is no one standard system in these fields which can be presented as the un-qualified universal system. The kind of plurality which emerges today is not merely quantitatively, but even qualitatively new, and it demands of us to re-envision our understanding of the universals. It is an era wherein plurality sets the stage to understand the universal, rather than the other way round. Second, the process that is known as post-modernity in literature, art, and architecture flowing into ethical, religious, and philosophical domains is experienced all over the world today. It is, as in the words of Francois Lyotard, the incredulity of meta-narratives, a radical interrogation of some of those master-narratives which had gone so deep into our individual, collective, and civilisational consciousness that we did not have the reflexive ability to think about them critically; but today, these master narratives have come under the scanner of reflexivity, and the central narrative which is being interrogated is what had been projected as the universal human rationality. The cultural underpinnings of this projected universality of human reasoning is emerging these days very forcefully. On the basis of these experiences, that secularity of human rationality which had an anti-religious stance and its self-assumed pre-eminence in matters public is also being interrogated today.

Against the background of the emergence of these two salient trends, theology itself becomes public, in the sense that theological language cannot be brushed aside as irrational, but is to be taken as a meaningful discourse relevant for a public conversation. It can present its truth to the public, and expect the public to engage with it in a wholesome manner. Its validity is ensured not so much by human rationality as by the public, which interacts or engages with it. As Max L. Stackhouse would put it, "Every theology, as proposal, has to meet the test of public reception—according to what manifests the truth, justice, and mercy of God and what the public can internalise from it and weave into the fabric of the common life to enhance their moral, spiritual, and material existence."[2] By allowing

---

[2] Max L. Stackhouse, *God and Globalization—Globalization and Grace* (New York: Continuum, 2007), 84.

the public to become the validating source, theology goes public in a characteristically new way today.

A public theology of mission is anchoring on certain characteristic features of the context today. Some of the salient ones are:

Context of World Religions

We are living in an era of world religions today. World religions do not stand for a world-enveloping imperial reality, but for a ubiquitous reality, found everywhere. Empirically speaking, every major religion today has obtained global presence and networks. The modern open societies have become thickly multi-religious, while the restrictive societies are beginning to feel the power of global networks of different major religions of the world. Paradoxically though, religions obtaining global magnitude come with a radical disclaimer to absolutistic universalising discourse on their religious claims. Being in the vicinity of multiple religions, every major religion today becomes sensitive to the presence as well as discourse of others. This sensitivity initiates relationality, mutuality, and a necessity for interaction. World religions are therefore not imperial in any sense, but relational in a fundamental sense.

Christianity has become one of the very powerful world religions today. It has its presence, in terms of all its major denominations, in almost all the countries of the world, except perhaps in the Middle East and in some other Muslim countries.[3] Such an emphatic presence, paradoxically though, does not generate a universalistic theological discourse, but, rather, diverse theological discourses richly informed by indigenous contexts or indigenous Christianities. The issues that Christianity grapples with are also locally characterised, rather than dictated from above. It has brought about a world church, or a communion of global Christianities[4] consisting of multiple layers and varieties of transnational networks, more in terms of networks of local churches.

This new context of world religions and global Christianities necessitate a new theology of mission from Christianity. The new comparative theology proposed by a section of Christian theologians[5] today is a mark of the new context of world religions today. Similarly, we need to think of a new theology of mission for the contemporary world.

---

[3] Sebastian Kim and Kirsteen Kim, *Christianity as a World Religion* (London: Bloomsbury, 2008).
[4] Felix Wilfred, *Christians for a Better India* (New Delhi: ISPCK, 2014).
[5] Frank Clooney is one of the prominent proponents of the new comparative theology in the context of the discourse on world religions. Francis X Clooney, S.J., *Comparative Theology—Deep Learning Across Religious Borders* (UK: Wiley-Blackwell, 2010).

Context of Accentuated Experience of Exclusion

Yet another context that is relevant to public theology of mission is the subtle but accentuated experience of social and economic forms of exclusion human beings are experiencing today. In a country like India, the subaltern sections of people suffer from age-old forms of social and economic exclusions, along with patriarchal oppression if they are women. Caste-based social discrimination has kept the subaltern people away from the ambit of civil liberties, which are some of the central features of a democratic public sphere; endemic poverty has kept a considerable number (at least one third) of the Indian people below the poverty line and away from economic opportunities; and the deeply entrenched patriarchy has kept women away from public spheres. Today even amidst global opportunities, the exclusion of the poor from economic empowerment has got only accentuated, given the fact that the proportion of those enjoying economic prosperity is thinning down, creating a chasm between the rich and the poor; the traditional forms of social discrimination is getting reproduced even in the global contexts of migration.

A theology of public mission would confront these forms of exclusion. The core vision of Jesus's mission, the unfolding of the Reigning of God, is a mission to open the sites of life especially to those excluded in multiple ways—the sick, the social outcastes, the children and women, the poor, and so on. The experience of God, as mediated by the life and mission of Jesus, went forth to break all the barriers so as to open the gates of life to everyone. The Pauline mission sought to break the barrier between Jews and Gentiles so that everyone could receive the good news of salvation by faith. Whenever the church committed the sin of excluding a person or a people, there were regenerative initiatives or movements which emerged in history to break open the walls of exclusion. It is therefore a responsibility that rests upon the disciples of Jesus to continue to break the walls of exclusion so as to make the public sphere free and open.

Public Theology of Mission as...

Has the Christian mission in India ever been private? It has always been public, undertaken in the public realm, with the people in the public arena. However, the nature of public-ness has been characteristically self-assumed and one-sided. But today, the public world provides the ambience for a different way of being public—to be mutual and relational. The following are some of the ways in which it can be differently public:

Mission as a Public Conversation

A public Christian mission places everything in the gaze of the public, for understanding, responding to, and even making critique upon. It does not exclude anyone from the possibility of being responded to. Though it firmly believes in the uniqueness of its message, it understands in a fundamental sense that religious language, including its own, put forth in the public by several religious traditions, can communicate beyond their particular traditions. With this basic realisation, Christian mission presents its vision as a public statement. It presents its goal of transforming the contemporary society, characterised by multiple sinful closures, to be a society that can experience the divine mystery, by way of opening itself up to freedom of life. In presenting this vision, it announces its faith in the divine grace that comes through the person and message of Jesus Christ. While doing so, it beseeches God to give it the humility and openness to free itself from obstacles of triumphalism and assumption of superiority of truth. Its claim on a unique revelation, it believes, can be publicly communicated and conversed meaningfully.

Mission, thus, becomes a public conversation. It is a conversation, different from the inter-religious dialogue in that it does not seek to convince the other of the truth that one has realised, but seeks together the truth as co-seekers, and does not confine to sharing or exchange of religious truth-claims, but engages the political implications of the truth-claims which affect the life of the whole creation; "political" here would mean the fundamental process of collective-decision making, and not just the politics of representation. Politics is the space that expresses the collective will of the people, a space where different others experience a binding between them, and even beyond them to the ultimately transcendent God.

When we undertake this public conversation, say in a civil society group or in a platform of the political society, we follow the virtues of genuine conversations. It is to express our faith, without getting stuck within personal fideism, and it is to become confident of expressing the position of our faith in the public, without relegating it to the private sphere. As Max Stackhouse puts it: "A public theology ... differs from those forms of fideism that assert purportedly universal and absolute beliefs on the basis of a presumed infallibility of one or another tradition's scripture, or on the basis of any materialist fundamentalism or humanistic metaphysic that denies the possibility that transcendence could or should be the resource in life or thought."[6]

Mission as Making the Christian Values Public

Public theology of mission is to propose to the wider public to imbibe those Christian values that we consider the best of Christian witnesses. Christianity, for example, has been privileging all through its history the

---

[6] Stackhouse, *God and Globalization*, 78.

value of service to humanity as an integral part of its faith. Such is the integration of its faith and service that it considers loving God impossible without love of neighbour. It has endeavoured to live this faith-based service all through its history. Christianity in India has been, and is known for its service to the people of India. It is known in particular for the service it has rendered to the lowly, the marginalised, and the subaltern people of India.

Service to others, especially to the lowly, is then, a pristine faith-based value of Christianity. How does the wider public respond to this? Has it meaningfully understood this service? Perhaps not yet! It is quite perceptive of Felix Wilfred to point out to the fact that the caste-based consciousness of the Indian society might treat Christian service to others as nothing but the caste-based duty of the Christian *shudra* to serve others.[7] It means that Christian service is not appreciated for its faith-based value, but only for fulfilling a caste-based duty, which is but incumbent upon them. This socio-religious attitude not only belittles but also de-radicalises the Christian vision of service. Service to the subalterns, as part of the Christian vision, is nothing short of aiming at the total liberation of humanity from its bondages. It would imply, in the Indian context, the liberation specifically from bondages imposed by the sinful system of caste. The Indian contextual theology of Dalit theology has brought out this point very poignantly to the Indian Christian mind.

It is time that Christianity endeavours to bring home this point to the Indian mind as well. The Christian ideal of service needs to be put across to the Indian public as part of its public mission today. Even while acknowledging the appreciation that emerged for the kind of service rendered by a saintly person like Mother Teresa of Kolkata, we need to initiate a debate upon the value of the abiding service Indian Christianity has made to the emergence of the subaltern people of this land. This is not to look for accolades, but to propose such a service to others as well.

Mission as Making Public Values Christian

It is not merely in giving, but also in receiving that public mission obtains its significance. Christianity in India needs to make some of the quintessential values of the public its own. For example, democracy is the best of public values that an open society endeavours to cultivate. The church needs to cultivate this value of democracy within its inner space too. Participation of the members of the church in its decision-making process is a desideratum for the recognition of the church as a public person. The long-standing imbalance of power between laity and clergy, men and women, rich and poor, with closures along the lines of caste, language,

---

[7] Wilfred, *Christians for a Better India*, 72.

region, and so on, should be rectified in order for the church to become a genuine public institution. By way of nurturing inner democracy, the church should promote the growth of public sphere within its body too. Public sphere is the space where discussions and debates take place in an atmosphere of freedom of opinion. The church needs to form several forums where such discussions and debates can take place. Growth of such forums will have direct bearing upon the quality of public sphere, and eventually the quality of democracy practised within the church.

The church, in the era of public mission, must also place itself under economic, ethical, and other important forms of auditing from independent agencies. Shedding its image of being a pampered organisation under the cover of a charitable organisation, it must submit itself to external auditing of its financial accounts; by way of evaluating its moral standards, it must submit itself to ethical auditing to see whether it is genuinely committed to the values and objectives that it stands for; by way of reviewing the efficient management of human resources, it must submit itself for an auditing in this regard too; and, by way of evaluating its impact upon the wider society, it must undertake a social auditing as well. The list can continue. By applying all these forms of auditing, the church will emerge as a public organ, through a process of maturing in transparency and public interactions.

The leadership of the church will have to grow more steadily in the public value of democracy, transparency, and accountability. The church leadership should measure up to the leadership in the civil public arena. Those who occupy these positions must regularly update themselves in leadership skills and qualities, and improve upon their standard of performance. Those that cannot perform should have the humility to leave the opportunities to others. These are some of the public values in relation to the exercise of leadership which the church should also cultivate within itself.

Mission as Commitment to Common Good

Commitment to common good is becoming extremely precarious today. A world dominated by corporate business houses, forms of moral relativism, and the process of individualism creates extreme ambiguities as regards the common good. Private enterprises with motives of profit, sectarian demands camouflaged under identity discourses, salience of corrupt and unmeaning immoral practices in the public arena, and the dissipation of collective forms of living including family life due to extreme forms of individualism have only obscured the vision of common good. It is in this context, Christianity, along with other religious traditions of the world, needs to promote a clear commitment for common good.

The Catholic Social Teachings rest upon a relevant vision of the common good. Similarly, the World Council of Churches too incorporates the vision of common good in its teachings. While we acknowledge the way different denominations of Christianity have endeavoured to highlight the value of common good, we are called upon today to become aware of the way different religious traditions too promote common good in their own unique ways. Our public mission today is to serve as a catalyst to bring together the visions of different religious traditions on common good so that there can be a synergy between them. Such endeavours must emerge out of our deep convictions that different religions are equally valuable sources of the moral consciousness of humanity.

Endeavouring to bring the religious traditions around the vision of common good is an effective way of re-generating the public sphere with moral values. It will simultaneously address the two important concerns of public theology by making religious plurality meaningful and the secular public morally sensitive. Religious plurality is something vibrant, while religious pluralism is anaemic. Religious plurality can live in active efforts to bring different religions together for common good. Similarly, the secular public sphere can be healed of the dominating evil spirits like crass individualism, ruthless competition for profit, violent clashes between identity-related ideologies, and so on.

SITES OF THE PUBLIC THEOLOGY OF MISSION

Public Sphere as the Site of Public Mission

Public theology of mission cannot be pursued without the availability of a public sphere, a domain which lives in discursive practices like conversation, contestation, interrogation, negotiation, etc. Generally, it is the civil society where such practices take place. To the extent these practices are effective, to that extent they transform the social systems for better freedom, equality, dignity, and well-being. There is no gainsaying the fact that historically, Christianity contributed significantly to the emergence of a discursive public, by introducing the printing press, publication of classics, imparting modern education to the wider public, and so on. A historic contribution worthy of Indian Christianity is that it has enabled a section of the subaltern people of India to gain the ability to participate in the discursive public sphere of India. However, the strength of this contribution seems to be weakening today: the political sphere, media space, educational sphere, bureaucracy, and other public systems have come to be dominated by the dominant sections of the people of India. It is indeed a challenge to empower the subalterns to participate in the contemporary public sphere, especially with their agenda for social justice.

Public Issue as the Site of Christian Mission

There was an era when Christianity considered its primary site of mission the religious others, who had to know about the religious truth that it was proclaiming. Then came a time when it thought that all have their own truths, and that everyone needs be enriched by the other through dialogue. Today, the public theology of mission proposes that we, the different others, shed theological and ethical lights on every public issue so that the whole of humanity can be guided for taking the right decision. For example, bio-ethical issues today need the light from different religious others, and they cannot be just left to the wisdom of the so-called professional medical community, which is not free of its own vested interests; or, the political vision of a ruling party, or the political economy of a particular time, or the decisions of the government which affect the sentiments of different religious others need to be discussed and debated in public, and we must be prepared for such a debate.

Yet another important factor that dominates the contemporary life is technology, including the advanced information technology. Jürgen Habermas spoke about the domination of our life-world by the systems of modernity. Technology is one such system that dominates the ambience not only of our actions but also of our thinking, sensing, feeling, and so on. Such a dominating presence of technology conditions our way of being in the world today, our fundamental experiences related to intimacy, aesthetics, ethics, and transcendence. The world of technology, in spite of its positive contributions, works on many occasions to create closures in our thinking and imagination, if we are not critically alert to its dynamics. Technology can create "heaven" on earth, by substituting the reverence we have to an eschatological future heaven. It can, as Paul Tillich cautioned against the danger of creation of humans as automatons in an industrial world, approximate us to robotics. Un-proportionate growth of technology can lead to sinful exploitation of nature, including the biology of humanity. It is against this undue dominance of technology that religious traditions have to enter into the public arena with their voices of wisdom and faith.

Mission to the Modern Public Sphere

Modernity has achieved some fundaments for our public life. Through its different features, including the modern mass education, it has created the ambiences for the practice of public interactions and discourses; by bringing in the constitutional democracy and the rule of law, it has introduced the possibility for the practice of public virtues of equality, justice, liberty, and fraternity; through its communication technological advancement, it has opened the channels of communication across space and time; by bringing an element of economic power to the marginalised, it has made them assertive to stand for their dignity; by introducing modern political processes like representative politics and elections, it has empowered wider sections of the people to participate in the public processes; and so on.

However, the same modernity has also worked to embed an instrumentalist reasoning in the modern mind; induced craze for power, comfort, and temporary success; introduced unmeaning and ruthless competition for opportunities, that human beings damage their sensitivity to others; introverted the human consciousness upon humanity itself, debilitating their capacity for transcendence; and so on. In the Indian context, modernity has not matured so as to actualise its stated ideals of individual liberty, economic parity, equality, and so on; it has, according to some scholars, become a fractured modernity',[8] benefitting only a middle class, positioning itself, with the cultural power, between the elite and the poor. Some scholars speak also of a retro-modernity in the Indian context.[9] It means that the proverbial python of the Indian caste system co-opts modernity in such a way that its anti-modern ascriptive hierarchy is adjusted, and not eradicated; the irrational ideology of purity-pollution which includes and excludes people at various layers of the public is radicalised with the support of the fractured modernity rather than being done away with; different castes compete with one another to upgrade themselves in a hierarchical system, rather than demolishing the empire of caste; it generates retrograde casteist organisations rather than opening up the public.

Such "fallenness of modernity" needs to be redeemed by connecting it to the depth dimension of life and to the transcendent dimension of the Divine. This can happen in the best possible way by opening the fountainheads of deep running cultural streams and connecting to the wellsprings of transcendence, the fountains of religious experiences. Our public mission is to serve as a catalyst to bring about a synergy between the modern public sphere and the fountains of religio-cultural wellsprings.

Mission to the Global Public Sphere

Public mission is a mission to bring faith to the heart of the public, which is nothing but the public space that keeps opening up at different sites of the contemporary global world. It opens up at the meeting points of different cultures, traditions, religions, ethical doctrines, social systems, economic endeavours, political boundaries, and so on. In short, it opens up when different others encounter one another. In our increasingly migratory world, these encounters have become an order of the day. People

---

[8] Sanjay Joshi, *Fractured Modernity—Making of a Middle Class in Colonial North India* (New Delhi: Oxford University Press, 2001).

[9] Manuela Ciotti, *Retro-Modern India—Forging a Low-Caste Self* (London: Routledge, 2010).

migrate primarily for livelihood, but when they do so, they carry with them their cultural traditions, social identities, ethical values, and religious practices. And there begins a process of encounter, and it challenges one to open oneself to the other, and individual encounters become collective encounters, and challenge every group to open itself to the other. These openings are the fountainhead of the new public spaces being created everywhere in the global world. When these public spaces are converted into sites of discussion and debates leading to collective decision-making, they become the new public spheres of the contemporary global world.

These public spheres are filled with potentialities and challenges. They take us beyond restrictive borders; open new avenues for the creative spirit of the humans to blossom; break open some of the long-standing ascriptive ties like caste, race, patriarchy, and so on; create economic opportunities for wider sections of people; bring in inter-cultural fecundations; promote inter-religious dialogue for peace and harmony; and so on. On the other hand, they also make the public sites vulnerable to the emergence of multiple forms of the fear of the other—inimical stereotyping, ethnocentrism, clash of civilisations, religio-cultural fundamentalism, and terrorism. It is indeed a challenge to garner the potentialities, while arresting or weakening the negative features.

Mission to the global public would endeavour to study and become aware of these global publics which open up in our local vicinities; identify the various potentialities as well as the challenges; organise the human resources available in the vicinity to garner the potentialities and arrest the negativities; bring together various movements of the people for the rights of the marginalised and oppressed; serve as a catalyst to bring together and synergise the different religio-cultural traditions of the neighbourhood; and, ultimately serve as the channel of imparting the experience of faith in the transcendent Divine. It is this faith that will ultimately promote the positive potentialities and heal the negativities of the new publics.

Adopting a Subaltern Location in Civil Society

Christianity is a significant player in the Indian civil society. As mentioned earlier, Indian Christianity has made a historical contribution to the birth of the Indian public sphere, and to the making of the rudiments of democracy. More recently, Indian Christianity has been present in the civil sphere in newer ways. By being a voluntary agency to undertake social welfare schemes, community health programmes, disaster management programmes, and conscientization programmes, Indian Christianity has been meaningfully present in the civil sphere. It continues to involve in human rights issues and in advocacy roles for the empowerment of the subaltern people, which are the relevant ways of doing public theology in India.

A Christian public theology in India would locate itself within this subaltern concern and converse with multiple religious others to bring to birth inter-religious contextual theologies for the empowerment of the subalterns. It would explore the meaning of Indian secularism too from the vantage point of the empowerment of the subaltern people of India. Lest it becomes an elitist theology of the burgeoning middle class, Indian Christian public theology needs to make conscious efforts to stay with subaltern concerns.

SALIENT ISSUES IN THE INDIAN PUBLIC THEOLOGY OF MISSION

A public theology of mission becomes a relevant theology by addressing the pertinent issues of a given context. The following are some of the pressing issues, I surmise, to be addressed by this theology in the Indian context:

Strengthening the Indian Democracy

Wherever there is creative and healthy public theology, there will also emerge a healthy system of democracy. India is yet to mature as a country with a substantive form of democracy. According to a democracy audit of countries across the globe,[10] India comes at the 52nd position, leaving much to be desired.

Christianity has been a major player in bringing Indian democracy to birth. Starting with its contribution in ensuing an Indian renaissance by bringing to light the Indian classical religio-cultural and philosophical heritage, with its contribution to the silent revolution of the subaltern classes of people by educating and imparting awareness of civil and human rights to them, with its contribution to the post-independent nation-building, and with its solidarity with the poor and the marginalised for their economic and social empowerment, Christianity has indeed played a significant role in nurturing the rudiments of democracy. Needless to say, as mentioned earlier, that Indian Christianity has contributed also to the emergence of a public sphere in India by way of introducing the print media, and then being present in the contemporary media world. These contributions make Indian Christianity even more responsible for the continuing growth of Indian democracy, in spite of the fact that Christianity is only a minority community in India.

Evangelical Christianity is one of the fastest growing religious phenomena in India. What will be the relationship between this Christianity and democracy in India is an important question for the public theology today. There are scholars who defend the suitability of

---

[10] http://www.worldaudit.org/democracy.htm as per March 2018 data, accessed May 5, 2018.

evangelical Christianity for democratic processes.[11] David Lumsdaine, for example, argues that, "The embrace of evangelical Christianity has often enabled poor and marginalised people to have greater prosperity, self-confidence, and civic skills and a more vital associational life and has consequently pushed societies toward more open and democratic processes".[12] Evangelical Christianity bases itself solely upon the biblical revelation, thus democratising the sphere of Christian faith on the basis of the holy text, enabling every individual, regardless of her ascriptive ties, practise Christianity on their own. This possibility of receiving the biblical revelation individually, legitimated with special gifts of the Spirit, contributes to the emergence of individual agency in societal relationships, and this motivates the individual to participate in the public sphere, resulting in the strengthening of democracy.

However, an important element in evangelical Christianity is persuasion in mission, which might ensue in argumentative conflicts with other religious traditions leading to unmeaning strife in the public sphere. And, again, it seems to go well with the rising middle classes, and can therefore forget the disparities being created by the market-led world in educational and employment opportunities. Democracy cannot be meaningful if it is creating newer forms of disparities and exclusions.

Religious Conversion in India

Religious conversion has been a perennial issue confronting especially Christians in the Indian context. Right from the time of the missionary era, conflicts and controversies have existed in this regard. However, the more recent and the contemporary times have added their own specific challenges. The phenomenon of nationalism, a political child of modernity, has engulfed the debate in a paralysing manner. Nationalist leaders and organisations of various hues have found fault with conversion, treating it as a de-nationalising force among Indians. Gandhi said, "If I had power and could legislate, I would outlaw proselytising".[13] Some provincial States went so far as to legislate upon anti-conversion laws right at the dawn of the Republic of India, fearing that the Scheduled Castes and Tribes of India would convert to Christianity. The amendments made to Hindu personal laws by *The Hindu Marriage Act (1955)* made inheritance of property by converts impossible, and the Presidential Order of 1950 denied the benefits of reservation to Christians of Scheduled Caste origin, which deterred Hindus from converting.

---

[11] David Halloran Lumsdaine, *Evangelical Christianity and Democracy in Asia* (New York: Oxford University Press, 2009).

[12] Lumsdaine, *Evangelical Christianity and Democracy in Asia*, 3.

[13] Cited in Bhagwan Josh, "Conversion, Complicity, and the State in Post-Independent India", in *Christianity and the State in Asia—Complicity and Conflict*, eds. Julius Bautista and Francis Khek Gee Lim (New York: Routledge, 2009), 97.

The contemporary era has given salience to religio-cultural nationalism as a framework for the practice of democracy in India, and this has resulted in the emergence of the Hindutva Right with its majoritarian politics. While majority of Hindus have fewer problems with religious conversion per se, the Hindutva Right which is posing as the representative of Hinduism provokes controversies and conflicts. It needs be noted, however, that a feeble voice among the Hindutva Right demands debate upon conversion, while the majority of the Hindutva Right harbour grudge against it and inflict violence upon Christians, their places of worship and religious symbols. The magnitude of such violence keeps rising day by day. The hegemonic ambience created by the Hindutva majoritarian rule against the minorities keeps generating strife and acts of violence.

Christians respond in various ways to violent incidents related to conversion. They show their solidarity with the victims of violence by visiting them; they mobilise economic support necessary for re-building the lives of the victims; they make representations to civil and political authorities to ameliorate the conditions of the victims; they demonstrate publicly against the violence done to them; they organise various initiatives for bringing back inter-religious amity in the locality of violence; they take legal course of actions to seek protection under the freedom of religion clause of the Constitution; and so on. These ways have become the general pattern of responding to violence related to conversion. Such responses are necessary and effective in the immediate context. Along with these incident-specific responses, Indian Christians need to think also of those which make long-term impact too. Say, for example, entering into the civil sphere more actively to arrest the emergence of fundamentalism of various hues would be a substantive way of doing public theology.

Freedom of Religion

One of the important concerns of public theology in the Indian context is the interpretation of the freedom of religion clause in the Indian Constitution, a clause closely associated with the issue of conversion. The clause, adopted from similar rights given in the Universal Declaration of Human Rights, reads as: "Subject to public order, morality and health ..., all persons are equally entitled to freedom of conscience and the right freely to profess, practise, and propagate religion" (Article 25. 1). The bone of contention is the word "propagate", which was introduced into the Constitution after much debate in the Constituent Assembly.[14] While there should be no problem for the private "professing and practising" of religion, it would become a real issue when it comes to the right of propagation, which is a public activity. As noted earlier, some provincial

---

[14] Sebastian Kim, *In Search of Identity—Debates on Religious Conversion in India* (New Delhi: Oxford University Press, 2003).

governments sought to protect themselves against the implications of the clause by legislating upon anti-conversion laws, attaching such pejorative motives as "fraud, coercion" and so on.

We need to discuss the meaning of the freedom of religion clause in a new context today. We need, first of all, to ask the broader question of the relevance and meaningfulness of this clause to a democratic system of politics. The core question is, "Whether democracy stands to gain or lose when the Indian citizen exercises her/his right to propagate in the right and genuine sense her/his religion?" Any mature democracy should respect the freedom of conscience to choose one's religion, practise it, and even propagate it, without causing problem to law, order, and public morality. Indian Christianity needs to work towards protecting this freedom and help democracy mature. Public theology will continue to shed light upon the meaningfulness of this clause in varying contexts.

Relationship with Other Religions

Relationship of Christianity with other religions has been a major concern in the Indian context. For a very long time, it had been informed by various theologies of religions. Starting with traditional exclusivism, Christianity in India has held positions on inclusivism and pluralism. What has been the core dynamic in holding these positions is an initial projection of a statement of truth regarding other religions and then endeavouring to follow it meaningfully. Indian Christianity has bothered less to listen to others on their views of other religions, has instead been more concerned to present their own stances to others.

The dynamics of public theology demands that Christians relate with other religions interactively and inter-subjectively. The truth of Christianity needs to be tested in the public arena, in multiple acts of public conversations. The most relevant form of conversation is forging an embodied relationship with others. It is in being involved in actual forms of relationships with people of other faiths, that Christians will evince respect and understanding towards others. An effective way of being involved in such relationships is serving as a catalyst to bring together multiple others (religions) in various networking for common good.

Living with Minority Identity and Rights

It is a well-known fact that Christians in India preferred the minority rights to communal representation in the post-independent Indian parliament. Christian leaders were more concerned about ensuring the religio-cultural rights of Christians, while foregoing the opportunity to send representatives to the legislature. Minority rights, they thought, would enable the Christians to cultivate their religio-cultural traditions and live by them with freedom and dignity.

Living with minority rights has come under serious strains today.[15] Religio-cultural nationalism, relentlessly pursued by the majoritarian political forces, is choking, ignoring, and even antagonising the religio-cultural traditions of the minorities. History is being re-written at several nodal points to impose a history that suits the majoritarian politics; religio-cultural traditions of the minorities are not given their due place in the educational stream; and, historical monuments of the minorities are being erased or replaced with others.

These suffocating experiences of the minorities bring back the question of the need of their voice being heard in the legislature, the political decision-making body. This is one of the salient concerns that the Indian public theology of mission will have to grapple with. While Indian Christianity does not want to become sectarian in any sense of the term, it also needs to legitimately voice out its concerns in proper forums and seek redress. For example, the alarming statistics given out in the Chennai edition of the *Deccan Chronicle* dated October 4, 2015, carried a news item with the caption, "Many undertrials belong to Islam, Christianity". The content reads that,

> According to the National Crime Record Bureau, almost one in two undertrials in Tamil Nadu belongs to either Muslims or Christian communities. Though Christians and Muslims comprise 6.12 per cent and 5.86 per cent of the state's total population, the two communities together account for about 48 per cent of the undertrials in the state. Of the total 9,034 undertrials, Muslims and Christians comprise 1,867 and 2,538 prisoners respectively. Mr. A. Kathir, executive director of Evidence, said that this data indicate the presence of discrimination in law enforcement.

Needless to say that this is very shocking to the minority communities in Tamil Nadu; it is indeed an alarm to minorities all over India. The question is, "How do we account for such a data?" Are Christians and Muslims more criminal than others in Tamil Nadu? One always thought that the Christians who have benefitted much out of the educational system would be more civilised and less of a criminal than others. But the data implicate precisely the Christians! Is there any agenda of criminalisation involved? The sad thing is no one has reacted or commented upon it!

These and other discriminating acts that the Christians have to bear bring in a gloomy picture of the condition of minorities in India. However, Christians will face it with a public theology that will imbue them with inner strength and vision. The ultimate strength and inspiration for doing public theology come from the empowering presence of the Spirit of God.

---

[15] As this text is being prepared for publication, a debate has come up in the media regarding an observation of Cardinal Oswald Gracias that there is a growing anxiety among the Christians regarding their security.

The Bible witnesses to the Spirit of God who has been active with the prophetic minority, who have played significant roles in guiding the history of the people. The First Testament dwells upon a number of instances wherein the prophets, a minority within Israel, wielded critical power to lead, guide, judge, and even publicly correct the rulers of the times. They were effective also in leading the general population out of their enslavement to oppressive human masters and supernatural idolatrous powers.

Jesus, the prophet par excellence, manifested the prophetic power in enkindling the hope of a minority, and that too a marginalised minority of Palestine! The little flock, the small but intimate group of apostles and disciples who gathered around him, followed him, and was with him in his mission, death, and resurrection, was a miniscule powerless minority, but a minority which became a publicly significant force especially in the days after the resurrection. The early Christians, a small group that took to a different way of life, though hunted down by the powers that be, grew to fill up the Roman Empire with their presence and with their gospel. They were an open minority, open to the Spirit of God who continuously was journeying with them in history, and opening the future with immense hope.

Growing up to be such a prophetic, open, and dynamic minority should become the goal of Christians in India. Indian Christians should steer away from minority complex on the one hand, and triumphalism on the other. While the former can induce a sense of victimhood, the latter can estrange them adversely from others. By being an open minority, they need to bear witness to the presence of the creative Spirit of God in their life—both private and public. By being a dynamic minority, they need to face the challenging issues confronting them today.

Affirmative Action to Christians of Dalit Origin

Obtaining the benefits of affirmative action to Christians of Dalit origin is yet another important concern for Christian public theology in India today. The issue is that Christians of Dalit origin are denied by the State the benefits of affirmative action envisaged in the Constitution for the socially depressed classes of people, who have been historically wronged by the caste-system. The benefits are that these people can avail certain privileges in education and employment, when it comes to competing with others. While these privileges are available to Dalits in general, they are denied to the Dalits who practise Christianity. The reason being given is that Christians do not accept the caste-system, and therefore the provision of affirmative action does not apply to them.

But the church in India has been demanding that the Christians of Dalit origin should not be discriminated against on the basis of their religion, and that they should not be denied those privileges accorded to the depressed people in general.[16] Such a denial, first of all, would amount to discriminating Christian Dalits on the basis of their religion; second, their condition as Dalits has not improved substantially even after embracing Christianity. They are discriminated against even within the church. And therefore, their struggle continues. Doing public theology in India would imply that one joins in with their struggle.

By Way of Concluding

The event of Christian mission has journeyed through various stages in history, acquiring various shades of meaning and implications. The signs of the times today give us a call to join in with the Spirit of God at the public sphere.

Public theology of mission primarily is a response to the presence of the Spirit of God in the public sphere, where conversations between religions, ethical doctrines, ideologies, systems, and movements take place beyond narrow boundaries. It arises generally at the interface between civil and political spheres within the framework of democracy.

Doing a public theology of mission would then mean strengthening the bonds of democracy in a given political system, and treating the public sphere as the site of mission; presenting our values to the public, and conversely, imbibing some of the pristine values of the public; standing for the fundamental rights provided by democratic systems; networking with other religions and movements for common good, and so on. It would ultimately mean joining in with the Spirit of God who opens the sinful closures of the public so that the public can mediate life in freedom for the whole of creation.

---

[16] Felix Wilfred, *Dalit Empowerment* (New Delhi: ISPCK, 2007).

4

FAITH AND CULTURE: A CHRISTIAN *POIESIS*

Cultural Experience Today

In one of the super-singer episodes in a TV reality-show, an eight-year old girl sang a famous classical song with awesome dexterity—fine rendering in terms of the grammar of music, modulation of voice, expression of emotion, and the like. The entire audience watching it was enthralled. One of the judges of the performance, getting up to give a standing ovation, said, "It is unbelievable that you, at your age, could perform like this ... you all belong to a new age, a magical age".

Cultural sites have opened up today a sort of magical possibility for human beings, who have begun to perform with excellent standards, not just on the cultural platform, but also in political, economic, and social fields with the power and facility of cultural resources. Politics witnesses to meteoric rise of individuals from their condition of sheer absence of socio-economic capital to become leaders of major countries, all due to their cultural capital. Celebrated achievements of individuals are recorded in the economic field, aided by the processes of knowledge-economy—perhaps the most powerful outcome of the interfacing of the symbolic and the material. Women, who have been domesticated for millennia together, witness to a relatively greater degree of freedom and empowerment on account of their performance born out of cultural abilities. The educational field witnesses to similar experiences: a good section of those educated in professional fields are emerging from the hitherto excluded communities, and we hear news of a son of a vendor, or daughter of a coolie obtaining state level ranks or international accolades. All these point to the "truth" of the utterance, "yours is a magical age", an age borne by the wings of the cultural capabilities of human beings!

Experience of Freedom

There is a strong discourse today which holds the view that the present cultural facilities give an experience of great freedom, which is an *opportune moment* for the human being to grow. This is a freedom from undue ties of traditions and closed-up communities which have bounded the individuals so far. The spirit of neo-liberalism, emergent upon a liberalised economic process, and the condition of postmodernism are the important ingredients in the making of this cultural experience. The human person, by participating in the process of globalisation, is said to be transformed into a cosmopolitan person; and it is said that this cosmopolitan individual acquires a *reflexive* capacity, whereby she is able to transcend the local ties, and manage the local and the global in a dexterous manner as to constitute her personality with greater measures of confidence. This section of people, in point of fact, is said to be the leading cultural agents in the world of globalisation—receiving, transferring, transmuting, and hybridising the local and the global cultures. And they are said to become reflexive individuals, being more and more enriched by the opportune moment.

Marginal Cultures Moving to the Centre...

Yet another significant aspect of the contemporary cultural experience is opening up of a space for the hitherto subjugated knowledges. Indigenous cultures, the embodiments of indigenous knowledges, find themselves brought to the fore more and more. Their legitimacy, validity, significance, dynamics, characteristic features, and so on, are coming to light not just in a manner of valorisation, but by way of asserting their own right to exist amidst diversity of cultures, and by way of contesting the hegemony of dominating cultural traditions. These are the ways in which the periphery to centre movement is taking place in the postmodern cultural world today. This is the opportunity the marginalised sections of humanity are experiencing in today's world.

Intensified Struggle

However, the present cultural experience has also brought in a moment of intensified struggle for the vast majority of people, especially for those who are in the periphery, living under conditions of powerlessness. The neo-liberalism attendant on globalisation premises itself upon increasing competitiveness, but does not take into account the differentiality of locatedness and the disparity that prevails on account of socio-economic and political capitals. The Indian case is a typical example. The twenty-five to thirty percent of people who live below the poverty line (now as per the multi-dimensional poverty index, it is 41 percent[1]) and the socially subaltern communities are situated in economically and socially disadvantaged

---

[1] Suresh D. Tendulkar, *Report of the Expert Group to Review the Methodology for Estimation of Poverty* (New Delhi: Govt. Of India, Planning Commission, 2009), e-copy http://planningcommission.nic.in/reports/genrep/rep_pov.pdf, accessed on May 26, 2018.

positions. Over against this context, the culture of competition, attendant on the logic of the market, induces a struggle in the lives of the people in disadvantaged positions. It offers them a utopia of opportunities, but not real possibilities. The nation-states which began to offer some securities to the disadvantaged people are getting weakened by the pressures of globalisation and the situation consequent upon it pulls the carpet from below the feet of the subaltern people. This creates tension and frustration, and has rendered the present moment of intensified struggle.

An Experience of Rootless-ness?

An observation by Arjun Appadurai, one of the leading theorists on cultural globalisation, is worth noting: "The world we live in now seems rhizomic, even schizophrenic, calling for theories of rootlessness, alienation, and psychological distance between individuals and groups on the one hand, and fantasies (or nightmares) of electronic propinquity on the other. Here, we are close to the central problematic of cultural processes in today's world."[2] Appadurai is making a valid point in observing an emerging rootlessness for the contemporary individual. Increasingly losing the foundations—be they nation-states, ideologies, religious beliefs, philosophies, traditional communities, and even industry-based securities, the individual is at a loss. And, the masses, caught in the vortex of consumerism are experiencing an alienation from their humanity. The logic of the market, which Pierre Bourdieu calls the "tyranny of the market", generates a consumerist culture, at the heart of which is the logic which privileges profit over people.[3] It generates false aesthetics, ethos, values, ideals, and philosophies that serve this logic of consumerism. It progresses with relentless strides to enshrine itself as the normative cultural experience human beings have to have everywhere in the world. This causes a *consumerising of the self* or commoditising of the personhood today.

New Paradigm of Violence

A number of those who reflect upon the phenomenon of violence today do point to the role of culture in the production of violence. Michel Wieviorka speaks about a new paradigm of violence wherein the cultural resources have become the fountainhead of violence.[4] He calls it a new paradigm because it characteristically differs from earlier phases when class (bourgeiousie-proletariate), economic (First World-Third Worlds), regional (West-East) and other such systemic divisions served to organise

---

[2] Arjun Appadurai, *Modernity at Large—Cultural Dimensions of Globalisation* (Minneapolis: University of Minnesota Press, 1996), 29.

[3] Noam Chomsky, *Profit over People—Neoliberalism and Global Order* (New York: Seven Stories Press, 1999).

[4] Michel Wieviorka, "The New Paradigm of Violence", in *Globalization, the State, and Violence*, ed. Jonathan Friedman (Walnut Creek, CA: Altamira Press, 2003).

conflicts. Now, in their increasing weakening, new ones such as ethnic, religious, linguistic, and so on, begin to serve as resources of violence. The Huntington thesis of clash of civilisation takes this new paradigm into consideration.

These, then, are some features of the cultural experience of humanity today. They open a horizon of hope even while engendering a chain of closures on the other; they free the individuals from oppressive ties, help marginal cultures to emerge, and so on, on the one hand, and intensify the struggles of existence, induce rootless-ness, engender violence, and so on, on the other. It is against this experience of emerging possibilities and alienating contradictions[5] that this essay searches for the way the Christian faith can be meaningfully related to culture. In what sense can the gospel engage effectively with culture to heal the contradictions and bring harmony to the contemporary world?

FAITH AND CULTURE AS MANIFEST IN JESUS

Faith as manifest in Jesus is an event[6] of good news, unfolding through encounters between the Christian tradition as lived out in Christian churches on the one hand, and the concerns of socio-economic and political freedom manifest in cultural and religious expressive and latent forms on the other. It is an event wherein the Divine irrupts, and the human, in terms of its longing for freedom, erupts,[7] and thereby a manifestation of divine energy leading to liberative praxis occurs. It is an on-going event, unfolding through space and time, expanding the space of life in freedom. The Christian tradition embodies the primordial witness to the event of good news, wherein the person of Jesus, a mystic-prophet, becomes the site of encounter between the Divine and the world, a world as experienced by the human medium.

Jesus experienced the transcendent Divine, Abba, from within the Jewish culture, as a marginal Galilean Jew. The way he interacted with it has great significance for our theology of culture today. As Sebastian

---

[5] Some social theorists have pointed out this heightened contraction as symptoms of late capitalism. And they have also named the present-day post-modern culture, as the cultural logic of late capitalism. Jameson Frederic, *Postmodernism—the Cultural Logic of Late Capitalism*? (UK: Duke University Press, 1992).

[6] "For Tracy, the event and person of Jesus Christ—in the immediacy of experience mediated by the tradition (which is normed by the expressions of Scripture), developed and corrected by historical and literary and social criticisms, and correlated with our present situation—is the prime analogue for theological imagination." James J. Buckley, "Revisionists and Liberals", in *Modern Christian Theologians—An Introduction to Christian Theologians Since 1918*, eds. David F Ford and Rachael Muers (New York: Blackwell, 2005), 217.

[7] Sebastian Kappen, *Jesus and Cultural Revolution—An Asian Perspective* (Bombay: BUILD Publication, 1983).

Faith and Culture

Kapppen points out, it was a time when Jewish culture was filled with cult, law and apocalyptism, an indicator of the shrinking of real freedom.⁸ This had brought about fundamentalist tendencies within the Jewish culture, whose beneficiaries were none but the priestly classes. Apocalyptism, as Kappen understood it, was a manner of seizing or foreclosing the future in the name of the Divine. As such, the Jewish culture had lost its radical freedom and creativity. Its implication was that the priestly class, in conjunction with the powers that be, had spread its net of hegemony over the Jewish world, thereby holding the people under its cultural power.

It was in this context that Jesus announced the message of radical freedom, the Reign of God. He interrogatively took on the culture of seizure or closure of the Divine, thereby opening a horizon of freedom wherein the poor, marginalised, and the oppressed could experience the empowering presence of the Divine. Interrogation of the Jewish culture occurred in him in the very manner in which he situated his life within the culture of the time. As Lucien Legrand points out, Jesus identified himself with the "accursed", the "people of the land", who were a "mixed lot of simply honest souls … of poor people struggling to make both ends meet…"⁹ Though struggling, they were people who could express their dissent in not so insignificant ways. "They were rather inclined to oppose the harshness of absentee landowners by hook or by crook (Luke 16: 1–8), by laziness (Luke 12:45), or by plain violence (Mark 12: 1–9)."¹⁰ Identification with these people brought about an earthy freedom to Jesus, which he evinced in his words and deeds. As Legrand continues, "From within the culture he belongs to and in which he was born, he transcends the cultural … set patterns".¹¹ This freedom became a prophetic freedom in Jesus by which he transcended the cultural conditioning, and emerged to be a radical prophet. "Humanly speaking", as Legrand notes, "Jesus belongs to the race of the creators who open new dimensions of human existence, of the poets who invent new languages, of *the prophets and mystics* who enter the divine sphere and transcend the human perspectives in their commerce with the Divine. They are undoubtedly people of their own times and are an expression of the culture of their land. Yet they go beyond it and become, in the midst of their own generations, the explorers of new horizons of being".¹² So was Jesus and his experience of rooted transcendence, which occurred as an event interrogating the closures.

---

8   Kappen, *Jesus and Cultural Revolution*.
9   Lucien Legrand, *The Bible on Culture—Belonging or Dissenting?* (Maryknoll, NY: Orbis Books, 2000), 95.
10 Legrand, *The Bible on Culture*, 95.
11 Legrand, *The Bible on Culture*, 112.
12 Legrand, *The Bible on Culture*, 112.

It would be instructive to see some instances where Jesus interrogates the cultural closures. Aesthetics is a core component of any culture, and it would do well to see how Jesus experienced, as for example, this inner core of culture. Jewish culture had its own approach to beauty and ugliness, which was intimately linked to its religious experience. Right from its ancient days when it was constituted in the post-exodus context, "being without blemish" (Lev 22: 21–22) was considered as something worthy to be dedicated to God. A person with any deformity was considered unworthy to go near the tabernacle of God, and was positively prohibited. Similarly, a person with illness like leprosy was also considered a person with deformity. We see Jesus exhibiting enormous inner freedom in relating to such personalities, and radically subverting the Jewish rules of purity-pollution. He touches a leper, touches the blind man with clay made out of spittle (John 9: 6), dines with sinners and a short-statured Zacchaeus, and so on. There is radicality in the way Jesus as a Jew interrogated the Jewish cultural aesthetic conditionings, and opened up the cultural closures. This experience of Jesus demands of us a praxis of culture, which would redeem it from its contradictions, and open a divine horizon for us.

Cultural Paradigm of Life

Christian theology, the wings of faith, for a long time in history, had considered philosophy as the privileged companion to journey with. While theology was the queen of sciences, philosophy was considered her handmaid, functioning as a discipline that raised human consciousness to universal and normative dimensions. Today, we find a move away (or we have moved?) from philosophy and a turn towards culture. The move is borne out of a deep realisation that we as humans are less and less capable of universal judgements, and more and more embedded in our cultural worlds. This realisation led to the cultural-linguistic turn that had occurred in Western philosophy through existentialism, phenomenology, and linguistic philosophy.

The cultural turn is immense, multidimensional, and deeply consequential. It has impacted heavily upon philosophy, religion, knowledge, communication systems, social relations, identities, politics, and even economic activities. As we know, Ferdinand de Saussure (1857–1913), with his pioneering lectures in linguistics, signalled the cultural turn in the realm of philosophy. His basic insights like linguistic self-referentiality, arbitrariness of significations, origin of meaning from differences in signs, and so on, brought to light the deeply embedded linguistic net within which we think, communicate, and act. Structural anthropologist Levi-Strauss followed the exploration with making a linguistic analysis of kinship relations and showed the linguistic binaries in which human consciousness and relationships were cast. While he shed much light upon the linguistic structures that determined the human consciousness, the hermeneutical turn in phenomenology pointed out to the indispensable act of interpretation human consciousness is involved in, in any cognition or encounter with reality. The home of this interpretative act is nothing but language, and Martin Heidegger could call it the house of being. The subsequent developments which led to a post-structuralist phase of Western philosophy only strengthened the case for the centrality of language in human perception, understanding, and encounter with reality. The analytic philosophy, associated with philosophers like A.J. Ayer, Jane Austen, and Wittgenstein further strengthened the case for the linguisticality of human existence. All these developments in Western philosophy made us realise that the cultural-linguistic turn was not anything of a choice, but the very manner or the only manner of human consciousness, or the very condition of possibility for human perception and communicative behaviour.

Such a radical cultural-linguistic turn in philosophy had its deep impact upon the field of knowledge. In addition to the fields of anthropology, folkloristics and linguistics, a new discipline of cultural studies came into existence. It began to explore the vital role culture played in epistemologies, historiographies, politics, gendering, social relations, and economy. The epistemological nodes like objectivity, rationality, universality, and so on, were deconstructed to disclose their cultural origins and affinities. As a result, different cultures, especially the cultures of the periphery came to claim validity for their unique culture-based rationalities and knowledge-systems.

Culture, then, became the focus of thought and action. Its role was realised to be more than a medium, more than the fund of artistic creations, more than something that evaporated into thin air; it was as substantial as any system could be in terms of its enduring hold over individual and collective life. There were those who went to the extreme of saying, there is no life outside culture (akin to "nothing outside the text" of Derrida), no meaning to life beyond those created by different cultures, and so on. Culture came to be understood as the arena of life, wherein people experienced meaning, purpose, identity, self, and others.

Culture, thus, came to stand for a vital process of life of the whole of humanity, and not just of an aristocratic elite civilised stratum, nor even just that of the creative artists. It became the very reality with which social, economic, and political negotiation and contestation took place. It was a process, rather than a product. As Sheila Greeve Davaney would put it,

> In contrast to earlier notions of culture as the deposit or accumulation of knowledge or meaning produced by elites, or as a body of beliefs and values shared by all members of a group such as a nation or religious

community, culture now is viewed as the dynamic and contentious process by which meaning, and with it power, is produced, circulated, and negotiated by all who reside within a particular cultural milieu.[13]

It was the process whereby human beings created their identities, involved in politics, and so on. Thus, culture came to be understood as the very matrix of human life, an indispensible and inescapable reality, engulfing all our life-experiences, and being the house of our being.

CULTURE AND FAITH

In a context wherein culture is realised as the very paradigm of life, how can we meaningfully discuss the relationship between culture and faith? Can the flourishing of culture be taken as an indication of the manifestation of the power of faith and transcendence?; or, is it an indication of an Immanentism in faith? These are some of the vital questions while relating culture to faith.

One of the early systematic attempts within Christianity to relate faith to culture was made by Richard Niebuhr during the fifties of the twentieth century. In his publication titled, *Christ and Culture*, Niebuhr discussed the famous five typologies of "Christ against culture", "Christ of culture", "Christ above culture", "Christ and culture in paradox", and "Christ the transformer of culture". Even though the typologies suggested by him are relating Christ to culture, it will not be less appropriate to read faith analogously in the place of Christ. The first type stands for a dichotomous approach, wherein faith and culture are opposed to each other. It would imply that faith operates entirely in a different sphere than culture, and the latter, as a human creation, is inadequate to express or mediate faith. The second type, on the contrary, considers faith as part and parcel of culture, and that culture can not only mediate but also nurture faith in the right way. The Western liberal thought is a typical example of this variety, and some leading philosophers like John Locke and Immanuel Kant looked for religion within the limits of reason (culture) alone. Between these two opposing poles, going analogically with Niebuhr's typology, we can think of three intermediary types as "faith above culture", "faith and culture in paradox", and "faith as transforming culture". Faith above culture would stand for an approach that it is the sublime culture, that is, culture that nurtures spiritual orientations, rather than crass mundane culture that can mediate or nurture faith. This position believes in culture to be a channel of faith, but, however, a refining of culture through the very cultural capabilities (like right reason) is necessary to make it capable of faith. The position

---

[13] Sheila Greeve Davaney, "Theology and the Turn to Cultural Analysis", in *Converging on Culture—Theologians in Dialogue with Culture and Criticism*, eds. Delwin Brown et al. (Oxford: Oxford University Press), 5.

on "faith and culture in paradox" suggests that faith and culture work dialectically, challenging as well as enriching one another. One will undergo either of the experiences, even though one will not be able to be fully conscious of their identities; they work paradoxically. And the final position "faith transforms culture" suggests that faith can work as a transformative catalyst, whereby culture is renewed.

Paul Tillich thought through the relationship between faith and culture through an existential analysis. Faith, for him was, the "directedness of the spirit towards the unconditioned meaning", while culture the "directedness of the spirit towards the conditioned form";[14] religion, the medium of faith was the substance, while culture the form; faith the ultimate concern, while culture the form that expressed the ultimate concern. Tillich thought of a dynamic unity between the two: "The unity of religion and culture as a unity of unconditioned meaning-import and of conditioned meaning-form."[15] He named this unity as thenonomy, by which he meant, the "fulfilment of all cultural forms with the import of the Unconditional".[16] A theonomous relationship seeks to synthesise autonomy and heteronomy at a point of unconditionality; while autonomy, autos+nomos, the site of a perennial conflict between the hubris of the self and the nomos of the objective order, tends to be self-sufficient, heteronomy may lead to postulation of unmerited externalities, bordering at times even upon the demonic. Culture, in its mere autonomous form, can become absolutist and self-enclosed, and in its mere heteronomous form, can become a reified fetish, dominating over the cultural sense. It is a theonomous relationship of the two, which can heal the extremes of autonomy and heteronomy, and bring about a creative and liberative experience of culture.

The industrial culture that came to be the epitome of modern culture was indicted by Tillich as alienating and estranging the human from its very being. The industrial work culture, dominated by heavy automatic machines, rendered the humans too automatons, bereft of creativity and spontaneity. This secularist orientation of industrial culture, the source of consumerism, was directed towards immediate profit, thereby losing its capacity for being directed towards the unconditional, the transcendent. It is in place to note Jürgen Habermas's observation that technologically advanced media, which came to dominate the modern lifeworld, made humans as mere consumers and not producers of opinions, thereby incapacitating them for creative responses to the public sphere.

Tillich's understanding of the relationship was from an existentialist perspective, trying to go beyond the then prevalent structuralism. For

---

[14] Paul Tillich, *What is Religion?*, ed. James Luther Adams (New York: Harper Torchbooks, 1969), 72.
[15] Tillich, *What is Religion?*, 74.
[16] Tillich, *What is Religion?*, 74.

him, a culture directed towards the unconditional can well connect itself to faith, the very domain of the unconditional; however, when culture is directed towards conditionalities, absolutising certain immediacies, it may as well disconnect itself from faith. Tillich needs to be appreciated for helping us imagine a theonomous relationship between culture and faith, which is relevant for our times. A theonomous relationship, I surmise, is open-ended, futuristic and explorative, unlike the autonomous or heteronomous ones. Niebuhr's fourth type, that is, "culture and faith in paradox" may well be taken to point towards a theonomous relationship wherein faith and culture, as far as humans can consciously experience or perceive, can be held only in a paradoxical relationship.

Faith and Culture in the Post-cultural Turn Era

However, the typologies of Niebuhr or the existential analysis of Tillich may not stand the test of the cultural-linguistic turn philosophy of knowledge has taken and has brought to our awareness the inescapable language-riddenness of our experience of reality. Accordingly, faith and culture can no more be held as two points in a relationship, as if human beings have the capacity to transit from one to the other. We have no location to stand outside of our cultures to speak about our faith. Our discourses on faith, be they scriptures, traditions, symbols, religious ethical teachings, and so on, are ultimately cultural-linguistic creations, coming down to us from generations past. They may not be mere linguistic codes bereft of history, aesthetics, morality, and so on, but, are events of the linguistic creativity of human beings manifest across space and time.

The lightning effect of the cultural-linguistic turn began to impact upon Christian theology, which began to realise its task as not so much explicating and stating eternal truths, but as exploring, describing, innovating, and presenting the intricate role, functions, and dynamics of religious experiences and traditions as cultural events. Theology began to speak less in terms of essentialism, universalism, and absolutism. Its very location as outside of culture became a matter of criticism, and a cultural paradigm of theology began to unfold. What was possible as regards the practice of Christian faith, as Graham Ward put it, was creating a cultural imaginary of Christianity, a cultural *tour de force* of Christianity. Language is the very fibre of faith, and the activity of creating religious sign-systems is faith in action, having the potential to bring about changes in our social, political, economic, and cultural systems. Culture can be self-reflexive and self-dialectical.

In this context, there were those who began to speak about the end of theology—end of a philosophical theology that claimed to relate to truth and God beyond the linguistic system. But others responded to it more positively. Gordon Kaufman, for example, re-imagined theology not as a reflection upon eternal truth claims, but upon the "sense" of God, that is experienced in living out religious beliefs and practices. Theology became a processual reality, an on-going event, a linguistic formation or textures of significations, constituting a Christian habitus. Habitus, in the theory of Pierre Bourdieu, would mean a system of dispositions which operate in an individual or a collective, propelling to decision and action. Accordingly, a Christian habitus would be a system of Christian disposition, a product of the Christian cultural *practice*.

At this juncture, responding to this realisation, there emerged theologies like theological realism, liberal revisionist, post-liberal, and Radical Orthodoxy. Theological realism held on to the possibility of relating to the object of theology, God, in spite of the criticism of linguistic philosophy; Revisionist theology took on board the cultural-linguistic turn, cultural limits, and argued for "shaping up Christian practices and teachings in dialogue with modern philosophies, cultures, and social practices",[17] hermeneutically revising the beliefs/doctrines held by a religious community as an exercise, for example, in public theology; George Lindbeck and Hans Frei related directly to the cultural-linguistic paradigm, and understood the nature of Christian doctrine as an intra-textual cultural practice. They emphasised the importance of situating ourselves within our faith-tradition, and explore life, purpose, and so on; Radical orthodoxy went to the extent of demanding from a Christian a radical rejection of secular reason so as to situate herself within the Christian tradition.

FAITH AND THE CULTURAL IMAGINARY

In this new context, Christian theology, as a title from the *American Academy of Religion* puts it, may be said to be converging on culture.[18] The cultural paradigm of theology envisions theology not primarily as a cognitive task of proving the truth claims of Christianity, but a stream of *discursive practices*, whereby the Christian gospel is contextually described, liturgically celebrated, commitments proposed, guidelines given, negotiations with other beliefs undertaken, and so on. This discursive practice, different from cognitive ontological and subjective-expressive theologies, emerges as a *Christian poiesis*—a Christian thought-action of transformation. *Poiesis*, with its etymological meaning "to make", stands for an action that transforms and continues the world, an action which reconciles thought with action.

---

[17] Buckley, *"Revisionists and Liberals,"* 213.
[18] Delwin Brown, et al., *Converging on Culture—Theologians in Dialogue with Cultural Analysis and Criticism* (Oxford: Oxford University Press, 2001).

Graham Ward, one of the prominent theologians of the cultural paradigm, proposes to understand the Christian discursive practice as a project, a *poiesis*, that creates its own cultural imaginary, in dialogue with others in the public forum, and become a transforming event of good news amidst various cultural imaginaries. Ward uses the phrase cultural imaginary, associating it with the phrase of social imaginary used by Charles Taylor who said, "The social imaginary is not a set of ideas; rather, it is what enables, through making sense of, the practices of a society".[19] By practices of society, Taylor points to the way ordinary people practice their lives, in certain context, with a certain imaginary, formed out of a set of symbolic resources. Ward, on the other hand, speaks of the cultural imaginary, because "our conceptions of social order are culturally governed".[20] He applies this concept of cultural imaginary to the Christian theology of discursive practice, which, situated within the Scripture-based Christian tradition, would produce the hope and desire for the eschatological perfection of humanity in Christ. It will propel a culture of desire, which is an antidote to the culture of satisfaction, which is, according to him, "A culture where aesthetics have become anaesthetics, because what it aims at is the erasure of desire: that is stasis (or death)".[21] This Christian *poiesis* will transform cultures even while being transformed self-reflexively by being an overlapping power of socio-economic and political processes. It aims at interrogating the many cultural closures which mask social, economic, and political oppressions, and open up a horizon of freedom for life on earth.

Can the Christian tradition of faith be meaningfully pursued as a cultural imaginary in the Indian context? I think there is a new energy in such an understanding, as it is related to mission—mission to self and others. First of all, it allows for a revitalisation of our memory of the Christian tradition of faith as an emancipatory inheritance to the whole of India. As mentioned in earlier chapters, the contributions made to India, in terms of a cultural Renaissance, and the social reform through its subaltern humanity, comes as a narrative inheritance from which we can continue to nourish ourselves. Second, such a cultural approach can help open the discursive potentialities of indigenous Christianities in the Indian soil. Christian tradition can emerge in its enriching varieties as it is manifest in the life-worlds of the people. It is heartening to note that the cultural imaginary of the gospel, in dialogue with different cultures, has brought forth different cultural forms of Christianity, as witnessed to in the creative formations of indigenous Christianities all over the world. Even while

---

[19] Charles Taylor, *Modern Social Imaginaries* (Durham: Duke University Press, 2004), 2.
[20] Graham Ward, *Cultural Transformation and Religious Practice* (Cambridge: Cambridge University Press, 2005), 160.
[21] Ward, *Cultural Transformation and Religious Practice*, 164.

scholars speak about Christianity as a world religion, they acutely become aware of the cultural embeddedness of local Christianities. The powerful presence of folk and popular Christian traditions within different denominational churches, especially within the Catholic church is for all to see. They are involved in a dialogue of life with the gospel of Jesus Christ. While there is mutuality between them, we find also the dynamics of resistance, interrogation, and re-interpretation in their dialogue of life. The gospel has also dialogued with many non-Christian leaders in India with whom the inspiration is visible. Raja Ram Mohan Roy, dialoguing with the Unitarian Church, emerged as a votary of the moral-teacher-Christ, and became a witness to the gospel through his campaign against social evils; Keshab Chander Sen, through his Church of New Dispensation, put forth very insightful Christian theological reflections; Gandhi acknowledged publicly the Christian inspiration for his doctrine of non-violence; Mahatma Phule and Ambedkar critically acclaimed the role Christianity played in the lives of the subaltern people; similar appreciations, appropriations, and other aspects of dialogue of the Christian gospel are being explored these days, as part of the effort to understand indigenous Christianities.

Third, such a perspective can also be a source of futuristic hope, as lived out in communities of Christian faith, especially lived out amidst contemporary challenges. We can speak of an Indian Christian *poiesis*, but in an inter-textual hermeneutics of life, constituted along with the religio-cultural others, from the locations of the subalterns. This will make the gospel of Jesus an effective contributor to the process of healing the present day contradictions.

Christians must be known by their culture, whose manifestive attributes are dynamism of faith as an ongoing enthusiasm for life, a deep sense of dignity of humankind, a communicative practice which respects the other and engages with the other in dialogue, an unfaltering commitment for community living, a zeal for justice, and a force of creative spirit. These attributes will be the fruits of a Christian's faith in a transcendent God.

Faith as Cultural Imaginary in the Public Sphere

As it has been discussed in Chapter 2, one of the theological discourses that has re-emerged during the contemporary cultural paradigm is public theology, which finds its relevance in the context of what is spoken of as public religion. A central claim of public theology is that the very language of theology is public in the sense in which it applies to the language of any other discipline. This assertion brings up the issue of the crucial relationship between religious language and public reason. While the classical secular European society defends the Enlightenment reason to be the universal public reason, the post-secular society has severely questioned its validity and capability to serve as a universal public common ground across cultures; and, in the post-linguistic-cultural realisations, modern rationality itself has been deconstructed to expose its cultural underpinnings, thus opening the world to think of multiple modernities. In this context, the argument that the language of theology should translate itself into the universal rational language does not carry weight, and so, the communication of religious truth in the public becomes one of *conversation* between the comprehensive doctrines.

Looking at it from the challenge of plurality, Tracy suggests the method of *analogical imagination* as suitable for this conversation. "*Analogical Imagination* is a paradigm ... which works by picking a primary analogue, showing the unity-in-difference within and between analogues (their order, perhaps harmony, their variety and intensity, including dialectical negations), and risking the self-exposure of putting these similarities and differences in the public forum."[22] Every religious community will present its analogue, the core-symbol of its inspiration, its classic (as Tracy would name them), in the public forum, and undertake the conversation internally within their own semantic layers as well as externally with other analogues. It will be a process of circles of conversation in the public sphere.

The Christian discursive practices—its beliefs, narratives, ideals, commitments, and so on—together must be presented as its analogue for conversation with other religious and secular comprehensive doctrines. It implies that Christianity continues to shape up and refine its analogue in the light of self-criticism as well as criticism from others, and engage with others in terms of proposing overlapping consensus as well as negotiation. It means that Christianity involves itself in an act of hermeneutical re-visioning of its tradition in the light of emerging realities of life, and goes beyond an intra-textual nurturing to enter into an inter-textual encounter. It is this inter-textual nurturing, which makes the Christian tradition of faith, its analogue, vibrant and meaningful for today's context.

The Christian tradition of faith, the event of salvation as unfolded in Jesus Christ, must encounter other "events of salvation" as manifest in mystics and prophets of different cultures and religious traditions, and "prepare" the human to the experience of the "irruption of the Divine and eruption of the human". Our mission will be initiating an on-going process of "preparation" so that the Divine-human encounter can occur. Initiating a preparation will take place only from a location, and our conversation should emerge from our preferred location, our rootedness for transcendence. Jesus's gospel, its cultural imaginary, true to its biblical inspiration and historical commitment, must clearly locate itself within the world of the little ones, the preferential site of Divine manifestation.

---

[22] Buckley, "Revisionists and Liberals", 220.

Indian Christian theologians like Sebastian Kappen, who earlier embarked upon an Indian liberation theology based on Christian-Marxist dialogue, had begun to explore the cultural potentials of Christianity for social transformation. He understood Jesus to be a prophet who initiated a cultural revolution. Prophets are born, according to Kappen, when there is a crisis in culture, and they initiate a counter-culture which renews the culture in crisis and brings about social transformation. There is thus a dialectical relationship between culture and prophecy, and prophecy is the manifestation of faith. The prophet serves as the point or the cusp, in which the experience of suffering and oppression along with hopes and aspirations of humans *erupt,* and at the same time, the Divine as the answer *irrupts* by taking hold of the prophet. A prophet, thus, is the point of contact between faith and culture initiating a process of cultural revolution, and Jesus, according to Kappen, embodied the prophetic self-criticality and emerged as the cusp wherein he, on the one hand, represented the *eruption* of the aspirations and hopes of the people for a renewal of culture, and on the other, the *irruption* of the Divine to intervene redemptively into the human. Thus, there ensued a cultural revolution, born out of faith. A similar cultural revolution, Kappen thought, needed to be enkindled in the Indian context too, and the Indian counter-religious traditions could be the appropriate points of insertion for the Christian prophetic tradition to enkindle a cultural revolution in India.

The Christian tradition of faith will weigh on behalf of the little ones in the arena of public sphere, which is the formative field of cultural imaginary, as it relates to the sphere of politics. Public sphere is the arena where opinions, viewpoints, doctrines, and so on are brought to public conversation, and, contestation and negotiations occur as part of the process of decision making. The Christian tradition will contribute to create a new public sphere, constituted by associations, cultural organisations, social networks, inter-subjective interactions, and so on, which will weigh upon the political for the life and freedom of the little ones. This will continually redraw and refine the nature and dynamics of the public sphere and the democratic political process from the standpoint of the life-concerns of the subalterns.

By Way of Concluding

We are living in an era when violence is produced with cultural resources. What goes into religious, ethnic, regional, and linguistic identities of different others which come into conflict are cultural resources of humanity. The depth and width of culture and its power, including the home that it provides for the very human life on earth, are increasingly being explored today in fields related to culture, knowledge, and philosophy. They have brought home the truth that our experience of reality is language-ridden, and there is no life outside the cultural text. Against this new realisation, how we relate faith to culture gains importance. There was a time when Christian theology treated culture as an outside reality with which faith could be related in one way or another. But the new realisation demands of us a new way of understanding the relationship. It is at this juncture, the proposal of thinking of a Christian *poiesis*, a cultural imaginary, which is a practice of faith, performatively oriented, becomes meaningful. Accordingly, the Christian faith in the Indian context is to be understood in terms of the cultural imaginary it has constructed over the centuries, and which is being created today along with others in the public sphere.

5

NURTURING TRANSCENDENCE: CHURCH AND CIVIL SOCIETY

INABILITY FOR TRANSCENDENCE?

As observed in the previous chapter, Paul Tillich alerted us to the impending danger of the industrial society that was "choking" the creative spirit, by making the humans automatons, cogs in the wheel of the giant machine of industry. He pointed out the increasing existential inability of the human person to experience transcendence in a world that made them a routinised being, bereft of creativity. Going by the subjectivisation and horizontalisation of human consciousness that has taken place during the modern era, several other theologians and social scientists too have pointed out the increasing inability of human beings to experience transcendence during the contemporary phase of human history. Some have observed that the modern disenchanted ethos has irreversibly corroded the human ability for transcendence.

Surrounded by a form of modernity characterised by scientism, instrumentalism, atomic individualism, ruthless competition for socio-economic gains, and the will to power, religions too tend to lose their creative dimensions of transcendence today. Our world is facing some of the grave dangers on account of religion, or *irreligion*. Needless to say that religion-related violence, induced by religious identity politics and the co-mingling of the religious with the market-induced consumerist utopia, has become a real danger all over the globe today.

Violence in contemporary life has its specific character, which differentiates itself from earlier forms. Michael Wieviorka, a leading social theorist, would call it a new paradigm of violence[1] wherein identities come into clash. Wherever identities are vigorously organised, there emerges a sharply contrasted scheme of insider-outsider, and it serves as the framework for organising violence. Unlike the previous era, when the

---

[1] Michel Wieviorka, "The New Paradigm of Violence", 109.

insiders and the outsiders of organised violence such as war were situated across borders, today they live in close physical proximity to one another. As Veena Das observes,[2] the insiders of local-worlds, people who have been living side by side for generations, people who constitute the real life-world with immense social trust (the core component of social capital[3]), become the suspected outsiders and targets of inhuman brutality.

Unfortunately, religion emerges or has emerged to be one of the dominant categories to organise violence today. Starting with the so-called world religions to region-specific folk religious traditions, they are involved in identity-politics, oftentimes narrow and sectarian. How come religions, mediators of transcendence, are instrumentalised for narrow sectarian violent ends? How come religions, wellsprings of transcendence, become instruments of temporal power?

A religion that serves sectarian ends is nothing but an impaired religion, infected with the evil of immanentism. It is a retrogressive irreligion which arises from human aspirations for security, fame, and glory; it is irreligion which unmeaningfully temporalises our faith-experience; it is irreligion which compromises our deep and challenging faith with short-term goals of identity, power, and hierarchy; it is irreligion flourishing upon human vulnerabilities; it is irreligion serving selfish needs, rather than high moral goals; and, it is irreligion which ultimately closes the door against God.

Our post-industrial society,[4] a society of knowledge-economy, powered by knowledge systems, aided by the advanced Information and Communication Technologies is wounded too by the virus of immanentism. As a result, these systems too seem to induce counterproductive "closures" in the forms of stagnations of thought—fundamentalisms of various kinds, religious communalism, ethnocentrism, constrictive identities, and so on, triggering violent clashes. Such "closures" are being produced today especially in political and civil spheres of life, posing serious challenges to public life; and they keep producing or legitimising the

---

[2] "The violence in these areas seems to belong to a new moment in history: it certainly cannot be understood through earlier theories of contractual violence or a classification of just and unjust wars, for its most disturbing feature is that it has occurred between social actors who lived in the same local worlds and knew or thought they knew each other." Veena Das et al., "Introduction", in *Violence and Subjectivity*, eds. Veena Das et al., (USA: University of California Press, 2000), 1.

[3] For an exploration into social capital, Pierre Bourdieu, "The Forms of Capital", in *Handbook of Theory and Research for the Sociology of Education*, ed. J. Richardson (New York: Greenwood Press, 1986), 241–258; James S. Coleman, "Social Capital in the Creation of Human Capital", in *Social Capital—A Multifaceted Perspective*, eds. Partha Dasgupta and Ismail Serageldin (Washington, D.C.: The World Bank, 2000); Robert D. Putnam, "Bowling Alone: America's Declining Social Capital", *Journal of Democracy* 6, no. 1 (1995): 65–78.

[4] Daniel Bell, *The Coming of Post-Industrial Society* (New York: Harper Colophon Books, 1976).

idolatry of money[5] and the market along with various hegemonies, resulting in exploitative forms of social and economic exclusions in the wider society today.

Nurturing the Ability for Transcendence

It is in this context of increasing inability to transcendence and formation of multiple closures, that the church is called upon to nurture faith, the light of faith (*Lumen Fidei*) so as to rejuvenate humanity with the refreshing experience of transcendence. The *Compendium of the Social Doctrine of the Church*[6] observes that the church is the "sign and defender of transcendence of the whole person...and all humanity".[7] It is, as the *Compendium* discerns, in a transcendental reference to a "thou" that a person can define an "I", and therefore, only when in communion with the Transcendent Other that a person can experience a healthy subjectivity. With the experience of transcendence, the human person "comes out of himself/herself, from the self-centred preservation of his/her own life, to enter into a relationship of dialogue and communion with others".[8] This human person is "open to the fullness of being, to the unlimited horizon of being", which is God.[9]

This theological anthropology of the *Compendium* entrusts the church with a mission of being a "sign and defender" of transcendence, a mission which is at once historical and eschatological. It is, theologically speaking, a challenge to hold on to a creative and healthy tension between the Immanence and Transcendence of God. In their volume titled, *20th Century Theology—God and World in a Transitional Age*, Stanley J. Grenz and Roger E. Olson point out the struggle of Christian theology to maintain a "balance" between the Transcendence and the Immanence of God. According to them, it was the Enlightenment modernity that caused the

---

[5] *Lumen Fidei*, an encyclical of Pope Francis, issued in the year 2013, points out that the "opposite of faith is idolatry" in the life of Israelites, http://w2.vatican.va/content/francesco/en/encyclicals/documents/papa-francesco_20130629_enciclica-lumen-fidei.html, accessed May 26, 2018.

[6] Pontifical Council for Justice and Peace, *Compendium of the Social Doctrine of the Church*, e-copy 2004, http://www.vatican.va/roman_curia/pontifical_councils/justpeace/documents/rc_pc_justpeace_doc_20060526_compendiodottsoc_en.html#The%20Church,%20sign%20and%20defender%20of%20the%20transcendence%20of%20the%20human%20person, accessed May 26, 2018.

[7] Pontifical Council for Justice and Peace, *Compendium of the Social Doctrine of the Church*, 49.

[8] Pontifical Council for Justice and Peace, *Compendium of the Social Doctrine of the Church*, 130.

[9] Pontifical Council for Justice and Peace, *Compendium of the Social Doctrine of the Church*, 130.

major imbalance from their traditional classical balance.[10] While their observation has a point, I would like to surmise that what we can look for in the realm of faith is not a "balance", as if the faith experience can be humanly "balanced", but an experience of the creative tension between these two dimensions (Transcendence and Immanence) of the divine mystery. When we fail to open ourselves to experiencing this tension, we fall victims to our own manufactured "faith-claims", masking our vested interests. What we can be involved in, then, is an activity of opening ourselves up to transcendence, by way of experiencing the creative and healthy tension born out of the revelatory dialectics between the Transcendence and the Immanence of God.

When Pope Benedict XVI declared 2013 as the year of Faith, his concern was to regenerate humanity, by reclaiming faith in a transcendent God. The secular principle of organising the society along such binaries as secular-sacred, public-private, reason-faith, and so on, had progressively strengthened itself in the Western society through the processes of industrialisation and modernisation backed by scientific discoveries, Enlightenment thought and revolutions, and the political philosophies of liberalism. Basing on these processes, the Euro-American society had gone to the extent of strictly proscribing any role for religion in the public sphere—public institutions, political sphere, and so on, to the resultant effect of humanity getting estranged from its ability for transcendence, and of its sensitivity for ethical common good. Against this saturating secularity of the West, the Pope spoke of a project of new evangelisation to open the Western society to experience a revival of faith. He involved in debates with secular philosophers like Jürgen Habermas, who, after a period of being a votary of the secularisation thesis, began to acknowledge the role of religion for the moral regeneration of humanity.

Continuing with the concerns of Benedict XVI, the present Pope Francis, in his Encyclical Letter *Lumen Fidei*, speaks of recovering from out of its modernist rationalistic abandonment the Light of Faith, a light that can "illuminate every aspect of human existence".[11]

Resurgence of religion in our post-secular world and the emergence of public religion with all its challenges, then, form the new context to our mission of being a "sign and defender" of the transcendental dimension of humanity. Mere facts of resurgence of religion and emergence of public religion are no guarantee to the possibility of experiencing faith and transcendence, because the positivity of religion remains merged with multiple forms of idolatries based on money, market, fundamentalism, narrow

---

[10] Stanley J. Grenz and Roger E. Olson, *20th Century Theology—God & World in a Transitional Age* (Secunderabad: OM Books, Indian Edition published in 2004 [1997]).
[11] *Lumen Fidei*, No. 4.

ethnocentric identity formation, and the like. It is therefore a challenge to our faith to sift through the positive potentials of religion which will mediate transcendence to our humanity. This challenge can be met, not by church alone, but by all wellsprings of transcendence—religions, spiritual traditions, art and aesthetic traditions, cultural traditions, and all the well-meaning creative initiatives for common good. The arena that stands for all these traditions and initiatives is civil society, an autonomous sphere that generates the voluntary initiatives of human beings. Our church-based practice of faith, therefore, has to extend itself to the sphere of civil society, wherein multiple religious and secular ideological others can be brought into creative interactions so as to mediate transcendence to a world that is increasingly yearning for it.

Civil Society

The thought on civil society, from its earliest days, has stood for not one but different spheres of life and activities. The earliest idea of it is to be found in the writings of Aristotle, who spoke of it as *koinoniapolitike*, denoting the political community which represented the citizens of the Greek city-states. Since it was a sphere wherein the elite citizens alone took part, it did not become widely participatory, and therefore, it did not grow and spread through history. However, the idea re-emerged again during the modern era, when individuals, as agents seeking to free themselves from heteronymous powers, began to assert their place in the decision-making process. John Locke (1632–1704), one of the early modern political philosophers to formulate themes on civil society, thought of it again in the model of the Greek city-state, wherein aristocratic citizens alone freely participated in political decision-making. In his opinion, civil society was nothing but the very political society itself.

As the processes of modernisation unfolded, and as the capitalist mode of production took hold of the economic process, the civil space began to shift its terrain from the political to the economic sphere. The producers and the industrialists began to assert their freedom to pursue trade and mercantile activities without interference from the States—the monarchical States of the time. Hegel (1770–1831) appreciated their assertiveness, and considered these initiative taking, enterprising bourgeoisie as the pristine actors of civil society (*Burgerliche Gesellschaft*). With their rights for private property duly affirmed, these bourgeoisie were said to constitute an independent space, unfettered by the State.

It was this understanding of civil society that Karl Marx (1818–1883) and Antonio Gramsci (1891–1937) reacted to, and dumped hastily the whole idea of civil society as bourgeois. However, while Marx explained away the civil society as a mere super-structural reality, not having any substance of its own, Gramsci saw some value in it. He found it playing an effective role to maintain the hold of the ruling bourgeois class upon the consciousness of the working class people. His reflections opened up the thinking that since civil society was doing a substantive role for the bourgeoisie, it could do a similar role for the liberation of the proletariat as well. This insight gradually helped explore the role which the religio-cultural institutions were playing or could play in social and economic transformation.

The contemporary debate on civil society began by the last quarter of the twentieth century, when the world experienced vibrant actors in the form of movements and organisations, and cultural and religious institutions, which formed part of neither the political society nor the state nor of the economic system. These actors, across the nations, became a significant force fighting for the rights of the underprivileged, socially oppressed, and ethnically marginalised people. The world, therefore, came to recognise these forces, and began to classify the space these actors were occupying as *independent* and *autonomous* from the State, the political society, the economic productive system, and from the family institution as well.

It needs to be noted that well-known political theorists began to question the claim of independent, autonomous space of the civil society, pointing out to the domination of civil society by forces of exploitation and un-freedom as well. Neera Chandhoke, an important political theorist in the Indian context, spoke of the conceits of civil society.[12] Jürgen Habermas, in his influential work *Structural Transformation of the Public Sphere*, lamented that the once-prevalent public sphere, as found, for example, in the coffee houses of Europe had disappeared due to the colonisation of the life-world by the technocratic communicative systems of the capitalist world.

Civil Society: Contemporary Relevance

Braving these criticisms, the contemporary civil society activists and theoreticians find greater value in it, especially in our global age wherein the organised States are abdicating much of their responsibilities under the dictates of multinational corporate houses. They point out to some relevant aspects of the civil society meaningful for us today. They are: (1) *the dynamic aspect*: civil society as a *dynamic*, not a static, space *relatively* independent from the State, economic system, family and individual; (2) *voluntary aspect*: emergence in this space of voluntary initiatives or organisations which operate to strengthen the rights of the individuals and communities; (3) *participatory aspect*: people's participation in governance

---

[12] Neera Chandhoke, *The Conceits of Civil Society* (New Delhi: Oxford University Press, 2003).

and in collective endeavours for common good; (4) *democratic aspect*: formation of a public sphere that contributes to the strengthening of the democratic polity; and, (5) *value based society*: formation of a participatory democracy and egalitarian society based on justice. These aspects can be empirically seen in the following texts.

The quantum of NGOs, interest-based voluntary groups, faith-based voluntary organisations, religious organisations, professional groups, consumer protection groups, and so on, has increased significantly during the last quarter of the twentieth century. They unmistakably point to the presence of a relative degree of independence from the State machinery, economic systems, family units, and individual selves.

These voluntary organisations focus on the rights of the individuals as well as collective identities. Human rights discourse has been one of the salient discourses in the public sphere today; similarly, identity centred discourses based on language, region, religion, minority status, oppressed status, and marginal categories, too have emerged boldly during the last twenty to thirty years.

Focus on *governance*, rather than *government*, has been an important turn in the civil society discourse in the recent times. After a phase of concentration on human rights discourse, which seemed to stress the rights of the individual, a concern has emerged to strengthen the case for the participation of grassroots people in public governance in different ways. And all these efforts, needless to say, orient themselves towards the common good.

Public sphere is the arena where public debates take place, contributing to the formation of the general will of the people in a democratic polity. These debates, informed by knowledge and ethical consciousness, shape the political will of the people and enhance the quality of democracy. Media plays an important role in this process. While civil society is not identical with this public sphere, the latter is an important feature of a vibrant civil society.

Finally, a civil society stands for an egalitarian ideal, based on the values of liberty and justice. These values differentiate a people-based civil society from an elitist, bourgeois one. This distinction is vital, because we do find the emergence of an elitist civil society which pretends to be neutral, but caters to the needs of the middle and upper classes, inducing an amnesia of the poor and marginalised people of our society.

Religion and Civil Society

While these aspects turn our focus upon the spaces of civil society, contemporary times have produced much debate about the relationship of religion to civil society. On one end of the spectrum, we have voices which oppose a role for religion in civil society, and, on the other end, there are the rightist forces—theocratic States for example, which go about running governments under religious mandates. Thus, we have those who wish to totally dis-establish religion in the civil and public sphere on the one hand, and those who wish to establish it at all levels of State-making on the other. Between these two extremes, we have voices today which discuss the role of religion *within the framework of constitutional secular democracies.*

Richard Rorty, a well-known post-modern philosopher from the US, argues that religion is a conversation stopper in the public sphere and therefore inimical to civil society. His negative stance is based on the in-commensurability theory regarding the incompatible relationship between different religions, ideologies, or comprehensive doctrines.

The critical theorists, who initiated a re-thinking on the Enlightenment rationality, have taken a less antagonistic and a more positive look at the role of religion. Max Horkheimer, Theodor W. Adorno, Herbert Marcuse, and others of the Frankfurt school have pursued a qualified approach to religion, verging on a critical appreciation.[13] Jürgen Habermas, one of the well-known critical theorists of the twentieth century, has, as mentioned earlier, come around to a positive stance from his earlier stance of resistance to the public role of religion in the civil society.

In the Indian context, André Bétteille, a well-known sociologist, opines that "the well-being of civil society depends upon the emergence of open and secular institutions, and on their differentiation from each other".[14] He, for one, does not consider religion to be a healthy institution of civil society, though he himself acknowledges that "secular institutions and the culture of civility often lack the energy and vitality that come from unshakable religious faith".[15]

There are other scholars in India who are positive about the role of religion in the public sphere, and they re-envision or re-interpret secularism more dynamically. Rajeev Bhargava is one of the well-known proponents of open-secularism for India. He propounds the ideal of secularism as enshrined in the Indian Constitution as a positive doctrine towards religion, and oriented towards fulfilment of justice to the Indian people.[16]

---

[13] Eduardo Mendieta ed., *The Frankfurt School on Religion—Key Writings by the Major Thinkers* (NY: Routledge, 2005).
[14] André Béteille, *Democracy and Its Institutions* (New Delhi: Oxford University Press, 2012), 187.
[15] Béteille, *Democracy and Its Institutions*, 190.
[16] Rajeev Bhargava, *The Promise of India's Secular Democracy* (New Delhi: Oxford University Press, 2010).

It is interesting to note that some of the activist-scholars, for example, V. Geetha,[17] speak about the public role of faith as well, especially as a transformative potential for the subaltern people.

That the danger of religious fundamentalism is looming large in the Indian context is a real challenge to be reckoned with. An extreme reaction to this danger would be to rigidify the doctrine of secularism, and refuse any role for religion in civil society or public sphere. On the other end, going by the general resurgence of religion in the public sphere, people can become fundamentalist about the public role of religion. While the hardcore secularists should realise the positive potentials of religion, the fundamentalists should respect the dynamic autonomy of the public sphere, constituted by multiple others.

Church and Civil Society

It is in this context that the church is called upon to play an inspirational and prophetic role to mediate transcendence through civil society. It may well be surmised that church and civil society are kindred concepts, having a historical affinity to one another. Originating with Jesus and his itinerant followers, encountering the Divine in a poignant way in and through the death and resurrection of Jesus, receiving a powerfully affirmative spiritual experience at the event of Pentecost, an outwardly forward looking people became the nucleus of the early church. They progressively formed a community, whose nature and functions were quite distinct from the then existing groupings of people in the Palestinian context. This was a spirited community, living out an eschatological hope. The system of sharing (Acts 2: 44–45; 4: 32–35) that arose in the early church was a singular example of the spirit of participation and sharing that the community experienced. It offered an alternative model of community, gathered round the experience of the Spirit of God. There are many good examples in the life of the early church, which show how they went beyond ascriptive hierarchical ties. The most notable one was the ability of the early church to go beyond the boundaries of Judaism by deciding not to impose the practice of circumcision upon the non-Jewish Christians coming from the Hellenistic world. The definitive proclamation of Paul in his letter to the Galatians (3: 28) that there is no discrimination as Jew, Gentile, slave, male, female, and so on, was the typical spirit of the community of the early church.

This alternate community inspired a living based on the two-fold principles of faith in a transcendent creator God and praxis of loving relationship among creatures. These principles, combination of a vertical and a horizontal dimension of faith, propelled a radical praxis of community,

---

[17] V. Geetha and Nalini Rajan, *Religious Faith, Ideology, Citizenship* (London: Routledge, 2011).

with an absolute sense of equality that broke down human-made hierarchies. Due to its radicality, it infused a unique vitality for egalitarian living though it was continuously sought to be domesticated by the dominant powers of the time. Birth of monasteries was a singular instance of the practice of this radical vision of community, when the institutional church went with the powers that be. Thus, the real church, the radical experience of community, journeyed along space and time, rejuvenated through the vibrant initiatives of prophetic individuals and collectives.

When Tertulian raised the question, "What has Athens to do with Jerusalem?", he was reflecting about an aspect of the relationship between faith and human reason—an important component of civil society. Athens, the symbol of the Hellenistic culture with its overbearing rational philosophical inquiry, did interact with the fertile faith of Christianity, and has guided the theological thinking[18] as well as the practice of faith for a long time in history. Similarly, Jerusalem, the fountainhead of Christian faith, has continued to serve not merely the Christian community, but the whole of humanity through the mediation of Christian religion and civilisation, with ever refreshing experiences of faith.

St. Augustine spoke of the church as a pilgrim community, journeying towards the city of God, even while partaking of the temporal realities of the earthly city. This temporal city, according to Augustine, was this world, the *saeculum*, the rudiment of the secular city to emerge later in history. The church was the very inspiration to this earthly city, even while pilgrimaging towards the eternal city of God. Augustine was thus proposing the church to be an alternate community to the then existing Roman empire—a power that believed in self-glory.

The second half of the second millennium of the Christian era witnessed substantive events in relation to the journey of faith of the church. It was the epoch of modernity. Major events like scientific discoveries, Enlightenment thinking, French Revolution, and Industrial Revolution, gave birth to the era of modernity. During this era, Christianity, through its teaching centring on *Imago Dei*, played a vital role in bringing forth a consciousness of humanism. The Reformation movement played a vital role in propagating a sense of democracy—the political essence of modernity, by underlining the priesthood of believers (a decentralisation of the spiritual authority), and instilling confidence among the wider believing public to read, understand, and become able to receive the divine revelations without priestly mediation. The birth of welfare nation-states has much to do with the inspiration of the church as a community of sharers

---

[18] This interaction is very much evident in the formulation of the core Christian dogmas, and later on in the classical scholastic theologies, and more recently in neo-scholastic theologies.

of resources. Thus, the epochal events of modernity carried the abiding inspiration of the church, and the latter played its catalytic role as leaven in the flour.[19]

Modernity, with an embedded inspiration of the church, has gone about playing an empowering role as it spread throughout the globe during the colonial era. In *The Acknowledged Christ of Indian Renaissance*, M.M. Thomas has highlighted this aspect of modernity, befitting the Indian context. Needless to say that modernity went with the process of colonisation, a major event during the second part of the second millennium. Today, we realise more and more the ill-effects of colonialism. The post-colonial criticism has shed much light on this matter. But, a much qualified post-colonial criticism from the subaltern stance is yet to emerge. It will not be difficult to understand the fact that colonialism, and the aspects of modernity it spread, did result in the subaltern people waking up to challenge the ascriptive hierarchy, especially the caste hierarchy in India. The missionary endeavour did contribute to the spread of modern education, and spread of Enlightenment values like liberty, equality, and fraternity in the colonised countries. Democratisation of the sphere of education, inculcation of the Enlightenment values, enabling a public sphere to emerge with the aid of print media, empowering the periphery of the Indian society through various measures, and so on, were the ways through which the church contributed to the emergence of civil society in the Indian context. This contribution needs to be reinvented meaningfully today.

The church is a spiritual community with its faith in Jesus Christ, who, through the Spirit of God, is leading it towards a new heaven and a new earth. This spiritual sense of the community gives a transcendental dimension to the church, which in turn, gives it certain radical freedom from natural, political, and civil communities (societies). This transcendental dimension shares in the mystery of the Divine and gives us, as the *Compendium* points out, an intuition into the face of God. And this dimension, in an extreme paradox, cannot become a matter of our experience unless it becomes an aspect of the immanence of God with us. The very possibility of speaking and experiencing transcendence is rooted in the condition of possibility of speaking and experiencing the immanence

---

[19] It is also argued that this modernity is part and parcel of the exploitative system of capitalism. While granting that an aspect of this modernity, especially its calculative instrumentalist rationality goes with the profit-oriented capitalist motivation, I surmise that the whole project of modernity cannot be reduced to this instrumentalist rationality. One needs to situate oneself in a context to appreciate the various aspects of modernity. Looking at it from a subaltern perspective, especially as situated in the Indian context, the emancipatory aspects of modernity with its own specific kind of rationality, find their relevance. It is therefore fair to state that the Christian inspiration in modernity, that is, its communitarian and egalitarian elements, should not be brushed aside under the fallacy of an overarching generalisation of post-modernity.

of God. Experience of the exodus for Israelites was the condition of possibility for speaking about the creator God; Mosaic Law, for the Covenant of God; Davidic kingdom, for the messianic kingdom; incarnate God, for the pre-existent logos; repentance and transformation, for participation in the Reigning of God; the Cross, for Resurrection; human nature, for divine grace; earthly Jerusalem, for the heavenly Jerusalem; and so on. It therefore brings forth a paradigmatic revelatory dialectics between transcendence and immanence which becomes the very source of our experience of God. Accordingly, when we treat the church as a transcendental community, it becomes intelligible only when it becomes an immanent community that is a community in the society, here and now.

PRACTICE OF PUBLIC THEOLOGY

David Tracy speaks of three publics wherein public theology can be meaningfully practised: church, academy, and society.[20] I find these three domains relevant, *mutatis mutandis,* also for our Indian context. I am aware of the differences between the Western and Indian contexts. One major difference would be the very confidence of Tracy to place the church as one of the publics. In a society like ours, we will have to think of "religious/multi-religious publics" in the place of the church. However, since this particular reflection here is undertaken from the Christian perspective, I find it meaningful to speak of the church as a public.

1. Church is our home of faith. We draw our resources of faith from our faith-community, that is, the church. As a voluntary community based on faith, the church is an active player in the civil society, and this opens not only a wider site but also a dynamic possibility for the practice of faith. It can network with other voluntary organisations, and help create an interactive sphere, whereby spiritual energies, ethical sensitivity, and theological visions can be transmitted for transforming the wider society. It can help create an interactive sphere between the multiple religious traditions operative in a particular vicinity, and contribute to the creation of "community of communities",[21] consisting of various religious communities. It may even help create an interactive sphere between the so-called social groupings (communities in the Indian societal sense), and help them get liberated from in-ward looking ethnic closures and become

---

[20] David Tracy, *Analogical Imagination—Christian Theology and the Culture of Pluralism* (London: SCM Press, 1981). Sebastian Kim, another important proponent of public theology in the contemporary context, thinks of six areas of the public sphere as sites for doing public theology: state, market, civil society, academies, media, and religious communities. These sites are more differentiated than Tracy's scheme. However, I find Tracy's scheme more simple, and theologically congenial.

[21] Sebastian Kim, *Theology in the Public Sphere—Public Theology as a Catalyst for Open Debate* (London: SCM Press, 2011).

open communities to participate in the wider public in a healthy manner to build up the democratic polity.

In so far as it is part of the civil society, the church itself functions as a civil society within its own sphere. As is known, the primary trait of a civil society is the democratic public sphere within itself. The Indian church needs to establish this democratic public sphere within itself. First of all, every individual church needs to make itself people-based and democratic. It is the power of the people that is going to give every church the power to negotiate the wider democratic society, and bring meaning and vitality to itself. We need to therefore empower the people with theological education and various pastoral/institutional roles. Second, we need to establish a communicative sphere between the various individual churches, including the denominational and independent churches. We need to urgently forge this solidarity, taking into account the fact that all the churches together constitute the Indian church and all of us together share a common identity in the public sphere. And therefore, establishing and shaping up the inter-church communicative sphere is a manner of becoming an effective player in the wider civil society.

2. Academia is yet another public, an important component of the civil society. It is unfortunate that the contemporary academia seemingly serves the interests of the State or the economic system. As a domain of knowledge and wisdom, it must function in an independent autonomous sphere of the civil society. While the freedom of the civil society is meaningfully furthered by the academia, the latter's creativity draws its wisdom and commitment from the power of the civil society.

Indian church is a major player in academia, starting with the formal school education to the higher education and to the vast arena of non-formal education. With its centuries-old commitment in the field of modern education, the Indian church had imparted knowledge to a people, who had empowered themselves with this education; they became aware of their rights and dignity, and by demanding their civil liberties, civilised the public sphere of India to a large extent. To the extent it was involved in this process of humanisation, the Indian church was doing indirect public theology, mediating faith, and contributing to the unfolding of salvation (as M.M. Thomas would have it). However, the involvement in education has become rather dubious during the present times: whether the Christian involvement is contributing to mediation of faith that gives us an experience of transcendence or to a mere technological professionalisation (of a certain section which self-perpetuates its own comfort) which inhibits and impairs the human ability for transcendence is a critical question the Indian church has to ask itself. Its open-minded participation in the civil society will invite such questions from the wider society, and clarify its goals in the light of wider criticisms. This ability to interact with the civil society as regards its involvement in education is one of the ways in which the Indian church would do a very basic public theology today.

It has also its own sites of academia like the theological colleges, research institutes, departments of theologies, or religious studies, wherein it can effectively do public theology and mediate faith. Tracy would propose systematic theologies to be pursued in our academia as a way of doing public theology. Systematic theology is one by which we formulate our faith-claims and pursue their meaningfulness in wider publics shared by different denominational and religious others. In our contemporary context, where there are increasing numbers of denominational churches along with their own theologies and many religious traditions establishing their study centres or departments in the academia, it is the duty of the Indian church to systematically pursue public conversations with them in order to be able to mediate the vitality of faith in these circles.

3. Society at large is the wider public, Tracy suggests, a public theology should engage itself with. Wider public includes those spheres where we pursue social, cultural, economic, and political interests with the goal of common good. The wider public in India today is threatened by multiple closures! The most visible one is majoritarianism in politics, backed by religious nationalism and communalism.[22] Not merely a case of travesty of democracy, this closure threatens to revive the forces of social and cultural hegemonies, with a will to dominate over the public sphere. It means loss of freedom not only to the religious minorities, but to social minorities as well. The less visible, but, more substantive form of closure is the one caused by the market forces today. As if there is no development outside the market, the contemporary world is getting organised by the neo-liberal invisible hand which threatens the life-world of the people, with commercial urges entering even into the moral, ethical, aesthetic, and cultural veins of the people. The general humanity seems to lose the power to transcend the closures caused by these commercial impulses. Along with these two forms of closures, the age-old oppressive and discriminatory systems like caste and patriarchy, with the combination of residual feudalism (mainstay feudalism in many rural areas), get expressed in such uncivil acts like honour killing, rape, moral policing, and so on. These oppressive systems are further compounded by the increasing cleavage between the rich and the poor. These realities, sustaining a serious imbalance in socio-economic and political systems, present a fertile soil for the production of fatalism, deterministic thinking, reductionism, fundamentalism, and violent

---

[22] One of the recent works to reiterate the danger of majoritarianism is by Manjari Katju, *Hinduising Democracy—The Vishva Hindu Parishad in Contemporary India* (New Delhi: New Text, 2017).

reactionary forces. In this context, religion, otherwise a fountainhead for the experience of transcendence and faith, turns into irreligion.

It is in this wider public that the Indian church is called upon to play a public role in order to mediate Faith in a transcendent God of life, love, and justice. Pessimists would ask, what can a Church, consisting only of 2.4 percent of the population, do, in this ocean of humanity that India has. They must be reminded that it was only a minority of the prophetic community that guided the Israelites through its history; that a modicum of leaven could sweeten the whole flour; that the reigning of God is like the mustard seed or a seed that grows without being noticed. The minority Christianity has indeed contributed significantly, and can contribute significantly in the future. Its chosen arena must be the civil society, the site of transcendence for the whole of humanity. As the *Compendium* points out, it is the church that has given the theological anthropology to the very idea of civil society. It says, "... by her vision of man, understood as an autonomous relational being who is open to the Transcendent", the church has given an identity to the civil society. Presenting a human being with transcendental qualities, Christianity gave a human being an autonomous dignified self, morally responsible, realisable only in its relation to a transcendent God. The autonomous self was the reflection of the image of God, and its moral responsibility was engrained through a natural law. "This idea of the individual, which stands at the core of civil society, was pre-eminently a Christian idea."[23]

Christianity in India can, then, be a catalytic agent for constituting a religiously creative and ethically anchored civil society, which can mediate the transcendence to the whole of India. The local churches will not be only the parishes, but the whole vicinity inhabited by all God's people (*oikumene*). The local churches can involve in establishing interactive sites between religious and ideological others; they can bring together the voluntary initiatives of people for cultural creativity, economic parity, political participation, social justice, and peace. Thus, the Indian church can become a visible player in the civil society, contributing to the mediation of faith and transcendence.

By Way of Concluding

We are used to experiencing light through the windows—the interstices—of the massive structures of cathedrals. The interactive sites, provided by the multiple publics of the civil society, become the interstices through which the light of faith can shine upon humanity today. Inter-denominational, inter-religious, inter-disciplinary, inter-cultural, and

---

[23] Adam B. Selgman, *The Idea of Civil Society* (Princeton: Princeton University Press, 1992), 66.

inter-ideological sites are some of the interstices for the light of faith to shine forth. This light of faith will help not only the Christians, but also the whole of humanity, to journey as "pilgrim people" towards the future, with the refreshing experience of transcendence. As *Lumen Fidei* says: "Faith is truly a good for everyone; it is a common good. Its light does not simply brighten the interior of the Church, nor does it serve solely to build an eternal city in the hereafter; it helps us build our societies in such a way that they can journey towards a future of hope."[24]

---

[24] *Lumen Fidei*, No. 51.

6

RELIGIOUS PLURALISM AND DEMOCRACY

Theology of Religious Pluralism

Religious pluralism[1] has become a singular experience of our times. It is singular in the sense that it is both momentous and unique to our contemporary global world, which, unlike the unarticulated or less articulated religious plurality of the past, has come to actively constitute different religions and religious pluralism, impacting upon the dynamics of public life, and generating new prospects as well as challenges to the practice of democracy. This new religious pluralism is being explored from different perspectives today: sociology of religion explores the way this phenomenon impacts upon social relationships; psychology of religion investigates how it becomes an integral part of the experience of the self; political science deals with the way it intervenes into the domain of collective decision-making, throwing up new challenges and opportunities in national and international political practices; and, closer to our field of interest, theology of religion explores anew the salvific value of religious pluralism.

During the latter part of the twentieth century, when the public experience of religious pluralism was growing thicker, Christian theologians responded to it with theologies which sought to engage with religious pluralism beyond the then extant ecclesial frameworks of *exclusivism* and *inclusivism*. Exclusivism, beginning with the era of the strict principle of *extra ecclesiam nulla salus*, extends up to the contemporary far-right evangelism; and, inclusivism, beginning with fulfilment theologies (J.N. Farquhar's *Christianity—the Crown of Hinduism* being a typical example in

---

[1] The term pluralism is perhaps not adequate to signify the reality that we would like to discuss; it tends to stand for an ism, that is, a kind of constricted ideology, or for an unrelated parallel of religions; both these significations are not adequate to the reality of religious pluralism. Going by Raimon Panikkar's suggestion, I take religious pluralism to be that which stands "between unrelated plurality and a monolithic unity" which implies the human condition that "in the actual polarities of our human existence we find our being". R. Panikkar, *Intra-Religious Dialogue* (Bangalore: Asian Trading Corporation, 1984), 37.

India), has gone through christocentric, theocentric, and kingdom-centric approaches and extends up to the theological-anthropological schemes of anonymous Christians (Karl Rahner) or of the unknown Christ of Hinduism (early Raimon Panikkar). Both these frameworks were proposed from "within" the Christian claim of the absoluteness of its religious validity (validated by revelation) and the relative validity of other religions. Theologies of religious pluralism, on the other hand, began to approach the truth claims of different religions more openly. The documents of Vatican II (*Nostra Aetate* and *Ad Gentes*), for example, could speak of finding truth and holiness in other religions; Raimon Panikkar, in his later period, could speak of encountering other religions with radical openness; Jacque Dupuis could think of christocentric pluralism rather than church centric ecumenism; and, Paul Knitter could locate the relevance of religious pluralism primarily in terms of its ability to address the social evils of poverty and social discrimination.

This increasingly open theologising on religious pluralism is an ongoing vibrant theological activity pursued today not only by official theologians but also by lay, unofficial theologians, and by theologians of different religions too. Varieties of theological views are emerging in this regard. There are those like John Hick, Alan Rice, and others who stoutly defend the possibility and the necessity for a healthy theology of religious pluralism for our times. Contrarily, there are persons like Gavin D'Costa[2] who deny even the very possibility of a theology of religious pluralism, more for its illogicality, because, any theology, which premises itself upon a normative axis, according to him, will have to exclude or include others. We witness today also *ultra* neo-evangelical stances which totally deny any theological significance to religion in general and other religions in particular, and hold on to the irreconcilable superior truth of Christian religion. While such extreme positions do emerge, we have other voices which engage with the challenges involved in theologically responding to religious pluralism today. They probe how a theology of religious pluralism could be premised upon radical pluralism and yet not succumb to passive indifference; and, recognise the incommensurability of different religious traditions, and yet look for a pro-active, dialogical, interactive, and inter-subjective mutuality. They explore how religious truth and reality manifest themselves in categories of identity-difference, one-many, unity-diversity, universality-particularity, and so on.

Philosophy of Pluralism

This opening of the horizon of the theology of religious pluralism, when examined closely, would show that it has happened not in a vacuum, but

---

[2] Gavin D'Costa, *Theology in the Public Square—Church, Academy and Nation* (Malden, MA: Blackwell, 2005).

along with or in dialectical relationship with the unfolding philosophical perspectives on truth and reality, and on the modalities (knowledge-related) of experiencing them, cognitively or otherwise.

It is a matter of common knowledge that the modern era, as it emerged in the Euro-American context from the sixteenth-seventeenth centuries onwards, had taken to a mind-centric cognitivist approach to truth, reality, and knowledge. Modern rationalist philosophers like René Descartes adopted the method of doubting everything so as to arrive at truth and reality. Doubting everything was to be based ultimately upon an undoubtable thinking self, the *cogito* (*cogito ergo sum*—*I think, therefore I am*), which gave certainty to truth, reality, and knowledge. This rationalist approach postulated an eternal transcendental thinking self to provide certainty to the methods of the emerging modern sciences. The following phase of empiricism took the road to truth, reality, and knowledge with rigorous methods of experimentation, verification, and falsification—all premised upon the possibility of certainty rendered on account of the permanent thinking self.[3] And the subsequent Kantian philosophy too depended upon the certainty of the thinking self for the emergence of the autonomous self.

In the religious domain, it was the era of classical Western Christian missionary movements, initiated by the Catholics and followed up by the Protestants. Philosophically speaking, the former was anchored upon the Scholastic Christian philosophy, underpinned by the Aristotelian metaphysics, and the latter upon the modern rational realisations initiated by persons like Descartes, Berkeley, Kant, and others. Both, however, presented Christianity to foreigners (pagans, heathens, etc) as the sole embodiment of absolute truth and reality (supernatural reality of God), and beckoned others to see (convert to) the truth as contained in the Christian religion. The certainty of truth, reality, and knowledge, as found in this missionary Christianity, was based primarily on the reality of faith, but however, legitimised and nurtured by the classical epistemology and the modern sciences, oftentimes the positivist variety. Protestant Christianity was indeed in the forefront in endeavouring to synchronise Christian biblical truth with modern sciences, and the birth of liberal theologies and the historical critical methods of biblical exegesis and interpretation are worthy witnesses to this endeavour. The emerging Western Christian modern ethos, challenged as well as propelled by events like the French Revolution and Enlightenment, defended the absoluteness of its truth and sought to demonstrate it through scientific methods. Recognition of religious pluralism was treated as an anathema or a defeat to the truth of Christianity/the Bible.

---

[3] It is also of common knowledge that an empiricist like Bishop George Berkeley spoke of God as the Super Mind that designed and maintained the empirical world.

The heydays of Euro-American modernity (eighteenth-nineteenth to early twentieth century), even while enshrining the rational self with further fortifications of empiricism, positivism, and so on, brought about philosophical movements of self-reflexivity in the forms of existentialism and phenomenology. Philosophical existentialism went beyond the postulation of metaphysical/ontological essences, and the phenomenological movement made a call to go to things in themselves, to the phenomena as they manifest themselves. These movements of reflexivity and self-criticality rendered the reified certainties of truth, reality, and knowledge questionable, and opened the horizon for more explorative approaches. Truth, knowledge, and self came to be understood less as fixed, eternal, and intransigent and more as dynamic realities. Further on, the linguistic turn in philosophy enlightened the role played by language in the experience of truth, resulting in linguistic structuralism, and later, post-structuralism, problematising the very possibility of representation of truth and reality (crisis of representation). The ensuing knowledge-related movements of deconstruction and constructivism contributed significantly to the decentring of metanarratives of truth, knowledge, and self.

In the realm of religion, when various religious traditions began to cross borders and exist along with Christian religion in the Euro-American context, pluralism began to dawn upon the Western ethos as an irreversible fact of life. Experiencing different religions, with their own philosophical, social, and cultural universes, was a new phase in the history of the modern West. How to make meaning out of the different religious traditions and their claims for truth and validity became an important concern. Study of religions, as scientific exercises (*religiowissenschaf*), arose in the academic field, and phenomenology of religion as a method came to support such studies. Comparative study of religion, collecting huge religious data from across regions, classifying them, and looking into them for common features/patterns of the sacred /the holy became a dominant orientation of the study of comparative religions. These phenomenological studies endeavoured to describe the religious phenomena as they manifested to religious-insiders rather than evaluate them from the perspective of outsiders. As Martin Heidegger put it, phenomenology meant "to let that which shows itself be seen from itself in the very way in which it shows itself from itself",[4] and phenomenology of religion approached religion to show itself from itself. As a method, phenomenology of religion tried to focus upon the intentionality of religious consciousness both in terms of the intentional act (*noesis*) and the intentional object (*noema*), and tried to bring to light the attributes of the intending consciousness that existed across

---

[4] As cited in Merold Westphal, "Phenomenology of Religion", in *The Routledge Companion to Philosophy of Religion*, eds. Chad Meister and Paul Copan (New York: Routledge, 2007), 733.

traditions. By identifying such transcendental consciousness, Edmund Husserl endeavoured to show the objectivity of consciousness and thereby establish phenomenology as an objective science.

However, the science of hermeneutics followed up upon the phenomenological study of religions, and showed that hermeneutics was not a dispensable activity, but the very way of being in the world. Philosophical and theological hermeneutics, as disciplines of study, explored further the dimensions of interpretative experiences of reality, religious truth, and so on. Hermeneutical existence is radically inter-subjective, in the sense that it constitutes itself necessarily in relation to the other. In the light of hermeneutics, different religions obtained interpretative meaning for their practitioners in their own right. And this opened up space for religious pluralism in the domain of religious truth, reality, and knowledge. Differences therefore came to be understood not as inadequacies, but different embodiments of truths.

The contemporary moment is being characterised as the postmodern era, and the postmodern philosophical variants are making a virulent critique of the classical metaphysical metanarratives, including the grand metanarrative of the Enlightenment rationality. They question the epistemological systems of knowledge which work on a dichotomised subject-object logical distinction, which is identified as the root-cause of the emergence of instrumental rationality. Instead, they foreground the indigenous modes of knowledge as valid forms of knowing. Emergence of neo-social movements like feminist, ecological, and civil society groups begin to function with new understandings of knowledge. The new religious movements of the contemporary era, and the innumerable cultural universes brought to light by the global media, seriously interrogate such rationality-based binaries as subjective-objective, religion-superstition, secular-religious, and private-public. This postmodern era gives further legitimacy to plurality of truths, undergirding religious pluralism.

Religion and Democracy

How does religious pluralism exist in a democratic polity is the question that concerns us here. It has many sub-questions to be addressed: Can religion be at all an ally to democracy? If it can be so, how can it relate itself to a secular liberal democracy that has come to be the epitome of political practices today? If it can relate positively with a secular liberal democracy, how can the reality of religious pluralism engage with it? And most pertinent of all, how can democracy and religious pluralism come together in the Indian context? are the important questions to be addressed here.

During the modern era, democracy began to be newly constituted with the emergence of the initiative-taking traders and entrepreneurs, who negotiated for their power or influence in decision-making in economic activities. It was more a form of direct democracy whereby the members participated directly in the act of decision-making. However, down through the centuries, the decision-making process extended itself beyond the realm of economics to cover wider public concerns dealing with security, liberties, rights, duties, common good, and so on. The participants too extended beyond the select enclaves of people (aristocrats, entrepreneurs, etc) to the wider population, who gradually gained the right of franchise. As the participatory agents increased, democracy became a representative democracy, to be exercised through the institutions of parliaments or democratically elected individuals.

One may have several questions as regards the efficacy of such representative democracy for collective decision-making. However, the wisdom embedded in the political practice of democracy that humanity has come up with cannot be undermined, nor can its substantive value be underestimated. A major critique of hitherto existing democracy has been, and rightly so, that it has so far been a political ideology of the ruling class of capitalists or a pliable instrument in the hands of fundamentalists, dictators, and retrogressive agents of power-mongers. In the place of this apparently vulnerable and inefficient system, some well-meaning individuals advocate even benevolent dictatorships as right forms of political rules. Needless to say that these criticisms, in spite of being true in several contexts, cannot hold absolutely against the sublime value humanity can attach to the political practice called democracy, which embodies a simple but deeply significant wisdom of equal participation in decision-making for collective living. The fact that such an equal participation has not come about all over the world cannot nullify the singular importance of the principle. It is on the other hand, incumbent upon everyone to nurture this ideal, by renewing it contextually, enhancing its quality, even while challenging the negativities accruing upon it. Relating democracy to religion during the contemporary era, in an analytical and critical manner, is one way of nurturing the ideal, clarifying several misgivings and criticisms, while promoting positive potentials of the interface.

There are several objections to the coming together of religion and democracy. First of all, there is the argument in terms of the difference in domains: while religion concerns itself with the other world, that is, guiding people to achieve salvation, otherworldly liberation, and so on, democracy is about this world of temporal concerns (*vyavakarika*), that is, dealing with matters of power, politics, decision-making, and economics of this temporal world. These two worlds do not meet, and if at all they meet, they do so in an individual's private self, which cannot be meaningfully counted for public political activity. Second, a kindred argument of the foregoing one is that religion and democracy have incongruent authorities as power-centres: while religion arises out of and is being legitimated by a transcendental/supernatural power-centre, represented by an individual or institution with absolute authority, democracy originates from and is being legitimated by a horizontal societal power, constituted by a participatory or representative process of decision-making for common good. People who draw upon religion may legitimise their arguments upon the transcendental source of God, and it may play truant in a historical and secular debating forum. Third, the languages of religion and of secular democracy are not intelligible to each another. Richard Rorty, as mentioned earlier, argues that religion is a conversation stopper in public political fora, because, the language of religion is neither verifiable nor falsifiable, and therefore, it is impossible to make an argument with a religious language in a secular decision-making forum. Moreover, the nature of religious language is generally absolutist, and therefore, tends to exclude different others in a common forum, and can turn divisive and sectarian rather than promoting life in public. Fourth, religion goes with a passionate commitment, and the history of humanity is sadly characterised by wars, strife, and acts of terror supposedly born out of religious convictions, and this does not augur well for democracy or a rational public sphere. These are some of the main arguments against relating religion to democracy.

On the other hand, when we go by actual history, we realise that the development of democracy has had much to do with the practice of religion. The modern form of democracy has had much to do with the event of Reformation and its essentials like *sola fide, sola gratia,* and *sola scriptura,* which have religiously nurtured individuality and autonomy, have in turn contributed to the emergence of the ideals of citizenship endowed with human and civil rights. The biblical account of human beings created in the image and likeness of God contributed further to the dignity of the individual. These Reformation impacts have had much to do with the birth of modern democracy in the Indian context as well. The Protestant missionaries to India, infused with the Reformation ideals of individuality and the Enlightenment ideals of equality and liberty, undertook to be involved in the civilising mission, which meant modern mass education, working for abolition of slavery, and other forms of indignities suffered by the subaltern people, raising the consciousness of civil liberties, and so on. It would then mean that religion, the Protestant Christian religion in particular, has been contributory to the emergence of modern democracy, which continues to relate itself to religion in a context-specific manner. The liberal theory of democracy has dealt much with the place of religion in a modern state.

Religion and Liberal Democracy

It was against the violence unleashed by wars of religion in Europe that democracy as a modern political system was constructed. The first substantive reflection upon the treatment of religion in this democratic polity came from John Locke, in his *Letter Concerning Toleration* (1689). He argued forcefully for distinguishing "the business of the civil government from that of religion, and to settle the just bounds that lie between the one and the other"[5]; he did so in order to uphold the value of liberty (absolute liberty, just and true liberty, and equal and impartial liberty—in his words). Demarcating the boundary, he believed, would protect the liberty even for conscientious dissent by individuals and communities of conscience, and result in equality and peace in a society organised by the modern democratic State. The separation principle of Locke needs be situated against the background of a process of establishing of religion in the newly emerging Protestant States in Europe. For example, John Calvin (1509-1564), one of the forerunners to lay the foundation for the Protestant Christian religion, committed "to civil government the duty of rightly establishing religion"[6] because he, being true to the principle of *sola scriptura*, took the civil authority to be ordained by God.

As history went on to show, establishing religion at the State level had serious problems not only for religious pluralism (Christian denominations) but also for the then developing modernising forces of science and technology. John Locke had to, therefore, state forcefully the liberal principle of separation. The founding fathers of America, drawing much inspiration from Locke, implemented the principle of a wall of separation between State and religion, which, as given out in the First Amendment, meant neither establishing nor preventing the free exercise of religion in the modern State. Thus, the United States developed its own version of separation of State and religion, while France, through its political doctrine of *laicite*, implemented a rigorous version of the same.

The liberal democracy, as being practised today, has multiple variants: They begin with total denial of any role for religion in modern democratic politics and go through multiple variations to arrive at the opposite end point of accommodating religion in politics; that is, running a democratic government in a polity wherein religion is established substantially. We have countries like France, where there is total denial of religion in politics; countries like the United States, UK, Australia, Canada, and Scandinavian countries of Protestantism, wherein democracy goes with a predominant

---

[5] John Locke, *Letter Concerning Toleration*, in *Two Treatises of Government and Letter Concerning Tradition*, ed. Ian Shapiro (New Haven: Yale University Press, 2003), 218.

[6] John Calvin, "Institutes of Christian Religion", in *Calvin—Institutes of Christian Religion*, ed. John T McNeill (Kentucky: Westminster John Knox Press, 2006), 1485.

religion but freedom for religious pluralism is protected as a democratic right; liberal democracies like India wherein liberalism is enshrined in the Constitution, but majoritarianism seeks relentlessly to swallow it up; countries like Nepal, Bangladesh, Malaysia, Pakistan, Israel, and Iran where a particular religion is established within their variants of democracy.

Religion and Democracy in the Post-Liberal Era

That being the variations in liberal democracy, we are witness today to the phenomena of resurgence or vitalisation of religion, as discussed in Chapter 2. Corresponding to these, we are witness also to a revision of the philosophical approach to religious truth, especially in terms of its absolute-relative, universal-particular, and, one-many binary attributes. Religious truth is approached from different standpoints today. The traditional metaphysical standpoint that begins with the postulation of God as the absolute cause of everything, and then going on to speak about the attributes of God as eternity, infinity, sovereignty, omnipotence, omnipresence, and so on, has become *one of the* approaches to religious truth/reality today.

The salient features of the liberal worldview like rationality and secularity, and the assumption of their universality, normativity, and unilateral legitimacy have come under severe criticism today. Under the scanner of Lyotard's incredulity of metanarratives, these features have become non-normative and have opened up a post-liberal horizon for consciousness, experience, and political processes. Secularisation as a process of freeing human consciousness from mythical enchantments or secular ethos as one freed from religious imaginations are not concepts unquestionably agreed to anymore. In this context, we find extreme positions being proposed by advocates of radical orthodoxy[7] that there is nothing like secularity at all. On the opposite side, one finds a stream of scientific fundamentalists (e.g., Richard Dawkins) who claim that religious truth (God) is an illusion and that the earlier its disappearance, the better the human development. Between these opposites, scholars like Charles Taylor would think of the contemporary *secular age*[8] as one that is open to secularity as well as religion, without, however, contradicting one another.

The emergence and sustenance of different voices go to show that post-liberal ethos, as one that remains open to different viewpoints, and especially as one that considers religion on its own, as a *sui generis* reality, is gaining ground today. And this ethos relates itself to the political practice of liberal democracy as well.

---

[7] John Milbank, *Theology and Social Theory: Beyond Secular Reason* (Oxford: Blackwell, 1990).

[8] Charles Taylor, *A Secular Age* (Cambridge: The Belknap Press of Harvard University Press, 2007).

On the occasion of the dismemberment of the erstwhile Soviet Union in 1989, Francis Fukuyama, a policy maker in the US State department, posed a question, "The End of History?" implying that "the end point of mankind's ideological evolution and the universalisation of Western liberal democracy as the final form of human government"[9] had been achieved. He exuded the confidence that liberal political system, as a political ideology, had won for ever against any other form of political system. Though Fukuyama's claim was made on the basis of the absolute and universal value of liberal democracy for humankind, this value is yet to be fully actualised in history. In a recently published volume titled, *The Retreat of Western Liberalism*, Edward Luce, a journalist and commentator, argues that the West is experiencing today the regression of liberal democracy, as witnessed to in the salience of illiberal forces like ethnocentrism, racism, religious fundamentalism, and so on. Liberal democracy seems to be facing up to unprecedented challenges in today's post-liberal era. Religion seems to play a conspicuous role in these challenges. The way religious sentiment is sought to be exploited for an illiberal agenda of majoritarian politics, but through a liberal system, is the typical dilemma of liberal democracy today. Can liberal democracy and religion be anymore related meaningfully?

One of the latest support to relate religion to liberal democracy is offered by Cecile Laborde, an Oxford-based political philosopher, in her volume, *Liberalism's Religion* (2017).[10] She points out that there are two major camps that debate upon the liberal theory of religion today. One, the liberal egalitarian camp, whose central figure is John Rawls, and includes theorists like Ronald Dworkin, Charles Taylor, Christopher Eisgruber, Lawrence Sager, Jonathan Quong, and others. This camp dwells upon the continuing relevance of the liberal theory, and argues for a separation of the State not only from religion but also from every conception of good, or every comprehensive doctrine, without however, denying the possibility for exemptions. The other camp, which Laborde calls as critical religion theorists, consists of persons like Talal Asad, Stanley Fish, Saba Mahmood, Winnifred Sullivan, William Cavanaugh, and others, who are critical of the liberal theory, and point out to the mission impossible in distinguishing between State and religion. Laborde identifies three versions of this critique as *semantic*, *Protestant*, and *realist*: while the semantic criticism points to the lack of criteria for the identification of the very category of religion itself, the Protestant critique dwells upon the Protestant core embedded in the liberal theory and therefore its misfit for different contexts,

---

[9] Francis Fukuyama, "The End of History?", *The National Interest*, Summer 1989, at https://www.embl.de/aboutus/science_society/discussion/discussion_2006/ref1-22june06.pdf, accessed November 15, 2017.

[10] Cecile Laborde, *Liberalism's Religion* (London: Harvard University Press, 2017).

and the realist critique argues that the liberal principle in reality is more a sovereign State's prerogative to regulate religion rather than protecting State neutrality. Responding to these critiques, Laborde proposes that the liberal principle can still indeed be relevant, but in an interpretative manner, as one of a minimal secularism, which may even allow for establishment of religion, provided the State is justifiable, inclusive, and limited. And, on the other side, religion too needs to be disaggregated in terms of its beliefs, institutions, conceptions of good, and so on, so as to be established in a justifiable, inclusive, and limited State.

Religion and the Public Sphere

Granting that there is an increasing accommodation of religion in liberal polity, how do we envisage the actual manner of relationship of religion to democratic State? To put the question in another way, can religious views be related to public issues and policies? If yes, what is the actual process whereby they get related?

John Rawls, the well-known representative of the liberal theory, suggested a model of *translation* of religious or moral comprehensive doctrines into secular universal language, to join in the public political debate; and, considering the radical differences, he suggested an overlapping consensus between the incommensurable comprehensive doctrines to support liberal values like justice, egalitarianism, individuality, and so on.

Others propose a model of *conversation*. Jeffrey Stout, a proponent of this model, speaks of it as "an exchange of view in which the respective parties express their premises in as much detail as they see fit and in whatever idiom they wish, try to make sense of each other's perspectives, and expose their own commitments to the possibility of criticism".[11] Religious convictions can come together, as per this model, on their own, with their own idiom, without translating themselves into any universalistic language, and converse among them in relation to a common good, allowing themselves to be critiqued by the conversation partner as well as by the voice of the public.

Alasdair McIntyre, another well-known proponent of this model, develops a three-step approach to communicating convictions on a conversation model in a democratic polity: the first step for proponents of a particular tradition is to learn the tradition of the other, in the other's language; the second is for each proponent to present an account or history of the other in other's idiom of expression, from the other's point of view; and the third is to evaluate one's own tradition in the light of the other. These steps, according to McIntyre, when applied to a particular context,

---

[11] Jeffrey Stout, *Democracy and Tradition* (Princeton: Princeton University Press, 2004), 72.

will come up with common visions of public life, derived from plurality of traditions.

Where can these conversations take place is an important question too. Rajeev Bhargava would characterise the democratic political system as having three realms: ends, institutions, and policies.[12] The realm of ends deals with the goals of a democratic polity, institutions stand for such structures as parliaments, bureaucracy, and so on, and the realm of policies stands for the space of formation of general will wherein viewpoints on public concerns are expressed, debated, and represented. Relating religion or establishing religion at the realm of ends, as it happens in theocratic societies, would be antagonistic to religious pluralism and detrimental to liberal democracy; bringing together the realms of institutions and religion too would not serve the cause of an efficient administration; and, the realm of policy making, the civil and public spheres, including the judiciary, are those wherein religion can be related meaningfully with democratic political processes.

Civil sphere, a relatively free space that emerges between a family, a State and an economic system, and a space of independent initiatives in art, culture, and social welfare, oftentimes expressed through formation of NGOs, including faith-based NGOs, is congenial for religious conversations impacting upon political decision making. It is these conversations which are relatively better capable of arresting the formation of such retrograde forces as religious nationalism, majoritarianism, and fundamentalism, and nurture a substantive democracy.

RELIGION AND DEMOCRACY IN INDIA

It has become a cliché to say that India has been a land of religious diversity and tolerance. The upanishadic aphorism that *ekam sat viprabahudhavadanti*, meaning, reality is one, sages call it differently, is often quoted to argue for the validity of oneness as well as differences. The famous fable of blind men and the elephant is adduced to argue that, in addition to the fact of the incomprehensibility of reality, human perception is radically perspectival, and therefore, differences are germane to culture, civilisation, and religion. The Jaina doctrine of *anekantavada* (many-sidedness of reality) and its epistemology of *syadvata* (may be—that every judgement is conditional to certain perspective) give a philosophical grounding to the reality of pluralism—whether religious, cultural, philosophical, and so on.

---

[12] Rajeev Bhargava, "How Should States Deal with Deep Religious Diversity? Can Anything Be Learned from the Indian Model of Secularism?" in *Rethinking Religion and World Affairs*, eds. Timothy Samuel Shah et al., (Oxford: Oxford University Press, 2012), 73–84.

While Indian philosophers have thus highlighted an important theme of Indian philosophical and religious traditions, the historical study of comparative religion, as applied to the Indian religious terrain has unearthed the diverse independent religious traditions existing in the Indian subcontinent, and the more recent field of folkloristics has brought to light the innumerable folk and popular religious traditions which sustain the religious life of the multi-ethnic population of India. Romila Thapar, the well-known cultural historian, has time and again reminded us of the thesis that diversity of Indian religious traditions are anchored upon their social and ethnic identities, and therefore are independent and different from one another.[13]

While differences, reckoned in terms of comparative religion and cultural history, are grassroots realities of Indian religious life-world, they have obtained political significance in the recent times. Involvement of religious beliefs and practices in the political sphere has been an undeniable reality in the Indian subcontinent, or in most regions of the world. Emperors and monarchs have exercised their political power with the support, manifest or latent, from religious traditions. However, the change during our contemporary era is the supersession of emperors and monarchs with the modern State, and the polity is liberal democratic rather than traditional and hierarchical. Equality and liberty have become the cornerstones for political exercise within the framework of modern statecraft. The Indian modern State, which was gradually getting formed during the centuries of the British colonial era, got constituted finally as an independent modern State, with its own constitution, legislature, rule of law, judiciary, and bureaucracy. The modern State of India had to relate itself to the religious traditions of this land in a new way. It enshrined its vision of religion-State relationship in the Constitution under several sections, and especially under the fundamental rights in Articles 25–30 which relate themselves to freedom of religion.

The Constitution provided for a specific manner of State-religion relationship. It provided for a very robust freedom of religion (Art. 25), which ensured freedom of conscience, and the right freely to profess, practise, and propagate religion, subject to public order, morality, and health; the right to carry religious markers in public; the right for every religious denomination to establish and administer religious institutions (Art. 26); and, the right to manage its own affairs in matters religious. At the same time, it safeguarded the freedom of the individual not to be discriminated on the basis of religion (Art. 15), not to be compelled to pay any taxes whose proceeds would be used for promotion of any religion, or not to

---

[13] Romila Thapar, "Syndicated Hinduism", in *Cultural Pasts—Essays in Early Indian History* (New Delhi: Oxford University Press, 2000).

be required to take religious instructions in public schools (Art. 27–28), thus protecting the secular character of the public space. And, it duly provided for the rights of minorities, religious or linguistic, to establish and administer educational institutions (Art. 30). However, it gave the right to the State to intervene in religion, especially in Hindu religion, for reforming its practices, like throwing open the temples to everyone regardless of caste. Thus, the Indian Constitution has its own specificities, granting a robust freedom of religion, in terms both of individual and communities' liberty, even while granting the State the right to intervene for the sake of reform, morality, and public order.

Sarvepalli Radhakrishnan (1888–1975) gave one of the impressive paraphrases of Indian secular democracy as:

> Though faith in the Supreme is the basic principle of the Indian tradition, the Indian State will not identify itself with or be controlled by any particular religion. We hold that one religion should not be accorded special privileges in national or international relations, for that would be a violation of the basic principles of democracy and contrary to the best interests of religion and government... No group of citizens shall arrogate to itself rights and privileges which it denies to others. No person should suffer any form of disability or discrimination because of his religion but all alike should be free to share the fullest degree in the common life.[14]

Radhakrishnan's interpretation, perhaps, is one of the best expressions of the Indian vision of State-religion relationship. As Rajeev Bhargava formulates, it is a vision of contextual secularism, which is different from the US vision of wall of separation and the French vision of *laicite*, both of which seem to take a unilateral stance of suspicion against religion. Indian secularism, as given out in the Constitution, is positively oriented towards religion, protecting the religious rights of individuals and communities, even while protecting the State from the dominance of religion.

There were voices, which interpreted Indian secularism from the emancipatory concerns of the subaltern people of India. Ambedkar's version of secularism was the best example. The idea of a secular State, for him, was to achieve civil liberties, socio-economic, and political equity for the subaltern people of India. He was not against religions, neither was he a soft religious nationalist like Gandhi; he was indeed a secular liberal democrat, hoping that such a liberal democracy, based on the high values of equality, liberty, and fraternity, would ensure the emancipation of the subaltern people. His version of secularism was something of what Marc Galantar later called ameliorative secularism,[15] a variety that focused upon the

---

[14] As cited by Aswani Kumar Peetush, "Diversity, Secularism and Religious Toleration", *India International Centre Quarterly*, 6, no. 3/4 (2013–2014): 162.

[15] Marc Galanter, "Hinduism, Secularism, and the Indian Judiciary", in *Secularism and its Critics*, ed. Rajeev Bhargava (New Delhi: Oxford University Press, 1998), 268–297.

ameliorations of the conditions of the people, rather than being worried about neutrality, equidistance, and so on. This version of secularism has much value for us today.

While these visions of religion-State relationship are indeed admirable, the developments and discourses which take place on the ground are not worthy of emulation. Donald E. Smith, as mentioned earlier, made an assessment of the secular State of India, sixteen years after independence, in terms of the principles of citizenship, freedom of religion, and the separation of State and religion, and opined that India had a fair chance of emerging to be a mature secular state. However, in the years that followed, starting with the State of Orissa bringing up a Freedom of Religion Bill in 1967 and few other states to follow suit, the question of freedom of religion had been considered less under the principle of liberal democracy than that of a majoritarian hegemony. From yet other perspectives, some noted Indian sociologists of religion like T.N. Madan and Ashis Nandy have questioned the suitability of the Western modern doctrine of secularism for the Indian context.

The recent salience of rightist forces in Indian politics and governance has battered the life, nature, and functions of Indian secularism. There is, as we know, a project of hegemony at work, in the name of the majority of Indian people, to the very detriment of democracy. Romila Thapar has rightly warned us of this project, in her influential essay on syndicated Hinduism, as mentioned earlier. There are unmeaning agents of this project, operating from countries, which have granted them the freedom, precisely under the principle of liberal democracy. The work of Rajiv Malhotra is a case in point. One of his relatively recent books entitled, *Indra's Net— Defending Hinduism's Philosophical Unity*, is not so subtle an effort to construct the hegemony around the Vedanta-based Hinduism. It is a mythical net of Indra (probably consciously chosen to synchronise with the world of *internet!*) which weaves together the jewels of different religions. It is a typical example of the inclusive project, or the hegemonising project that the Hindutva forces are following to the detriment of religious pluralism.

Indian Christianity, Religious Pluralism, Radical Democracy

Finally, what would be Indian Christianity's approach to religious pluralism in the context of contemporary issues related to liberal democracy?— is the right question to discuss.

A typical issue generally perceived by Hindus to be problematic, if not anti-democratic, is that of religious conversion. Right from the early modern days of India, the Christian narrative of conversion has brought about reactions—violent, concerted, legal, and political. Such an important figure like M.K. Gandhi got himself embroiled in this issue as well, and the antipathy from several other nationalist, including cultural nationalist, leaders is part of the violent history of the question of freedom of religion in the modern State in India. There is a certain disconnect between the Christian narrative of conversion and its perception by the others. The Rajasthan Bill on Freedom of Religion, returned recently by the Centre, on the ground that it has, instead of speaking of prohibition of conversion by fraud, collated conversion with fraud itself speaks volume of the disconnect.[16]

One is left with a question as to why, after all, religious conversion is so inflammatory in the Indian context. One of the answers given by sociologists and scholars of religious studies is that religious conversion is disturbing not only the religious but also the social fabric of India. It is the disturbance of the caste-ridden social fabric, which is causing violent reactions from the outside others. Granting that this answer is very significant, the cause of conflicts related to religious conversion is also on account of the low level of consciousness of civil liberties and human rights that characterises the general Indian population. A liberal democracy can emerge in its strength only when the wider population is prepared for it. That a person holds a religious affiliation or changes it, is integrally part and parcel of the rights of a citizen, and if that is compromised, an important aspect of liberal democracy is compromised. Indian statecraft and democratic ethos need to go a long way to recognise the rights of an individual human person, and that process is arduous and multidimensional; it is not a matter to do with the right to religion alone, but to civil rights, economic rights, right to social security, cultural rights, associational rights, right to sanitation and health, and so on.

By Way of Concluding

Nurturing a substantive democracy that ensures the multiple rights of citizenship and communities, and the religious freedom not only to practice religion but also to relate with other religions and comprehensive doctrines, needs to be an important concern of Indian Christianity. Religious pluralism has to be continuously explored as a point of empowering relationship between different religions within the democratic polity. One of the meaningful ways of nurturing this religious pluralism would be to do a public theology of religion, which takes the public and the political process as constitutive of philosophical and religious truth. It would imply that theologising begins with a public practice of conversing with religious

---

[16] Vijaita Singh, "Rajasthan Conversion Bill Returned by Centre", *The Hindu*, 16 November, 2017, http://www.thehindu.com/news/national/other-states/rajasthan-conversion-bill-returned-by-centre/article20461261.ece, accessed June 5, 2018.

and ideological others, in a dialogical and dialectical relationship. The arena for doing this is the civil society, wherein different others can come together around a public cause (common good), with a public reason, hermeneutically enriched by different traditions and ideologies.

7

SUBALTERNITY AND RELIGION IN INDIA

Subaltern: The Concept, the Project, and Beyond

From the year 1982, when a *Subaltern Studies Project (SSP)* emerged with the initiatives taken by Ranajit Guha and his colleagues, the word "subaltern" became widely known in the Indian academic and civil spheres. As we know, the *SSP* itself did not invent the word, but took it from its earlier usages,[1] especially by Antonio Gramsci who used it during the early part of the twentieth century. Gramsci spoke of two layers of consciousness existing among the subaltern people: one which is their own, giving direction or meaning to their spontaneous activity of transforming the world through their labour, and the other which they take in (oftentimes through imposition) from those who exploit, oppress, and dominate over them. There is thus a layer of native consciousness which is free, autonomous, and emancipatory, and another a layer of alien consciousness, imposed from outside. This results in a contradictory consciousness in the subaltern mind. Gramsci spoke of the possibility of the subaltern classes of people to emerge as agents of their destiny only when they acquired critical consciousness, with the role played by organic intellectuals who shared the common sense of the people but converted it into a good sense characterised by historical critical thinking.

Having this Gramscian insight as the backdrop, the *SSP* researched upon the subaltern consciousness as well as their agency, and published in volumes (12 until now) known under the generic title, *Subaltern Studies—Writings on South Asian History and Society*. In the very first volume, Guha clarified the term subaltern as a "general attribute of subordination ... whether it is expressed in terms of class, caste, age, gender, and office or

---

[1] As David Ludden points out, "In late-medieval English, it (the word 'subaltern') applied to vassals and peasants. By 1700, it denoted lower ranks in the military, suggesting peasant origins. By 1800, authors writing 'from a subaltern perspective' published novels and histories about military campaigns in India and America". David Ludden, ed., *Reading Subaltern Studies—Critical History, Contested Meaning, and the Globalisation of South Asia* (Delhi: Permanent Black, 2001), 4.

in any other way".[2] Contrasting it with the term elite, which, according to him, stood for the "dominant groups, foreign as well as indigenous",[3] Guha used the term subaltern interchangeably with the term people, which stood for "the total Indian population"[4] differentiating itself from the dominant elite. The *SSP* revisited the then-existing writings on South Asian history to unearth aspects of subaltern agency that lay buried under the colonial, nationalist, and Marxist historiographies which were the major historiographical paradigms of the time. It focussed, during its initial phase, primarily upon acts of insurgence or rebellion by peasants against empires of control, the colonial empire in particular. It searched such documents as police records, administrative reports, personal diaries, and oral traditions to bring up the elements of peasants' agency that informed their native autonomous consciousness. Thus began a *project* of subaltern studies, which continues until this day with their publications to underscore the agency of the subaltern people.

While this project has initiated discussion and debate on aspects of subalternity primarily in academic circles, we find several social movements, human rights activists, civil rights advocacy initiatives, and organic intellectuals, pre-existing or existing parallel to the *project* and contributing in manifold ways for the empowerment and emancipation of the subaltern people in India. The work of Mahatma Phule during the nineteenth century and the contributions of B.R. Ambedkar during the twentieth century are two salient examples among the many. There are a good number of studies on them, independent of the *SSP*. They have shed more light upon the category of subaltern, treating the latter more emphatically within the Indian specific hierarchy of caste. Even the economic problem of poverty, the gender-related problem of patriarchy, the marginality of tribal people, and the multiple socio-political exclusions cannot be understood and eradicated without taking into account the way the caste-system works in the Indian society. Several studies have emerged today upon the continuing struggles of the people subordinated by the caste system, especially the most oppressed groups of people called by the generic name Dalits whose life-world, with all its victimhood as well as agency, becomes the anchor of subaltern studies.

---

[2] Ranajit Guha, ed., *Subaltern Studies I—Writings on South Asian History and Society* (New Delhi: Oxford University Press, 1982), vii.

[3] Guha identified the foreign dominant group consisting of sections like "British officials of the colonial state and foreign industrialists, merchants, financiers, planters, landlords, and missionaries", and the indigenous dominant ones at the national and regional levels, consisting of "biggest feudal magnates, the most important representatives of the industrial and mercantile bourgeoisie and native recruits to the uppermost levels of the bureaucracy," and the like. Guha, *Subaltern Studies*, 8.

[4] Guha, *Subaltern Studies*, 8.

SUBALTERN STUDIES AND RELIGION

"How has the *SSP* treated religion?" is a good question to begin our exploration of the interface between religion and the subaltern self in the Indian context. Gramsci, in the context of his thinking of the revolutionary action for socialist transformation, treated religion along with the common sense, both of which, according to him, could not produce the critical historical consciousness (individual and collective) necessary for the revolutionary praxis. Religion, according to him, could not be a critical and historical consciousness premised upon a coherent thinking, because religion went with a disconnect between thought and action, as he found in the creedal/institutional religion (rather than in religion in its confessional sense).[5] Gramsci was much worried that the institutional religion, as he experienced Catholicism in Italy, would always endeavour to keep the masses under its control and not allow them to acquire the transformative critical consciousness.

The volumes of *SSP* carried a few essays which had direct or indirect references to religion. In one of the pioneering essays, Partha Chatterjee, an important member of *SSP*, related the Gramscian understanding of subaltern consciousness to the reality of caste in the Indian context, touching upon the mediatory role played by religion.[6] He wrote that, "Subaltern consciousness in the specific cultural context of India cannot but contain caste as a central element in its constitution",[7] and that the centrality of caste in the subaltern consciousness worked in conjunction with religion. In order to explain this, he drew upon the arguments of Louis Dumont, as found in his well-known work, *Homo Hierarchicus*, wherein he had spoken of the caste system as premised upon the triple principles of hierarchy, separation, and division of labour, which were based on the tensive unity continuously being forged between the opposite principles of purity and pollution. In his own words:

> The three principles rest on one fundamental conception and are reducible to a single true principle, namely the opposition of the pure and the impure. This opposition underlies hierarchy, which is the superiority of the pure to the impure, underlies separation because the pure and the impure must be kept separate, and underlies the division of labour because pure

---

[5] In his own words: "... the problem of religion taken not in the confessional sense but in the secular sense of a unity of faith between a conception of the world and a corresponding norm of conduct". *Selections from the Prison Notebooks of Antonio Gramsci*, ed. and trans., Quintin Hoare and Geoffrey Nowell Smith (Hyderabad: Orient Longman, 1998), 326.

[6] Partha Chatterjee, "Caste and Subaltern Consciousness", in *Writings on South Asian History and Society*, ed. Ranajit Guha (New Delhi: Oxford University Press, 1989), 169–210.

[7] Chatterjee, "Caste and Subaltern Consciousness", 169.

and impure occupations must likewise be separate. *The whole is founded on the necessary and hierarchical coexistence of the two opposites.*[8]

While this co-existence was not easy, Dumont observed that it was the legitimating role played by the Indian *dharma* (universal religio-ethical code) that ensured its continuance. While relating this Dumotian insight with the Gramscian theme of the two layers of consciousness, Chatterjee opines that,

> Religions which succeed in establishing a dominant and universalist moral code for society as a whole can then be looked at from two quite different standpoints. For the dominant groups, it offers the necessary ideological justification for existing social divisions, makes those divisions appear non-antagonistic and holds together a potentially divided society into a single whole. For the subordinate masses, religion enters their common sense as the element which affords them an access to a more powerful cultural order; the element of religion then coexists and intermingles in an apparently eclectic fashion with the original elements of common sense.[9]

Chatterjee, thus, sees "religion in class-divided society as the ideological unity of two opposed tendencies—on the one hand, the assertion of a universal moral code for society as a whole and on the other, the rejection of this dominant code by the subordinated".[10] He goes on to add that, "It is the construct of dharma which assigns to each jati its place within the system and defines the relations between jatis as the simultaneous unity of mutual separateness and mutual dependence".[11] For the subalterns, it could be religion that works to construct an alternate *dharma* to overthrow the caste system; and we do find such instances of alternate religious traditions, operative among the people from the pre-modern through the modern to our contemporary era.[12] Our objective must be, as Chatterjee opines, "To develop, make explicit, and unify these fragmented oppositions in order to construct a critique of Indian tradition" of the dominant *dharma*.[13]

Chatterjee's analysis of the place of religion in the subaltern consciousness could be treated as a good example of the few cases where *SSP* treated religion in its exploration.[14] However, David Arnold, one of the

---

[8] Louis Dumont, *Homo Hierarchicus—The Caste System and Its Implications* (Chicago: University of Chicago Press, 1980), 43.
[9] Partha Chatterjee, "Caste and Subaltern Consciousness", 172.
[10] Chatterjee, "Caste and Subaltern Consciousness", 172.
[11] Chatterjee, "Caste and Subaltern Consciousness", 180.
[12] Starting with the *charvakas*, Jainism, Buddhism, *ajivikas*, the *saktas*, the *tantrics*, etc., the alternate religious traditions embodying dissent have continued to emerge in the Indian context.
[13] Partha Chatterjee, "Caste and Subaltern Consciousness", 185.
[14] For instances of Ranajit Guha's treatment of religion, see Ranajit Guha, "The Prose of Counter-Insurgency", in *Subaltern Studies II—Writings on South Asian History and Society*, ed. Ranajit Guha (New Delhi: Oxford University Press, 1986), 1-42.

seven founding members of the *SSP* collective, points out in a relatively recent essay published in a volume entitled, *New Subaltern Studies,* that "Subaltern Studies failed, at the outset, to take religion seriously enough".[15] This was because, according to him, "The initial Subaltern Studies' view was instrumental in the sense that religion was seen as a means of gaining access to, and locating evidence for, subaltern consciousness and collectivity", and not as a *sui generis* reality. Taking cue from Arnold's criticism, Aparna Sundar, in her study of the Catholic Church among the Mukkuvars of coastal Tamil Nadu, argues for the "primary mode of religious engagement" in cultivating such values as participation in public sphere, democracy, interrogating authority, and so on.[16] The church, in this case, becomes the arena for learning democratic values of participation, election, and democratic authority by which the people not merely enter into the wider public sphere, but continue to contest the lack of democracy and public sphere also within the church. Religious engagement, on its own, becomes the way secular ideals are nurtured. Thus, we see the emergence of a *New Subaltern Studies,* which approaches religion phenomenologically as a *sui generis* reality, without the modernist and instrumentalist biases. And this approach positions us in a meaningful way to study the relationship between the reality of subalternity and religion.

Exploring Subaltern Religions on their Own

It is instructive at this juncture to get to know that a good number of activist-scholars who, though not enlisted among the subaltern studies collective, have studied and contributed to the understanding of subaltern religion. Some selected examples are: G. Aloysius, *Religion as Emancipatory Identity—A Buddhist Movement Among the Tamils Under Colonialism* (Bangalore: The Christian Institute for the Study of Religion and Society, 1998); Saurabh Dube, *Untouchable Pasts—Religion, Identity and Power Among a Central Indian Community 1780-1950* (Albany: State University of New York Press, 1998); Manu Bhagavan and Anne Feldaus, *Speaking Truth to Power* (New Delhi: Oxford University Press, 2008); and, Gail Omvedt, *Seeking Begumpura—The Social Vision of Anticaste Intellectuals* (New Delhi: Navayana, 2008). These studies explore the emancipatory potentials of subaltern religions, on their own.

---

[15] David Arnold, "Subaltern Studies—Then and Now", in *New Subaltern Politics—Reconceptualizing Hegemony and Resistance in Contemporary India,* eds. Alf Gunvald Nilsen and Srila Roy (New Delhi: Oxford University Press, 2015), 269.

[16] Aparna Sunder, "Can the Subaltern Be Secular? Negotiating Catholic Faith, Identity, and Authority in Coastal Tamil Nadu", in *New Subaltern Politics—Reconceptualising Hegemony and Resistance in Contemporary India,* eds. Alf Gunvald Nilsen and Srila Roy (Oxford: Oxford University Press, 2015), 130.

The study by Milind Wakankar entitled, *Subalternity and Religion—The Prehistory of Dalit Empowerment in South Asia*, explores insightfully the saint-poet Kabir's verses as sites which render the transfigurations of the holy in the lives of the subaltern people. Observing the condition of violence wherein the Dalits were/are "thrown into" by the operation of caste, he notes the "co-existence of the experience of divinity and the experience of violence in daily life" of the Dalits,[17] who, however, refuse to submit themselves into "historically neutral and passive form of existence".[18] Such a refusal finds expressions in poets like Kabir in whose verses divinity and violence converge to construct a subaltern subjecthood. A mystical fountain gushing forth from the *sangamam* of Islam and Hindu traditions, brought forth a corpus of poems, which dwelt upon a transcendent formless God.

Such studies bear testimony to the positive relationship between religion and the emancipatory aspirations of the subaltern people.

SUBALTERN AND POST-COLONIAL STUDIES

It is in place here to clarify the relationship between kindred disciplines of the subaltern studies and the post-colonial studies. Post-colonial studies has been developing in literary criticism, historiography, philosophy, cultural studies, religious studies, and so on, for quite some time now.[19] Though thinkers like Achebe, Franz Fanon, and W.E.B. Du Bois have been bringing out the voice of the colonised in their literatures, it was the set of writings by diaspora writers like Edward Said, Gayatri Spivak, and Homi Baba during the second half of the twentieth century which came to be discussed in the academia as post-colonial writings. The central issue being debated here is the nexus between power (colonial power to be precise) on the one hand, and, knowledge, culture, art, religion, and so on, on the other. In his much debated work named *Orientalism,* Edward Said problematised the way the colonial creators of knowledge produced the knowledge of the Orient in such a way that they could instrumentalise it for their

---

[17] Milind Wakankar, *Subalternity and Religion—The Prehistory of Dalit Empowerment in South Asia* (New York: Routledge, 2010), 8.

[18] Wakankar, *Subalternity and Religion,* 7.

[19] Some of the important contributions to postcolonial studies include: Bill Ashcroft, Gareth Griffiths, and Helen Tiffin, *The Empire Writes Back: Theory and Practice in Post-Colonial Literatures* (London: Routledge, 1989); other often quoted studies by the same authors are Bill Ashcroft, *Post-Colonial Transformation* (London: Routledge, 2001), Bill Ashcroft, Gareth Griffith, and Helen Tiffin, *The Postcolonial Studies Reader* (London: Routledge and Kegan Paul, 1995), and Bill Ashcroft, Gareth Griffith, and Helen Tiffin, *Post-Colonial Studies: The Key Concepts* (London: Routledge, 2002); Ania Loomba, *Colonialism/ Postcolonialism* (London: Routledge, 1998); and Patrick Williams and Laura Chrisman, eds., *Colonial Discourse and Post-Colonial Theory: A Reader* (New York: Columbia University, 1994).

colonising agenda. Orientalism, then, was part and parcel of colonialism, and it was this that post-colonial studies explored as one of its targets. The perspective, later on, was applied to fields of literature, culture, art, and religion to critically examine the invisible hands of empires operative behind the texts which were/are produced in a given historical context.

Debates are on as to whether the very term post-colonialism is an appropriate one. There are those who dispute the relevance of the chronological connotation of the term. They point out to the fact that empire-building with the instrumentality of culture, religion, and knowledge-systems had pre-existed the types of colonialism which emerged from Europe from the sixteenth century onwards. There are others who argue that colonialism was not a monolithic category, experienced uniformly by the colonised people; there were variants of colonialism, which were resisted, responded to, or even appropriated by the so-called colonised people. Moreover, the way post-colonialism premised itself upon a commonality of the experience of colonisation starting with North America, Canada, and Australia, to the Global South countries from Asia, Africa and South America, homogenises the experience of colonisation without due consideration to the specifics of the varying contexts. For example, the Indian experience of colonisation, in a context of the hegemony of the caste, can never be equated with North American or Australian colonial experiences. And therefore, speaking of exploitation, oppression, and domination, even in terms of the epistemic empires, needs to be context-specific.

There are several aspects of convergence between the post-colonial and the subaltern studies. Both treat the subject as dominated over, and both discuss the subject's conditions of subordination in terms of her consciousness. For example, Gayatri Spivak, one of the pioneering trio of the post-colonial studies in academic circles, treats the conditions of subalternity as part of the post-colonial critique of coloniality and its empire in her famous question, "Can the Subaltern Speak?" The voice of the subaltern as the colonised, according to her, is irretrievably lost for contemporary historiography, and the subaltern consciousness, buried under layers of external consciousness cannot stand up. Despite the Spivakian provocative pessimism, the general thrust of post-colonial and subaltern studies is to highlight aspects of agency found among the subordinated or colonised in conditions of subalternity or coloniality.

However, the universalising tendency of post-colonial critique tends to leave the context-specific power-dynamics like caste in India easily elided. Accordingly, the subaltern approach to religions and their texts, as they have emerged in the Indian context, is unique and distinguishes itself from the post-colonial approach at least upon the following counts: (1) Subaltern studies in the Indian context deals with the question of subordination especially as it obtains in a hierarchical social condition characterised by the reality of caste, while postcolonialism looks at the universal reality of epistemic and cultural domination as they obtain globally in situations wherever empires are at work.(2) The reality of caste is more enduring across historical stages of life. The fact that the identity of caste is fixed by birth, and that one cannot wish for changing one's caste, speaks for the truth of its non-negotiability. But, the situation of being colonised, despite the fact that it leaves traces of subordination which are relatively difficult to erase, goes with less ascriptivity and systemic intransigence than caste. For example, identities based on race, colour, gender, and caste are more ascriptive and less negotiable than those based on empires, coloniality, first-third worlds, poverty, north-south, and so on. Collapsing the subaltern discourse into that of the post-colonial can happen only at the peril of making the emancipatory subaltern discourse dampened.

RELIGION AND THE SUBALTERN SELF IN INDIAN HISTORY

The argument of this essay is that subaltern religion which originates from the subordinated conditions of life can well be an emancipatory experience for the subaltern self. The Dalit self is the typical example of a subordinated self in the Indian context, and it would do well to explore the role of religion in the history of the experience of the Dalit self. Nothing can be more appropriate than taking a look at some of the occurrences of religion in the lives of Dalit individuals and movements:

1. Shankar Deva (fifteenth century) of Assam was a good example of a subaltern religious self.[20] Some of his verses, whose translation is given in the following texts, make a point that a person who eats dog's meat or is unable to execute ritual sacrifices because of ritual exclusions can do self-purification by singing the name of God:

   > The *mlechhas* who eat dogs purify themselves by singing the name of God.
   > The *Chandala* who only sings the name of *Hari* will properly execute the function of sacrifice...
   > That *Chandala* at the tip of whose tongue there is the message of Hari is to be placed in the highest estimation...
   > One is an ignorant boor who vilifies a *Chandala* who has sung the name of Hari.[21]

   Shankar Deva's "creed consisted essentially in *Namkirtan*, that is, keeping the memory of God in mind and heart, and expressing one's love and devotion to God externally by acts of praise and worship".[22]

---

[20] Stephen Fuchs, *Godmen on the Warpath—A Study of Messianic Movements in India* (New Delhi: Munshiram Manoharlal Publishers, 1992), 187.
[21] Fuchs, *Godmen on the Warpath*, 187.
[22] Fuchs, *Godmen on the Warpath*, 191.

Message of equality was an essential part of the religiosity of Shankar Deva. His followers "felt that they belonged to a community to which high and low were treated alike, where all treated each other as brothers and equals".[23] The Brahmins complained against Shankar Deva to the king that he "did not sacrifice to the gods; he did not observe the caste rules; and he treated the Brahmins with disrespect".[24] Shankar Deva withstood the persecutions, and finally became a well-celebrated subaltern saint to be remembered even to this day by festivities and other religious activities.

2. Ravidas was a pioneering saint-poet of the fifteenth century from the Chamar community in North India to give leadership to the Dalit Chamars to construct a new identity. He adopted the brahminic markers like the sacred thread, *tilak*, and so on, even while continuing to do his job as a cobbler. His very appearance challenged the Brahmins, and motivated the Chamars to take on a new identity. He chose poetry and religion as vehicles of social protest.

3. A nineteenth century illiterate mystic, Vaikuntasamy religiously treated the bodily selves of the Shanars, a subaltern community, for an experience of emancipatory identity. The mystic instituted rituals which treated the people bodily: a ritual known as *Thuvayal Thavasu* (washing penance) was a case in point. It was a context wherein the Shanars were considered "untouchable, un-seeable, and un-approachable", and were chased away from public places on account of these unmeaning restrictions. It was in this context that Vaikundasamy required them to undertake this *thavasu* (penance). Further on, in the same context wherein these people were violently denied the right to wear cloths to cover their upper bosom, there arose in his religious assembly a practice of "worshipping" God in a mirror, with a headgear on. It treated the bodily self of the Shanars with a poignant religiosity, which resulted in a liberated sense of the self.

4. Pundit C. Iyothee Doss (1845–1914) is yet another inspiring Dalit self that sought to interpret its existence into emancipation through its religiously oriented hermeneutical propensity. Spurred by a "deep faith in God",[25] he explored the *advaitic* vision not merely to satisfy his personal religio-philosophical quest, but also to find in it a remedy for the social discriminatory system. However, his struggle for a dignified social existence kept leading him to search for a more effectively transformative religion, and after reading a booklet given by a Buddhist bhikku, he was drawn to Buddhism, and that became his religious

---

[23] Fuchs, *Godmen on the Warpath*, 192.
[24] Fuchs, *Godmen on the Warpath*, 193.
[25] Gowthama Sanna, *C. Iyotheethasa Pandithar* (New Delhi: Sakithya Academy, 2007), 25.

home for life. The Pundit embarked upon the task of constructing a variant of Buddhism known as the "Tamil Buddhism", with the help of Tamil classical literatures. He involved himself in a life-time hermeneutical task of deconstructing the existing myths, *puranic* tales, and even popular religious practices in order to disclose their original Buddhist character and content which are liberative.

The religious pursuit of the Pundit went with a sense of enquiry and wisdom. He instructed his readers, or followers, to inquire into everything—beliefs, practices, and so on, until they got satisfactory answers to enquiry, experience, and sight. He treated experience and vision as two epistemological criteria for the truthfulness of claims—religious or otherwise. He said, "Buddha *thanmam* even if handed down by your great grandfather or grandfather, question it in your own enquiry and experience. If you realise its truth that it would lead to your descendent's, co-villager's and co-countrymen's welfare, then believe in it; but if found worthless in your enquiry and experience, leave it; that is why Budhha *thanmam* is named as the true *thanmam* (*meyyaram*)",[26] an enquiring religion.

The Pundit's spirit of enquiry shined forth in "deconstructing" some of the age-old puranic role-models, the role-model of Harichandra being the salient one among them. Needless to state the height of normativity this character had obtained in the popular Indian ethos for truthfulness. Gandhi is said to have learned his lesson of truthfulness from listening to the story of Harichandra. The Pundit was quite incisive in deconstructing this myth of the truthfulness of Harichandra. He published an article with the title, "The Story of Harichandra's Truthfulness and the Details of How He Became a Liar". He found this role-model characterised with umpteen number of lies, disloyalty to people, anti-women stances, and cowardice even to the extent of not being able to protect his wife. The Pundit was concerned about the concepts of truthfulness and lie that were being discussed in this *puranic* tale. He was agitated at the fact that Harichandra was extolled as a truthful king because he, through trial and tribulations, kept his word to the Brahmins, but, on the other hand, disgracefully denied the request of two women from the lowly community. This contradiction in the characterisation makes Harichandra a liar, and problematises the very neutrality of the concepts of truth and lie.[27] He accuses the proponents of the story of lacking in discernment of truth and lie, and of propagating such lies in order to manipulate and cheat the gullible.

---

[26] Sanna, *C. Iyotheethasa Pandithar*, 131.
[27] The Pundit contends that "it looks as if there are 'Brahmin truth and lies' on the one hand, and 'Paraiyar truth and lies' on the other hand", Sanna, *C. Iyotheethasa Pandithar*, 95.

The Pundit followed a uniquely linguistic approach, aided by his amazing skill to alliteratively search for the semantics of a given linguistic code, and by his grammatically informed wide knowledge of the classical Tamil literary corpus. It was laudable that he could trace out meanings from such classics as *Manimekalai, Sudamani, Pinkalai Nikandu, Veerasoliam, Seevakasinthamani, Tirukural, Silapathikaram, Gnanavetti, Muthurai, Korkaivendan*, and many more. It was not only the knowledge of the literary sources that gave the uniqueness to his linguistic approach but also a deep confidence in approaching reality through language. Whether it be religious or social domain, he believed in the power of the language to work out transformations. Perhaps, it was this core confidence which spontaneously oriented him towards a religious solution to social problems, rather than social remedies on their own. He worked with the claim that the genuine knowledge of the real and original meaning of the linguistic codes (words or phrases) would result in ethical behaviour and religious observances resulting in justice, peace, and harmony to the wider society, and to the oppressed in particular.

The way he made a fine critical comment on Christians, going by the interpretation of the word Christian (in Tamil) is a good example of his linguistic approach. He rightly interpreted the word Christian to stand for someone who dwells within Christ, who, in turn dwells in him.[28] Dwelling in Christ means dwelling steadfastly within the observance of the ethical teachings of Christ, which is nothing but "loving God, and loving one another as oneself".[29] After proposing this ethical orientation to being a Christian, the Pundit challenges the Christians whether they were really Christians, in the sense of dwelling in Christ. He finds a contradiction in them when they claim to be Christians, but call themselves as "Joseph Chettiyar, David Mudaliar, Savariappa Naidu, and so on". He poses a sharp question: "How to understand the legitimacy of those who call others as pagans, even while they themselves keep the Christian names but observe the pagan castes?" Can those who enter into Christianity, but yet observe caste be identified as real Christians? After posing such sharp questions, he gives a very pertinent piece of advice to the Christian priests based on a familiar

---

[28] கிறீஸ்த்தவன்: கிறீஸ்த்து அவன் – அவன் கிறீஸ்த்து என்னும் சிறந்த வாக்கியமானது கிறீஸ்த்து அவனுக்குள்ளும் அவன் கிறீஸ்த்துவுக்குள்ளும் அமர்ந்தவனே கிறீஸ்த்தவனாவான். அதாவது, அவருடைய நீதிப்போதனைகளுக்குள்ளும் அவருடைய நன்மார்க்க ஒழுக்கத்திற்குள்ளும் அமர்ந்து ஒழுகுபவனுக்குள் கிறீஸ்த்துவின் அன்பு குடிகொள்ளும். அவ்வகைக் குடிகொண்டவனை கிறிஸ்தவன் என்று கூறத்தகும். Iyothee Thasar, *Iyotheethasar Sinthanaigal—Religion and Literature: Hermeneutics*, comp. G. Aloysius (Palayamkottai: Folklore Resource and Research Centre, 1999), 99-100.

[29] Iyothee Thasar, "Christ as Christian, Christian as Christ", *Iyothee Thasar Sinthanaigal*, comp. G. Aloysius (Palayamkottai: FRRC, 1999), 97-99.

theme from the Bible: "Those who humble themselves will be exalted, and those who exalt themselves will be humbled"; accordingly, he says, when Christians consider themselves as high castes on earth, their status will be lowered in heaven, and so they need to be careful. He ends the section saying, "If there is one real Christian among thousand nominal Christians, the world will shudder, but, on the other hand, if there is not even one real Christian among ten thousand nominal Christians, the world will curse. Priests are the causes for both".[30]

The linguistic confidence of the Pundit needs more exploration, understanding, and appreciation. Being a literary scholar in Tamil, he developed a confidence that by tracing the original meanings of the words, one could construct a history, an ethics, a religion, and a programme for a movement. He deconstructed the existing hegemonic myths and *puranic* tales, and reconstructed Tamil Buddhism with the use of this method. In this endeavour, he integrated the modern spirit of enquiry, religious pursuit of high virtues, and so on. He needs to be understood in his own terms, and his approach to religion needs to be understood on its own. Wittgenstein said, "We are running against the boundaries of language when we speak religion"; Was the Pundit too running against the boundaries to express his subaltern self?

It is a case in point that the Pundit greatly appreciated the role played by the British colonisers. Every member of the Tamil Buddhist Society was enjoined to observe certain religious observances regularly, and one among them was paying obeisance to the British, because theirs was a reign characterised by justice, law, and compassion. In his own words: "The second obeisance is due to British officials who rule over us, because under their kind, just, and lawful rule, we live happily without fear of robbers, manipulators, deceivers, cattle, and diseases."[31]

The height of reverence he had accorded to the British cannot be understood even within a post-colonial paradigm, and it certainly needs a contextual subaltern approach. The Dalit critique has a more situated and nuanced approach to colonialism, rather than a one-sided rejection; it has to negotiate between multiple layers of coloniality in their actual contexts of existence; for them, the empire is not just a power emerging from the Western colonial powers, but also the

---

[30] Thasar, "Christ as Christian, Christian as Christ", 97-99.
[31] நம்மை ஆண்டுவரும் பிரிட்டிஷ் ராஜாங்கத்தோரை சிந்தித்துப் போற்றுவது இரண்டாவது பூசையாகும். அவர்களை ஏன் போற்றி பூசிக்க வேண்டியதெனில், அவர்களது நீதியும், நெறியும். கருணையு மிகுந்த வரசாட்சியில் சுகச்சீர் பெற்று வாழ்வதுடன் கள்ளர்பயம், காமியர்பயம், துஷ்டர்பயம், மிருகபயம், விஷவியாதி பயங்கள் யாவையும் அகற்றிக் காத்துரட்சித்து வருவதினால் அவர்களைப் போற்றி விசுவாசிக்க வேண்டுமென்பது அறிகுறியாம். Thasar, *Iyothee Thasar Sinthanaigal*, 431.

traditional, dominant hegemonies which cripple their lives in actual contexts of life.

5. *Ad Dharm*, emergent among the Dalits during the early part of the twentieth century, was a "movement in north-western India that aimed at securing a respectable place for the Dalits through cultural transformation, spiritual regeneration, and political assertion".[32] This "movement aimed at securing a distinct identity for the Dalits, independent of both the Hindu and the Sikh religions. Its central motif was that Untouchables constituted a *qaum* (community), a distinct religious grouping similar to that of Muslims, Hindus, and Sikhs, which had existed since time immemorial".[33] This "movement, led by Mangoo Ram, aimed at making Dalits realise their communal pride (*qaumiat*), religion (*mazhab*), and capability for organization (*majlis*), which had hitherto laid buried under the burden of untouchability".[34] It "brought about cultural transformation in the lives of Untouchables in Punjab through its emphasis on moral principles. Through promoting a moral code of conduct, the movement tried to bring a sense of self-respect to the state's Untouchables".[35]

6. Another good example of the subaltern self, pursuing an interpretative religious avenue for egalitarianism was Mahatma Phule (1827–1890). Phule believed in a Creator God—a God who created everything, to whom, we in turn have to offer our gifts in gratitude in the form of righteous conduct of treating one another with freedom, dignity, and fraternity. He wrote 33 *akhandas*[36] wherein he expounded the ethical conduct as a response to the Creator's gift of creation. In his *Sarvajanik Satyadharma Pustak*,[37] he presents these *akhandas* which dwell upon the criteria for the practice of righteous conduct. Some of the salient ones are:

- Those who admit that men and women have been born independent from birth and are capable of enjoying every right, can be said to practise righteous conduct.
- Those who do not worship the stars and stones, but have respect for the *Nirmik* (Creator) of the universe can be said to practise righteous conduct.

---

[32] Ronki Ram, "Untouchability in India with a Difference—Ad Dharm, Dalit Assertion and Caste Conflicts in India", *Asian Survey*, XLIV, no. 6 (2004): 900.
[33] Ram, "Untouchability in India with a Difference", 900.
[34] Ram, "Untouchability in India with a Difference", 901.
[35] Ram, "Untouchability in India with a Difference", 901.
[36] Phule used the term "akanda" instead of the existing word "abhanga", which means a devotional poetry.
[37] It was written by Phule in Marathi language, and its translation in English would be "Book of the Universally True Religion".

- Those who do not let other creatures enjoy all the things created by the Creator, but offer them in worship to the *Nirmik*, cannot be said to practise righteous conduct.
- Those who express gratitude to the Creator, who has created all things which we are using in this world, can be said to practise righteous conduct.[38]

Phule, thus, related faith in a creator God with the ethical duty of treating everyone as equal.

7. The early twentieth century *Satnami*[39] movement of the Chamar community in North India is yet another example for forging an emancipatory self through religion. They were worshippers of the "true name of God". Ghasi Das, who claimed a "divine mission and authority" to fight for the human rights of the Chamars, initiated this *Satnami* movement, for, as in the words of Stephen Fuchs,

> ... though the Chamars of Chattisgarh had abandoned their former dishonourable trade as tanners and leather-workers and taken to farming and at the same time strictly observed the traditional Hindu food taboos and rules of behaviour, the higher castes continued to treat them as impure castes with whom they wanted to have no dealings. This social discrimination the Chamars felt the more keenly since by hard work and frugal living they had become fairly prosperous and were in no way inferior to the other farming classes of Chhattisgarh.[40]

In this context, Ghasi Das, an extraordinarily spiritual man, initiated the *Satnami* movement by proclaiming seven precepts, which included "abstinence from liquor, meat, and certain red vegetables such as lentils, chillies, and tomatoes, because they had the colour of blood; the abolition of idol worship; ... the worship of one solitary and supreme God", and so on. "The *Satnamis* were bidden to cast all idols from their homes, to dispense with temples and fixed prayers, but they were permitted to reverence the sun, as representing the deity... caste was abolished and all men were to be socially equal...."[41] As Saurabh Dube, one of the early scholars to study this movement, opines:

> The close connection between divine, social, and ritual hierarchies located the Chamars at the margins of the caste order, and excluded them from Hindu temples. Ghasidas is believed to have thrown the idols of the gods and goddesses of the Hindu pantheon onto a rubbish heap. The rejection of these deities and of the authority of Brahman specialists of

---

[38] Archana Malik-Goure, *Jyotiba Phule—A Modern Indian Philosopher* (New Delhi: Suryodaya Books, 2013), 67.
[39] *Satnami* literally means "the true name".
[40] Stephen Fuchs, *Godmen on the Warpath*, 218–219.
[41] Fuchs, *Godmen on the Warpath*, 220–221.

the sacred, of temples and the Hindu *puja* (worship) offered in them was accompanied by the call to believe only in a formless god, *satnam* (true name). The new sect was called *Satnampath* and its members, *Satnamis*".[42]

This religious movement contributed much to the emancipatory experience of the subaltern self in the Chattisgarh region of North India.

8. B.R. Ambedkar (1891–1956), the exemplary subaltern individual to play a vital role in the formation of the modern constitutional State of India, turned to religion in his search for freedom to the subalterns. His search for a transformative religion landed him in Buddhism, which opened up a hermeneutical engagement for his self. In interpreting Buddhism, he envisioned a Dalit self, assertive, autonomous, free, and responsible. He took a conscious and bold decision to convert to Buddhism. At the time of conversion, he rhetorically said: "If you want to gain self-respect, change your religion; If you want to create a co-operating society, change your religion; If you want power, change your religion; If you want equality, change your religion; If you want independence, change your religion; If you want to make the world in which you live happy, change your religion...."[43]

Ambedkar's conversion brings to the fore certain questions. As Debjani Ganguly, a post-colonial writer has formulated: "How does one then read this paradox of a secular modern intellectual and political activist seeking recourse to rhetorical devices-genealogies, parables, tales-within-tales-that are the prerogative of men belonging to "archaic" societies?"[44] Ganguly herself attempts an answer: "Ambedkar's history-as-critique ... transforms the given dominant historiographical mode (i.e., Nationalist and Rationalist) from an *authoritative* one to an internally *persuasive* one."[45] The power and need of persuasion can much be appreciated in our post-linguistic-turn ethos that values the cultural power for transformation. Ambedkar intuitively took recourse to a source of cultural power with a transcendental reference (religion) that could propose a free self, capable of taking on the dominant self projected by the traditional Hindu religio-cultural system.

Ambedkar's encounter with religion brought home the awareness that religion is like a live wire, carrying a powerful stream of energy,

---

[42] Saurabh Dube, *Untouchable Pasts: Religion, Identity, and Power among a Central Indian Community, 1780–1950* (New York: State University of New York Press, 1998), 1.
[43] Debjani Ganguly, "History's Implosions—A Benjaminian Reading of Ambedkar", *Journal of Narrative Theory*, 32, no. 3 (2002): 334.
[44] Ganguly, "History's Implosions", 335.
[45] Ganguly, "History's Implosions", 335.

which can be both productive and destructive. It would imply that the political forces working for the emancipation of subaltern people address the religious question in an emancipatory way. Addressing them in this way is to find a right forum, which could be none other than a democratically provided space, the civil sphere. Religion, so as to enter the civil space, needs to disclose its ideal scheme and dialogue with different other ideal schemes. The ideal schemes of different religions can be judged not by their utility, but by the axiomatic principle of justice. That would be an enduring contribution Ambedkar would have made to subaltern studies. More about his philosophy of religion is discussed in the next chapter.

9. Conversion to Christianity and Islam was the other option the Dalit self-explored in its saga of struggle for freedom. In spite of the adverse impact of casteism within Christianity, one can still state that Christianity did offer opportunities for the social dignity of the embodied Dalit self. That Christianity mediated a sense of "touchability" of the body is a case in point. Its religiosity dwelt upon "healing" of the body (Jesus's touching of the lepers and healing is typical); its theology dwelt upon the possibility of the redemption of the "flesh"; its religious calendar gave importance to the "passion" and bodily resurrection of Jesus; the missionaries were meat-eaters, and therefore identified themselves with the meat-eating Dalits in dietary system; and so on. These aspects of engagement with the body and the religious provision of redemption by divine grace, could be said to resonate well with the aspirations for the "touchability" for the Dalit self. It is in place to note here an observation made by Mathew N. Schmalz in his account of the transformation of a "Dalit" Christian (John Masih) to become a charismatic Catholic.[46] He observes that "the most crucial aspect of

---

[46] Mathew N. Schmalz, "The Broken Mirror: John Masih's Journey from Isai to Dalit", in *Margins of Faith—Dalit and Tribal Christianity in India*, eds. Rowena Robinson and Marianus Joseph Kujur (New Delhi: SAGE, 2010). Schmalz studies John Masih's (a Dalit) religious vision which "reflect and embody his struggle to undo the place of untouchability. In his effort, he moves through a succession of spaces in which he progressively assumes or deploys new identities for himself" (187–188). "John's family and many Catholics felt they had attained a different kind of place in which they could experience a relative autonomy in their distance from their identity as Chamars" (189). John became a healer and practised a kind of Catholicism "that allowed him to use the power of words to effect the transformation of self. But John's transformation of self was not a simple change in public persona. Instead, it was an appropriation of an inspired and authoritative identity that could be deployed against the oppressive place of life as a Chamar" (190). "While John did not write poetry, he did have a large collection of aphorisms that he composed. Many of the aphorisms had clear Christian meanings: "if you become trapped 'in a cobweb', call out to The Lord... What unified all of these disparate aphorisms was their focus on general notions of selfhood or identity. Indeed, the sequentially numbered aphorisms constituted a record of John's own spiritual

charismatic Catholicism was its denial of untouchability. When John moved through the audience at prayer meetings, he laid hands on all who came within his reach. Once being of 'something' that defiled, John now became 'someone' who healed".[47]

Bodily experience of the self, or of an embodied self, is part and parcel of the life-reality of the Dalits. Their person has been constructed, reinforced, and reproduced within a *varna*/caste scheme of reality in terms of their bodily self. Their physic (raciality) has been essentialised through ritual, literary, religious, cultural, and social behaviour to the extent of being identified with an unvarying constant of impurity resulting in chronic untouchability; their bodies have been relentlessly reproduced as labouring bodies so as to be ready for rendering their physical labour to the maintainance of a society that is run by a "pure" bodied section of the people;[48] their dignity has been affronted with untouchability, unseeability, and unapproachability because of the empirical experience of the materiality of their bodies; civil liberties and their freedom of movement have been denied on account primarily of their physicality of existence. It is then nothing but an existential fact that the experience of self for the Dalit is singularly and more acutely pathetic than for other classes of people in India. Negativity in their living has got accumulated primarily in terms of their body, a thing that had/has become a predicament rather than a facility. A sense of being "imprisoned" in a world wherein the everyday aesthetics, religiosity, opportunities, and even ethics, smacks of a scheme of *varna*-based casteism is inescapable for the Dalits.

This pathos-filled condition of life generates a search among the Dalits for different avenues to exist, to have a meaningful sense of one's person, to strike respectful relationships, and so on. Religion had been an intimate ally in this search.

The subaltern individuals and movements mentioned earlier are some vibrant examples of the resurgent Dalit selves that manifested in the history of Indian religions. During the pre-modern and the modern periods, religion had indeed been integrated as a resource for the emancipatory project of the Dalit self. In the traditional context, against the school of *jnana-marga*, for example the *advaitic* philosophical systems, which presented a pursuit for an immutable universal ideal self (*atman*), a pursuit from which the subaltern people were excluded, the Dalit saints took to

---

epiphanies; they were flashes of self-knowledge arranged in a staccato testimony of insight" (192–193). "These aphorisms were not just tools for memory and mediation; they were weapons for controversy and contestation" (193).

47   Schmalz, "The Broken Mirror", 194.
48   Partha Chatterjee, "Caste and Subaltern Consciousness".

bhakti religiosity, premised on a relationality between the *bhakta* and the deity, and through their religious poems and activities, expressed a possibility for the Dalit self to present itself in history, or as per the Gramscian insight, to emerge out of the contradictory consciousness imposed upon them by the dominant.

During the modern era, various features of the Enlightenment got integrated with religion in the construction of the emancipatory Dalit self. Dr. Ambedkar was a good example. Enlightenment values of individual autonomy, equality, justice, liberty, and so on, acquired through the Western modern education, had matured in him to a level of inspiring radical protest against the demeaning social conditions of the Dalits. They made him a radical interrogator of the dominant religious myths which reproduced a hierarchical society. While coming out against the dominating Brahminic religion on the one hand, Ambedkar experienced the positivity of religion, in its emanicpatory dimension. It was the latter that steered his person towards an interpretative experience of Buddhism. Religion could be found to be at its best when it inspires a person or a collective to be involved in an interpretative experience of existence. Needless to say that most of the initiators of religions have been not founders in any juridical sense, but interpreters of existing religions. Ambedkar's interpretative confidence cannot be subsumed under an instrumentalist reasoning of a modernist self; but, it was a relentlessly searching self that came to religion, the wellspring of transcendence, to nurture the emancipatory identity of the Dalits.[49] Ambedkar, thus, in converting to Buddhism was fulfilling less a project of his modern self than entering into a decisive moment in his search for alternatives that could sustain the emancipatory selves of the Dalits. Ambedkar's modernity, thus, was an open-ended, subaltern modernity, that had radical openness to life, and to all that it offers, including the religious experience.[50]

Religion appears to be an interpretative potential for the subaltern self to take on the caste system, which remains deeply entrenched in the collective consciousness, with its own archetypal binary of purity and

---

[49] It is in place to note that a contemporary Dalit activist Jignesh Mevani quotes Ambedkar precisely on this point of connection between religion and caste as: "The root of the caste system is religion attached to varna and ashram; and the root of the varnashram is Brahminical religion". Ilangovan Rajasekaran, "You Can't Preach Self-Respect to Empty Stomachs—Interview with the Dalit Leader Jignesh Mevani", *Frontline*, 34, no.10 (May 13-26, 2017): 46.

[50] It is insightful to note the fact that in most of the cases of these subaltern leaders, saints, mystics, and movements, proclamation of faith in a supreme God went along with the ethical claim of equality between human beings. The one God becomes the source of a dialogically-forged universality of an egalitarian self. And this faith went with the denunciation of idols, rituals, and priesthood, which stood as the pillars of the caste-based hierarchical society.

pollution. The Western Enlightenment modernity empowered the Dalit-self up to a point, as it occurred in Ambedkar during his early development. However, it fell short of taking on the metaphysics of caste. Religion, on the other hand, with its metaphysical depth and transcendental ideal, could give the strength for an emancipatory identity to be situated in its alternate cosmogony and utopia. In its linguistic as well as embodied dimensions, religion came into relief as the subaltern self interpreted itself into emancipation.

Subaltern Religions and the Civil/Public Sphere Today

Thus, we find innumerable subaltern religious traditions, mediating an interpretative existence to the subaltern people of India. They continue to exist at the margins of the Indian society. Unfortunately, they do not seem to inform and engage the wider civil and public spheres effectively. This happens due to various reasons:

1. Nontextuality and Performativity: The subaltern religious traditions are mostly nontextual and performative, as they exist mostly in rituals, ceremonies, and symbols. Going into the genealogy of this nontextuality, one finds that it had been actively imposed upon the subaltern people by a brute denial of literacy and learning to the subalterns in the traditional *varnashramadhramic* society. Some attempts at bringing the performative traditions to texts do not get the aura of sacredness that the hegemonic texts have been enjoying for long in the Indian mind.

2. Co-option and Casteism: The subaltern religious traditions, though manifesting the subaltern self and agency through strategies of resistance, reinterpretation, and reconstruction of traditions, seem to get lost either by being co-opted into dominant traditions or by being pressured into service to uphold narrow ethnic and casteist pride and power.

3. Superstition and Fetishism: Sometimes, the subaltern religious traditions do turn out to be superstitious and fetish too. As they are not used to an ongoing revision of their traditions in the light of contemporary knowledge and wisdom, it so happens that their beliefs and practices become fossilised beliefs, that is, superstitions, generating fetish mentalities.

4. Subaltern religious traditions of dissent and resistance are generally not maintained and mediated in the wider public for the simple reason that they make the power seekers uncomfortable and insecure. For example, a voice of dissent emerging from a ferocious female deity could always be a matter of discomfort for a patriarchal male subject. Similar

instances can be causes for the dominant not to recognise them in the public.

These and other reasons make the subaltern religious traditions and their subjecthood being absent in the wider civil and public spheres. In their absence or relative reticence, what obtain salience are the traditions of the dominant, which continue to construct hegemony for the dominant and manufacture consent to the exercise of their power. Besides introducing hegemonic closures in popular consciousness, they deny the subjecthood to the subalterns in the public, and thereby effectively prevent their political agency from emerging.

It becomes therefore a necessity to actively promote the presencing of subaltern religious traditions in the civil and public spheres today. Their active presence would be a source and resource for the subaltern self to reclaim their subjectivity and emerge assertive in the public, leading to expression of their political agency too. It is a case in point that some subaltern leaders do understand the power of these symbolic resources more perceptively and accurately. We turn to one such perception as found in Ambedkar.

By Way of Concluding

Subalternity and religion are two realities which have much more insights to offer to humanity when explored in their own rights. The initiatives of the Subaltern Studies Project need to be extended to explore the aspects of subaltern agency expressed through the religious idiom. The varieties of examples, as reported from the Indian context, bear witness to the vibrancy and liberative potential of this interface. Unfortunately, these subaltern religious traditions are not brought to the gaze of the Indian public, much less to the Indian public sphere, leaving the space to dominant traditions which are poised for constructing their own hegemony. It is time we promoted the subaltern religious traditions to come to the public so as to represent the subjecthood of the subaltern in the wider Indian public arena.

8

AMBEDKAR'S PHILOSOPHY OF RELIGION AS A POLITICAL THEOLOGY

Dr. B.R. Ambedkar's involvement in or encounter with religion has been, for a very long time, an important theme of interest in Ambedkar studies.[1] Several researchers have explored and continue to explore this dimension, and have come out with meaningful insights. Not a few scholars describe Ambedkar's turn to religion as rational, secular, scientific, purely morality-based, and non-transcendental. Johannes Beltz, for example, observes that, "Ambedkar held Buddhism to be a social philosophy based on morality and science ... purified from all superstition, rituals, and theology, without any belief in God or worship in God, without prayers or sacrifices—Buddhism was nothing but morality... Ambedkar's most important innovation was in his viewing of Buddhism as totally secularist and anti-traditional".[2] In a similar vein, Valerian Rodrigues, in his introduction to the edited volume on the *Essential Writings of Ambedkar,* notes that:

> Ambedkar acknowledged the power of religion and upheld its need, but there is no place in his religion for God and the transcendent. He subscribed to a secular religion, moving away from established religions geared towards the sacred vis-a-vis the profane... He felt that since human beings are part of this world, the primary role of religion is to safeguard the moral domain. Religion deploys sentiments, feelings, and culture to secure the moral domain and make it universal.[3]

These and similar views on Ambedkar's approach to religion have been prevalent for quite some time now. They are predominantly sociological, and some anthropological, and a few even of religious studies but more from the perspective of history of religion, including the comparative

---

[1] Surendra Jondhale and Joahnnes Beltz, eds., *Reconstructing the World—B. R. Ambedkar and Buddhism in India* (New Delhi: Oxford University Press), 2004.
[2] Johannes Beltz, "Introduction" in *Reconstructing the World—B. R. Ambedkar and Buddhism in India,* eds. Surendra Jondhale and Joahnnes Beltz (New Delhi: Oxford University Press, 2004), 7–8.
[3] Valerian Rodriques, ed., *Essential Writings of B. R. Ambedkar* (New Delhi: Oxford University Press, 2002), 19.

religious approach. However, there are new approaches being adopted today in an open-ended and explorative manner so as to understand the reality of Ambedkar's encounter with religion as best as possible. Debjani Ganguly's attempt is a case in point. She contends that Ambedkar's religious experience, including his conversion, is "more often than not beyond the pale of sociological analysis",[4] and "In order to truly understand the significance of religious conversion from the point of view of the convert's life-world, one would have to engage with the phenomenology of faith and transcendence and their very singular manifestation in the individual lives of the converts".[5] Ganguly's view, along with several others who explore Ambedkar's religion from a post-colonial and a post-secular perspective, opens a new perspective to Ambedkar's encounter with religion. I use the term encounter to signify the orientation that occurred in Ambedkar towards religion. The term could point to the fact that religion engaged the mind of this modern individual who took on the dominant Hindu religious tradition in terms of a thorough-going critique, endeavoured to open a new religious horizon through the Buddhist tradition, desired the social freedom of a people in terms of a religious imagination and practice, and finally ended with an act of religious conversion. All these, and many more dimensions, can constitute the phenomenology of Ambedkar's religion. One therefore is invited to broaden the vistas of understanding in Ambedkar studies, especially those related to his encounter with religion.

I too would prefer to explore Ambedkar's encounter with religion in an open-ended manner. The contemporary context, characteristically different from the one Ambedkar experienced, is more than conducive to such an approach. Ambedkar lived in a time when the process of secularisation and the secular ethos attendant upon it had a sway of inexorability, and secularism as a political ideal, in spite of its differing shades, had a force of political correctness, appropriate to liberal democratic politics. Learning under John Dewey, a promoter of secular education, Ambedkar would have imbibed the vision and promise of secularism with much clarity and certainty. However, Ambedkar's secularism looked to be a distinctively different experience, opening itself up contextually, informed by the yearning/desire for the emancipation of a people yoked in the juggernaut of oppression. I would like to explore Ambedkar's encounter with religion and by implication his understanding of secularism, as it manifests in his writings on the subject of philosophy of religion. I do so with the concern of finding its relevance for today.

---

[4] Debjani Ganguly, *Caste, Colonialism and Counter-Modernity—Notes on a Postcolonial Hermeneutics of Caste* (London: Routledge, 2005), 156.
[5] Ganguly, *Caste, Colonialism and Counter-Modernity*, 156.

Ambedkar's Philosophy of Religion

Ambedkar, as a methodical thinker, begins with a clarification of the very concept of philosophy itself in order to undertake a discourse on philosophy of religion. He declares: "I am using the word Philosophy in its original sense, which was twofold. It meant teachings as it did when people spoke of the philosophy of Socrates or the philosophy of Plato. In another sense, it meant critical reason used in passing judgements upon things and events."[6] As a philosopher of religion, he engages in this twofold philosophical task: in his *Buddha and His Dhamma*,[7] he treats philosophy in its former sense, while in his *Philosophy of Hinduism*, he treats philosophy as a critical reflection centring round a normative axis.

Ambedkar's philosophy of religion, as a critical reflection, permeates most of his writings related to Hinduism, caste, and untouchability. Among all the works, *Philosophy of Hinduism* presents an open discussion of his philosophy of religion, and therefore I would base myself primarily upon this text. The major work, *Buddha and His Dhamma*, which emerged during the later part of his life (written in 1956 and published in 1957), too carries insights into his philosophy of religion. This work, as we all know, is a text that interpretatively brings forth Ambedkar's conviction on Buddhism, once he had embraced it or decided to embrace it. It carries, so to say, an intra-textual view of Ambedkar's philosophy of religion. On the other hand, *Philosophy of Hinduism*, a monograph written in 1941, carries the vision of an exploring mind, which dwelt extensively upon the concepts of philosophy, religion, and philosophy of religion, and related them also with the debating world outside of the Indian subcontinent, even while critically examining them.

Ambedkar makes it a point to differentiate philosophy of religion from the then popular European notion of comparative religion. Quoting Pringle-Pattison who treats philosophy of religion as an exercise to go beyond the multiple forms of religion to identify the common principles that underlie them, Ambedkar argues that such an exercise cannot be named as philosophy of religion. He differs not merely in terms of the methods followed in these disciplines, but also in terms of the insights or outcome emerging from them. For Ambedkar, every religion cannot be good or fulfilling the right role as a comparativist would opine; it could either be good or bad, and the task of philosophy is to differentiate the one from the other. "Everything depends upon what social ideal a given religion as a divine scheme of governance holds out."[8] It is that religion which

---

[6] B. R. Ambedkar, "Philosophy of Hinduism", in *Dr. Babasaheb Ambedkar's Writings and Speeches*, vol. 3, 4.
[7] Ambedkar, *Buddha and His Dhamma*, 4.
[8] Ambedkar, *Buddha and His Dhamma*, 5.

stands for equality, fraternity, and liberty which can be considered, according to Ambedkar, as a true and good religion. To arrive at this conclusion, Ambedkar follows a systematic method, beginning with clarifying what he calls the "dimensions" of philosophy of religion.

Three Dimensions of Philosophy of Religion

Ambedkar speaks of three dimensions of philosophy of religion, using the word dimension in a heuristic sense. They are: (1) religion (its nature and dynamics), (2) the ideal scheme propounded by a religion, and (3) the appropriate criteria to evaluate a religion.

Religion—its Nature and Dynamics

Ambedkar *understood* the potentials of religion in a deeper and substantive way than a secularist modernist mind would generally do. According to him, religion is a powerful force to sanctify a moral order and legitimise a social order; and it can be ignored only to the detriment of humanity. In his own words,

> Those who deny the importance of religion not only forget this, they also fail to realize how great is the potency and sanction that lies behind a religious ideal as compared with that of a purely secular ideal.... The practical instincts of man do yield to the prescriptions of a religious ideal however much the two are opposed to each other. The practical instincts of man do not on the other hand yield to the secular ideal if the two are in conflict. This means that a religious ideal has a hold on mankind, irrespective of an earthly gain. This can never be said of a purely secular ideal. Its power depends upon its power to confer material benefit. This shows how great is the difference in the potency and sanction of the two ideals over the human mind. A religious ideal never fails to work so long as there is faith in that ideal. To ignore religion is to ignore a live wire.[9]

Ambedkar sharply perceives the potential and power of an ideal over the real and of the religious ideal over the secular ideal. A secular ideal may be abandoned when not bearing fruit in terms of tangible material benefits; but a religious ideal, even if it goes contrary to earthly gains, continues to wield power over human person, as long as the person nurtures a faith in the ideal. That contrasting the secular and the religious in this manner comes easily to Ambedkar is itself an indication of Ambedkar's deeper perceptions on religion.

He then proceeds to explore the nature and dynamics of religion. He says: "I am using the word Religion to mean Theology."[10] He gives a functional understanding of theology as an act of "propounding an ideal

---

[9] Ambedkar, *Buddha and His Dhamma*, 20.
[10] Ambedkar, *Buddha and His Dhamma*, 4.

scheme of divine governance the aim and object of which is to make the social order in which men live a moral order."[11] It would imply, according to him, the theses "(1) That God exists and is the author of what we call nature or universe, (2) That God controls all the events which make nature, and (3) [that] God exercises a government over mankind in accordance with his sovereign moral law".[12] This theology, which he calls natural theology, thus, propounds an ideal scheme of divine governance, whose fundamentals lie with the belief in the existence of God and God's providential and moral government, the objectives of which are to construct an ideal society that exists in a moral order. The dynamics involved in religion or theology make it a positive act which constructs an ideal religious scheme of divine providence as well as the law of God for human living.

Ideal Scheme of Religion

The second dimension of philosophy of religion is the ideal scheme of religion itself. An ideal scheme is "What is the fixed, permanent, and dominant part in the religion of any society".[13] Ambedkar believed that every religion has an essential core, which is fixed, permanent, and dominant, and that can be known by a proper enquiry of the philosophy of religion. Finding the ideal scheme of religions in India is not an easy task. He points out Max Muller's observations about the Indian religious terrain which presents its difficulty because religions of all hues, coming from the past and present, exist together in India; primitive, ancient, and modern—all remain merged together. However, Ambedkar observes that this difficulty can be overcome by introducing a concept of positive religion, by which he meant a religion propounded or taught by sages or teachers in terms of a distinct set of doctrines, as distinct from religion which subsists only in rituals and ceremonies. Accordingly, Christianity's or Islam's *ideal scheme* could be easily identified and examined. Hinduism too, according to Ambedkar, is a positive religion that has its *ideal scheme* given out in its sacred texts, especially in the *Manusmriti*. Identifying and evaluating this ideal scheme of Hinduism is the work of the philosophy of Hinduism— says Ambedkar.[14] He then goes on to find appropriate criteria for the evaluation of religion.

Criteria to Judge Religion

Ambedkar's search for appropriate criteria, which he considers the third dimension of philosophy of religion, begins with identifying the revolutions religions have undergone in history. As he puts it, "To me, therefore

---

[11] Ambedkar, *Buddha and His Dhamma*, 5.
[12] Ambedkar, *Buddha and His Dhamma*, 5.
[13] Ambedkar, *Buddha and His Dhamma*, 5.
[14] Ambedkar, *Buddha and His Dhamma*, 5.

it seems quite evident that the best method to ascertain the criterion by which to judge the philosophy of religion is to study the revolutions which religion has undergone".[15] The first one occurs, according to him, in dismantling or disrupting the empire of religion. There was a time when religion had a dominating presence in human consciousness to control such different spheres as astronomy, biology, anthropology, politics, and so on. These different fields of knowledge had to follow the dictates of religion. It was the opening created by science and the process of secularisation that threw the first stones upon this empire, and brought about greater freedom for human consciousness. While this being an external revolution perceivable in the open domain, Ambedkar considered yet another revolution, the internal revolution, as the greatest of all revolutions and the most appropriate to help identify the criteria for evaluation of religions.

He deemed this internal revolution as concerned with the emergence of the very idea of God, the relationship of God to society, relationship of society to individual, and the relationship of individual to individual. In his own words, this "revolution touches the nature and content of ruling conceptions of the relations of God to man, of society to man and of man to man".[16] It is best seen, according to him, in the "differences which divide savage society from civilized society",[17] which have brought about immense transformation in the nature of religion. Religion in the savage society, according to Ambedkar, is found in the rites, ceremonies, taboo, magic, fetish, and so on, and that these are always related to the most elemental aspects of life like birth, puberty, marriage, and death.

While this concern is found in all religions including the savage religions, what are not found there, according to Ambedkar, are the very *idea of God* and the relation of God to morality. As he puts it, "In the first place in the religion of the savage society, there is no trace of the idea of God. In the second place in the religion of the savage society, there is no bond between morality and religion. In the savage society, there is religion without God. In the savage society, there is morality but it is independent of religion".[18] From a religion without God, and morality without religion, it needed an *internal revolution* to introduce the idea of God in religion, and associate religion to morality. Without going into the speculation of how the idea of God emerged, and how religion got associated with religion, what can be functionally observed, according to Ambedkar, is the fact that in the civilised society God comes into the scheme of religion, and morality gets sanctified by religion. He calls it the first stage of religious revolution.

---

[15] Ambedkar, *Buddha and His Dhamma*, 7.
[16] Ambedkar, *Buddha and His Dhamma*, 8.
[17] Ambedkar, *Buddha and His Dhamma*, 8.
[18] Ambedkar, *Buddha and His Dhamma*, 10.

And the second stage, according to him, is the revolution that occurred within the civilised religion itself, differentiating *the ancient* from *the modern*.

- The first difference relates to how God is treated in the ancient and modern societies. The ancient/antique society considers God as one among the humans, as fallible as humans, as benevolent and malevolent as any mortal could be, and God and humans are bound in a kinship relationship; but in a modern society, God is freed from this human kinship. As Ambedkar writes, "In ancient society men and their Gods formed a social and political as well as a religious whole. Religion was founded on kinship between the God and his worshippers. Modern society has eliminated God from its composition. It consists of men only".[19]

- The second difference relates to the way how God becomes a transcendent reality, freed from community bonds. In the ancient society, God owned a community and a community owned a God. There was mutual responsibility towards one another's protection. A community had an exclusive possession of a God, and God had an exclusive choice of humans. The Judaic understanding of God bound in a covenant to one chosen people is a good example of this ancient idea of God. But, in the modern religion, God is freed from community-based exclusiveness and becomes a universal God, transcendent, and supernatural.

- The third point of difference "has reference to the conception of the *fatherhood* of God. In the antique society, God was the Father of his people but the basis of this conception of fatherhood was deemed to be physical".[20] "In modern society", as he continues, "The idea of divine fatherhood has become entirely dissociated from the physical basis of natural fatherhood".[21] The consequence of this change is

    > a tremendous difference in the nature of God as a Governor of the Universe. God with his physical basis was not capable of absolute good and absolute virtue. With God wanting in righteousness the universe could not insist on righteousness as an immutable principle. This dissociation of God from physical contact with man has made it possible for God to be conceived of as capable of absolute good and absolute virtue.[22]

---

[19] Ambedkar, *Buddha and His Dhamma*, 12.
[20] Ambedkar, *Buddha and His Dhamma*, 13.
[21] Ambedkar, *Buddha and His Dhamma*, 14.
[22] Ambedkar, *Buddha and His Dhamma*, 14.

- The fourth point of difference is that in the ancient society, one's nationality went with one's religion. One could not change one's nationality, without changing one's religion, and vice versa. Religion and nation remained fused together. But, in the modern society, change of religion is independent of the nation, and there can be many religions in a given nation.

- The fifth point of difference, according to Ambedkar, is related to the necessity of knowledge about the nature of God. In the ancient society, one was not expected to know the nature of God but only to know what rules to obey, how to go about the customary laws, and so on; but, in the modern society, there is a quest to know the nature of God so as to believe in God.

- The sixth point of difference is related to the place of belief in religion. In ancient society, religion was a matter of *practice* of rituals; but in modern society, it develops into a *belief-system*. In ancient society, a practice is followed up from other practices, but in modern society, a belief comes in to explain the observance of any practice.

- The seventh point of difference is related to personal conviction in religion. In the ancient society, religion was part of the organised society, and practice of religion took place as a collective endeavour; but in modern society, religion turns out to be a matter of personal conviction.

- The eighth difference relates to God's relationship to society and individual, and God and society's relationship to individual. In the ancient society, what was expected from God were earthly blessings, like good harvest, sufficient rain, protection from adversities, and so on, and not any spiritual blessings; again, these earthly blessings were sought by a community, wherein the individual was part of; the individual could not directly beseech God to receive blessings, but only as part of a collective; the collective sought the welfare of the entire collective, and not so much of the individual as individual; if the individual suffered, it was considered a fault of the individual, but not of the community. God was the protector of the entire community. But in the modern religion, God's relationship to individual is direct, and God's blessings can accrue to an individual, regardless of the society.

Ambedkar considers these differences as a result of an unparalleled internal revolution of religion, far greater than the external revolution wrought by science and secularisation. The impact of this internal revolution, according to Ambedkar, is as follows:

By this revolution, God has ceased to be a member of a community. Thereby, he has become impartial. God has ceased to be the Father of Man in the physical sense of the word. He has become the creator of the universe. The breaking of this blood bond has made it possible to hold that God is good. By this revolution man has ceased to be a blind worshipper of God doing nothing but obeying his commands. Thereby, man has become a responsible person required to justify his belief in God's commandments by his conviction.[23]

Based on this discourse of revolutions in religion, Ambedkar proceeds to propose the criterion to evaluate the validity of a religion. He opines that the ideal scheme of divine governance as found in the ancient religion had the society as its subject, and the individual was to serve the maintenance of the society; it was a form of *utility* principle at work. But the revolution has brought about a change due to which, the subject of divine governance is the individual, and the principle with which the relationship between God and the individual, and society and the individual, is envisaged is *justice*. It is the principle of justice to human beings that should become, according to Ambedkar, the criterion to evaluate the philosophy of any religion.

RELIGION OF EQUALITY

It is in searching for a religion with the principle of justice that Ambedkar arrives at the door of Buddhism. It can be well argued that Ambedkar, in his *Buddha and His Dhamma (BD)*, discoursed upon religion with a different semantic than what he did in *The Philosophy of Hinduism (PH)*. While in PH he identified religion with theology, in BD he came to differentiate the two while arguing that *Dhamma* was not a religion, but "analogous to what the European theologians call religion".[24] The reason he gave to do so was to argue the point that *Dhamma* was a social philosophy of justice, concerned with societal living, while religion was something personal, concerned only with private life. In his own words, "Religion, it is said, is personal and one must keep it to oneself. One must not let it play its part in public life. Contrary to this, Dhamma is social... Dhamma is righteousness, which means right relations between man and man in all spheres of life".[25]

Ambedkar goes further to expound the social bearing of *Dhamma* by relating it to governance or any government. As he writes, "Society cannot do without Dhamma ... For Dhamma is nothing if it is not an instrument

---

[23] Ambedkar, *Buddha and His Dhamma*, 18.
[24] Ambedkar, "Religion and Dhamma", in *The Essential Writings of B. R. Ambedkar*, comp. Valerian Rodrigues (New Delhi: Oxford University Press, 2002), 58.
[25] Ambedkar, "Religion and Dhamma", 58.

of government".[26] It would mean that Ambedkar envisioned *Dhamma* to be a philosophy of the polity, a philosophy characterised by, as he would say, the two corner-stones: *Prajna* and *Karuna*, the former meaning understanding/knowledge and the latter love.[27]

In the *Philosophy of Hinduism*, Ambedkar proposed *Dhamma* as the doctrine of ultimate equality to be replaced with the hierarchical principle of inequality found in Hinduism. *Dhamma* is the theological ideal of social, economic, and political equality, whose name in the art of politics is democracy. The essence of democracy for Ambedkar is not so much the rule of the people as the condition of equality established by a government. Ambedkar critiqued parliamentary democracy because it bothered too much about liberty but not about equality. There must be a balance between the two. In his own words, "Parliamentary democracy developed a passion for liberty. It failed to realise the significance of equality and did not even endeavour to strike a balance between liberty and equality, with the result that liberty swallowed equality and has made democracy a name and a farce".[28] Ambedkar saw *Dhamma* as the effective ideal to bring about a balance between the two.

The earlier narration of Ambedkar's encounter or engagement with religion is a pointer to the fact that Ambedkar was exploring religion and continued to be a seeker all through his life. A certain characteristic openness, as found in several subaltern leaders, is to be found in Ambedkar. Treating religion in terms of a project, emancipatory though, borne out of the modern consciousness of self-confidence, was only an aspect of his exploratory journey towards emancipation.

It is here Ambedkar's intuitive realisation of the value of religion comes in. What sustains a casteist society is not just an external structure of caste. Louis Dumont, in his *Homo Hierarchicus*, argues that it is ultimately the religiously sanctioned scheme of purity and pollution, which maintains and reproduces a casteist society. A religiously sanctioned scheme of purity and pollution can be overcome only by the power of a good religion. It is with this quintessential realisation that Ambedkar stands out as a social philosopher of religion.

Concluding Remarks: Ambedkar's Political Theology

Ambedkar was the architect of the Indian Constitution, a document that envisions a substantive democracy, providing for the free and dignified life of every citizen in India. He involved himself heart and soul in sculpting

---

[26] Ambedkar, "Religion and Dhamma", 59.
[27] Ambedkar, "Religion and Dhamma", 59.
[28] Ambedkar, "Democracy", in *The Essential Writings of B. R. Ambedkar*, comp. Valerian Rodrigues (New Delhi: Oxford University Press, 2002), 62.

this document, even while involving himself in the broad political arena for the emancipation of the subaltern people. While this political involvement was afoot, the turn to religion occurs in Ambedkar. It is not that he was not religious earlier; in fact, going by his childhood accounts, one comes to know that religion was introduced to him early on by his parents. However, religion now occurs to him as an integral part of his political praxis. His religious turn was indeed the flame that emerged in the political furnace of the time. It was deeply integrated with the social angst of the oppressed, the enlightened vision for an emancipated India, and the creative religious *mythos*—expressed in a critique and a proposal (a critique of Hinduism, and a proposal of Buddhism).

Ambedkar's turn or encounter with religion has a lesson for us today. India, though projected to emerge as a world power, suffers deeply from several ills—social, economic, political, and cultural. That section of people who bear the brunt of all these ills is the Dalit (conglomerate) subalterns. While their suffering goes unabated in spite of some well meaning remedial initiatives, factors which endanger the latter are looming large in the horizon today. A religious right which tries to sweep their grievances under the carpet imposes a hegemonic scheme of religion upon them. It would mean that the subalterns are brought back under the ritually sanctioned hegemonic symbolic system, from which they have endeavoured for centuries to free themselves. Several well-meaning political forces, who work for the emancipation of these subalterns, are either reluctant to address the religious question or fail to recognise the magnitude of the problem.

It is in this context that revisiting Ambedkar's philosophy of religion gains significance. Ambedkar's encounter with religion brought home the awareness that religion is like a live wire, carrying a powerful stream of energy, which can be very productive and at times destructive too. It would imply that the political forces working for the emancipation of subaltern people address the religious question in an emancipatory way.

Addressing them in this way is to find a right forum, which could be none other than a democratic civil sphere. Religion, so as to enter the civil space, needs to discourse upon its ideal scheme and dialogue with different other ideal schemes. The ideal schemes of different religions can be judged not by their utility, but by the axiomatic principle of justice. This judging is both internal and public. An internal judgement would be a self-examination or a self-criticism of a tradition by its practitioners, and the public would be in terms of a conversation in the public, in the civil sphere, and in a parliament of traditions. These self-examinations or conversations would hinge on the credentials of religions to be demonstrated upon the norm of justice. That would be an enduring contribution Ambedkar would have made for an enlightened, ethically sensitive, free and just society.

Thus seen, Ambedkar's philosophy of religion, as part of his encounter with religion, could be treated as an exercise in political theology. This exercise comprises of his writings not only on religion but also on caste and untouchability, of his vision of the nation as found in the Constitution, and finally of his decision and the act of conversion.

9

BIBLICAL HERMENEUTICS: A SUBALTERN PERSPECTIVE

Introduction

A subaltern interpretation of the Bible has been proposed by biblical scholars, theologians, and activists for more than three decades now. It has been an effort to encounter the liberative potentials of Bible for the emancipation of subaltern people. It has meant or continues to mean reading of the Bible in dialogue with subaltern peoples' historical experiences, religio-cultural traditions, and socio-political initiatives so as to contribute to the emergence of an egalitarian free society. This effort will continue to be relevant, not only until the time when the subaltern people experience wholesome liberation but also till the time when the human tendency to subordinate, dominate, and exploit the other is healed radically. It would do well therefore to sustain this effort by continuously reading the Bible through the eyes of the subalterns.

This chapter is premised upon the core concept subaltern, whose provenance and semantics have been discussed in Chapter 7. Without going into the details of it here, this essay begins with the basic premise that subalternity as a condition of life generates the subaltern consciousness, which, in spite of a contradictory consciousness, yearns for a life of liberation and expresses it through religio-cultural traditions. These traditions, in spite of being suppressed by or co-opted into dominant traditions, continue to live on along the margins of the society. When these traditions encounter the biblical tradition, both can fecundate each other and bring about a liberative hermeneutics.

Subaltern Christian Theology

We find several Christian theologians deriving theological insights from studies on subaltern religions or emancipatory concerns of subaltern people.¹ These studies, though not directly focused upon biblical interpretations, do involve, directly or indirectly, biblical interpretations from the subaltern perspective. In his work entitled, *Dalits and Christianity—Subaltern Religion and Liberation Theology in India*, Sathianathan Clarke makes a creative effort to bring out christological reflections upon a subaltern symbol (drum) with a good theorising on the category of subaltern religion. He understands subaltern religion as the locus of subaltern subjectivity as well as the "locus of divine-human encounters, within the overall dynamics of subjection by and subordination to the mechanisms of the caste system".²

Peniel Rajkumar, concerned about the practical efficacy of Dalit theology, explores as to what made Dalit theology ineffective to the extent of not being able to abolish the practice of caste even within Indian Christianity. The attempt of Dalit theology to identify the Dalit person with the victorhood of God in the biblical narrative of Exodus or with the victimhood of God in the person of Jesus Christ is, according to Rajkumar, inadequate to take on the caste-system. A descriptive theology of this sort, according to him, does not impute the guilt upon an agent, and therefore, does not inspire effective actions for liberation. He would, therefore, suggest a prescriptive theology, which would motivate actions of resistance and protest against the oppressors.

Several other Dalit theologians³ and many theological research institutions explore subaltern religions with a perspective that is non-reductive and non-instrumentalist. They recognise the role of religion in constructing emancipatory identities and in inspiring the subaltern people for liberative action. These studies do provide us with the ambience for pursuing a subaltern approach to biblical hermeneutics.

---

[1] Sathianathan Clarke, *Dalits and Christianity—Subaltern Religion and Liberation Theology in India* (Delhi: Oxford University Press, 1998); Clarke, "Subalterns, Identity Politics and Christian Theology in India", in *Christian Theology in Asia*, ed. Sebastian C. H. Kim (Cambridge: Cambridge University Press, 2008), 271–290; Felix Wilfred, "Towards a Subaltern Hermeneutics", in *Asian Dreams and Christian Hope—At the Dawn of the Millennium*, ed. Felix Wilfred (New Delhi: ISPCK, 2000), 245–266; Felix Wilfred, 'India and China—Sites for Asian Subaltern Theologies", in *Margins—Sites of Asian Theologies*, ed. Felix Wilfred (New Delhi: ISPCK, 2008), 95–117; Felix Wilfred, "Postcolonialism and the Subalterns: Implications for Theology", in *Christians for a Better India*, ed. Felix Wilfred (New Delhi: ISPCK, 2014), 325–343.

[2] Clarke, *Dalits and Christianity*, 8.

[3] Dalit theologians, starting from the pioneers like Arvind Nirmal, M.E. Prabhakar, Devasahayam, James Massey, and Mohan Larbeer, down to contemporary theologians like Arul Raja, Peniel, and Joseph Dayam Prabhakar, have approached the potentials of religion positively.

Post-Colonial Biblical Studies

As noted earlier, subaltern studies have a kindred discipline in the post-colonial studies, which, though originating in the field of literature studies, has been adapted to biblical studies by biblical scholars for quite some time now. They examine the biblical texts to identify the traces of the empire (Roman, Egyptian, etc.) embedded in the text and to unearth the counter-narratives or resistance-narratives found in them. As R. Sugirtharaja, one of the leading scholars to apply it to biblical studies, puts it, the perspective is "a critical enterprise aimed at unmasking the link between idea and power... It is a discursive resistance to imperialism, imperial ideologies, imperial attitudes, and their continued incarnations in such wide-ranging fields as politics, economics, history, and theological and biblical studies".[4] In his book titled, *The Bible and the Third World—Precolonial, Colonial and Postcolonial Encounters*,[5] he shows how the Bible functioned as a marginal/minority text during the pre-colonial era, as an imperial text during the colonial era, and how resistance to its imperiality emerged during the postcolonial era in the form of liberation, Dalit and other subaltern hermeneutics. He makes it a point to distinguish the postcolonial hermeneutics from the Latin-American liberation hermeneutics. As he puts it, "There is a danger in liberation hermeneutics making the Bible the ultimate adjudicator in matters related to morals and theological disputes. Postcolonialism is much more guarded in its approach to the Bible's serviceability. It sees the Bible as both a safe and an unsafe text, and as both a familiar and a distant one".[6] Liberation hermeneutics, though privileging the liberation of the poor, suffers, according to him, from its modernist framework in proposing positivistic absolutist truth-claims, basing singularly upon the Bible. Postcolonial hermeneutics, on the other hand, endeavours to free itself from modernist uni-linear knowledge-claims, and tries to base itself upon the idea and praxis of liberation originating from peoples' collective unconscious, which in turn, originates not from inspiration hidden or latent in the Bible, but from praxis of "democratic dialogue between text and context".[7] However, both the hermeneutics converge on the concerns of the liberation of the poor and oppressed, though one privileges the discursive praxis while the other an activist-praxis.

---

[4] R. Sugirtharaja, *Postcolonial Reconfigurations: An Alternate Way of Reading the Bible and Doing Theology* (London: SCM Press, 2003), 15.
[5] R. Sugirtharaja, *The Bible and the Third World—Precolonial, Colonial and Postcolonial Encounters* (Cambridge: Cambridge University Press, 2004).
[6] Sugirtharaja, *The Bible and the Third World*, 259.
[7] Sugirtharaja, *The Bible and the Third World*, 262.

John Dominic Crossan, in his book, *God and Empire—Jesus against Rome: Then and Now*,[8] pitches Jesus's nonviolent revolution against the violent civilisational domination of the Roman empire in Palestine during the life of Jesus and of the American empire today. Empires hold others under their subjection by military, economic, political, and ideological powers, and Jesus inspires Christians to resist the dynamics of the empire.

Elisabeth Schussler Fiorenza, in her work titled, *The Power of the Word—Scripture and the Rhetoric of Empire*,[9] applies the postcolonial approach to the Bible, from a feminist perspective. She contends that the anti-imperial early Christian literature, like the Pauline literature and the book of Revelation of the NT, in spite of developing an anti-language (language that subverts domination) against the Roman imperial power, continues to re-inscribe domination by using imperial imageries like the Lordship of Christ, or Lordship of G*d[10] so as to perpetuate the patriarchal order, wherein the female is made to call her husband her Lord and Master. Fiorenza's difficulty is not "simply with the Roman Empire as the historical context of the emerging early Christian movements, but with the residual, mostly unconscious, biblical inscriptions of empire and its subordinating power over".[11] Her postcolonial reading, thus, focuses upon the continuing dynamics of the rhetoric of empires as they work, for example, in male-female relationships. Her endeavour in postcolonial biblical hermeneutics is, then, to explore "methods and approaches of conscientisation, detoxification, and decolonisation that would allow wo/men to critically name and adjudicate such imperial biblical inscriptions in the interest of constructing a scriptural ethos of radical democracy, which provides an historical alternative to the language of empire".[12] As she paraphrases,

> We find a series of texts in the Christian Testament (CT) which demand submission to the *kyrios*, the emperor, as well as to the head of the household, the lord, slave master, father—that is, to the elite propertied male colonizer. These texts which are classified as household code—a label derived from Lutheran teaching on social status and roles (Standerlehre)—are concerned with seemingly three sets of relationships: wife and husband, slave wo/men and master, and son/children and father. However, it must not be overlooked that in each case it is the kyrios/father—the head of the household—to whom the members of the household owe submission. The central interest of these terms consists in bolstering the authority of the

---

[8] John Dominic Crossan, *God and Empire—Jesus against Rome: Then and Now* (New York: HarperCollins, 2006), e-book.

[9] Elisabeth Schussler Fiorenza, *The Power of the Word—Scripture and the Rhetoric of Empire* (Minneapolis: Fortress Press, 2007).

[10] Elisabeth Schussler Fiorenza writes God, replacing the "o" with an *, in order to break the overload of patriarchal semantic layers accrued upon the usage of the word "God".

[11] Fiorenza, *The Power of the Word*, 7.

[12] Fiorenza, *The Power of the Word*, 7.

kyrios, the pater familias, by demanding submission and obedience from the socially weaker groups—wives, slaves, and children and the whole community.[13]

Richard Horsely is yet another scholar who has contributed much to the postcolonial reading of the Bible, by drawing insights from James Scott. The salient themes of James Scott have been the hidden transcript and public transcript of those who live under conditions of subordination like slavery, caste, and race.[14] Hidden transcripts stand for actions, done in private, which would subvert or question the authority of those in power; and, public transcript are those actions, stereotypical and ritualist, which show obeisance to authorities in public. Those who live under conditions of subordination are said to adopt overt compliance as public transcripts, but covert rebellion as hidden transcripts. The hidden transcripts are codes, which carry subversive messages, and they need to be decoded to get at their meaning. In one of his works, Horsely applies the category of hidden transcript to the biblical characters of Jesus and Paul to identify the art of resistance found in them.[15]

Thus, we see an array of scholars using the post-colonial lens to read the Bible. It would be in our interest to see how the subaltern lens has been used or could be used for biblical hermeneutics.

SUBALTERN BIBLICAL HERMENEUTICS

Biblical interpretation, as well-known, is centred upon three nodal points: author, text, and reader. What is problematic with these triadic nodal points is treating them as independent polarities centring round author, text, and reader. Perhaps, what is more appropriate is to say that these are three starting points for biblical interpretation, nay, any textual interpretation. By beginning from the vantage-point of either the author or the text or the reader, the hermeneut engages all the three components in any interpretation. The starting-point certainly has a privilege so as to open a new horizon of meaning; and to that extent, the starting point can be said to characterise an approach, but not so much as to become centred upon it, much less determined by it.

A subaltern hermeneutics, accordingly, starts from the location or context of the reader. She privileges the reader's life-world, so that it can become a window to the meaning of the biblical text. She approaches the text from a standpoint, and the standpoint is borne out of the struggles and

---

[13] Fiorenza, *The Power of the Word*, 151–152.
[14] James Scott, *Weapons of the Weak—Everyday Forms of Peasant Resistance* (Yale: Yale University Press, 1985); James Scott, *Domination and the Art of Resistance—Hidden Transcripts* (Yale: Yale University Press, 1990).
[15] Richard A. Horsley, ed., *Paul and Empire: Religion and Power in Roman Imperial Society* (Harrisburg, PA: Trinity International, 1997), 1–9.

hopes of the subaltern reader for a life in freedom. The text, though very central to the production of meaning, need not restrict the meaning-making process, nor obtain an authority which cares little for the life-world of the people. In the Indian sanskritic religious context, we see a decisive importance being given to the text and its authority, oftentimes to the neglect of the readers' context. Such a predominantly text-centred approach needs to be challenged by a reading which starts with the context of the reader.

Warren Carter's reading of Matthew's gospel is a good attempt at doing biblical hermeneutics from the location of marginality. Carter considers the Gospel of Matthew a counter-narrative, a "work of resistance written from and for a minority community of disciples committed to Jesus ... The gospel shapes their identity and lifestyle as an alternative community".[16] This community, which was living along the margins of the Roman empire, nourished its hope upon an alternate empire, the Reign of God, the hope of which was initiated by Jesus's mission, death, and resurrection. The Gospel of Matthew "mostly originates in social locations of weakness and cultural marginality, among a minority, from the poor".[17] The gospel, according to Carter, was a "work of resistance, written for a largely Jewish religious group... The gospel constructs an alternative worldview and community. It affirms a way of life marginal to the dominant structures".[18]

BIBLICAL HERMENEUTICS IN INDIA

India has been reading and interpreting the Bible for a very long time now. During the modern era, Raja Ram Mohan Roy (1772–1833), the father of modern India was interested in interpreting the Bible as a handbook of ethical teachings. He learned Greek and Hebrew in order to study the Bible in its original languages. Nehemiah Goreh (1825–1895) got trained as a scholar of biblical criticism. He took the Bible to be divinely inspired and revealed, and considered it to be occupying the status of the Vedas. Krishna Mohan Banerjea (1813–1885) tried to relate the Bible to Hindu scriptures, and thought that the Vedas came closer to Christianity than did the Old Testament. The cosmic figure of *Prajapathi*, who sacrificed himself in order to create the world was, according to him, closer to Christ, who sacrificed himself for the redemption of humanity. Banerjea opined that, "The Vedas confirm and illustrate Scripture traditions and Scripture facts ... Christianity fills up the vacuum ... in the Vedic account of the sacrifice, by exhibiting the true *Prajapati*—the Lamb slain from the foundation of

---

[16] Warren Carter, *Matthew and the Margins—A Sociopolitical and Religious Reading* (New Delhi: Theological Publications in India, 2007), xvii.
[17] Carter, *Matthew and the Margins*. xix.
[18] Carter, *Matthew and the Margins*. 1.

Biblical Hermeneutics

the world".[19] While these personalities were trying to replace the Vedas or vedic characters with the Bible or biblical characters, there were others who interpreted the biblical message in terms of the classical *jnana*, *bhakti*, and *karmamarga* traditions. A.J. Appasamy, for example, interpreted the Johanine text 10:30 from the perspective of the *bhakti marga*. Thus, several attempts to interpretatively relate the Bible to the Indian religio-philosophical traditions took place from the eighteenth century onwards.

SUBALTERN BIBLICAL HERMENEUTICS IN INDIA

However, a subaltern approach to the Bible may be said to emerge from Pandita Ramabai's (1858–1922) encounter with the Bible during the nineteenth century. Her very conversion to Christianity is supposed to have been inspired by reading Luke's Gospel and the episode of the Samaritan woman in John 4: 4–42. Her interest in the Bible grew to a great extent as to make her learn the languages of Hebrew and Greek to read the Bible in its original languages and to translate it into Marathi. For the inmates of *Sharada Sadan*, a home Ramabai founded for young widowed women, the Marathi Bible became an empowering source of faith in their condition of subordination.

However, a methodical adaptation of subaltern biblical hermeneutics may be said to emerge only with the birth of contextual theologies, the Dalit theology in particular. Drawing inspiration from the method of liberation theology, which interpreted the Bible in terms of the economic conditions of poverty, Dalit theology interpreted the Bible in terms of the social conditions of the caste system for the liberation of the Dalits.

SOME METHODOLOGICAL STANCES

The Dalit theological movement has made a very significant contribution in bringing out a series of volumes of Dalit Commentary on the Bible. Headed by the pioneering Dalit theologian James Massey, the *Centre for Dalit/Subaltern Studies* has been instrumental in making this great contribution to subaltern biblical hermeneutics. Massey proposes that by "Exploring the myriad themes like faith, revelation, inspiration, authority, word of God, incarnation, and so on, Dalit Bible *Commentary* should enable Dalit sensibility to enter into dialogue with the biblical word/text, making the Scripture more meaningful to their lives".[20] In order to do so, the *Commentary* suggests a Dalit hermeneutics methodology, which it claims to be of its own. "In the absence of any existing one", Massey says

---

[19] As cited in Jesurathnam, *Dalit Liberative Hermeneutics—Indian Christian Dalit Interpretation of Psalm 22* (New Delhi: ISPCK, 2010), 148.

[20] James Massey, "Preface", *One Volume Dalit Bible Commentary NT* (New Delhi: Centre for Dalit/Subaltern Studies, 2010), xvi.

that, "The interpreters involved in (the) project [had] have to evolve methods... based on their gained experience while working on the project".[21] Maria Arul Raja, a significant contributor to subaltern biblical hermeneutics, would opine that the "method of Dalit reading of the Bible has to be evolved in tune with the Dalit action for transformation and of the biblical passion for transformation".[22]

With this experience of the action for transformation, the interpreters are called upon to focus upon the way the Dalit world and the biblical world can inter-penetrate each other. "In this process, besides the role of social sciences, particularly the sociology and the culture have been recognised as most important influencing factors for the interpretations of the Scripture. The culture aspect is taken as part of the contextual realities of the two worlds, the Dalit world and the biblical world."[23] In approaching the biblical world, the *Commentary* adopts a dialogical-contextual-approach. In applying this approach to the NT, the *Commentary* points out that the role played by Greek philosophy in the formation of NT texts "not only created serious problem in the whole process of the interpretation of the Scripture, it also made such interpretation irrelevant for the Indian context in general and the Dalit context in particular".[24] Dalit hermeneutics, therefore, has to approach the Bible afresh, from the perspective of the Dalits, rather than the Greek philosophical perspective. By way of doing this, "The interpreters ... tried ... to find new approaches that could contribute to a fresh look at the Scripture: How could the worldview of royal consciousness, hierarchy, purity and pollution, and so on, be deconstructed and an alternative Dalit worldview in dialogue with the biblical worldview can be presented".[25] This Dalit approach to the Bible, Massey takes care to point out, is not to confine the Dalits to themselves, but to "expand them by becoming a spring board for integral liberation", which will "ultimately steer them towards the path to complete humanhood eventually establishing a Just Society".[26] Maria Arul Raja observes that when Dalits read the Bible as the word of God, "The inner world of Dalit sensitivities is activated with a fresh vigour. Dalit identities as victims, subjects, and community-builders are further empowered to pursue the agenda of building a new human society with an inclusive ideology".[27] Raja takes Dalit hermeneutics

---

[21] Massey, "Preface", xvi.
[22] Maria Arul Raja, "Towards a Dalit Reading of the Bible: Some Hermeneutical Reflection", *Jeevadhara* 25, no. 151 (1996): 31.
[23] Massey, "Preface", xvi.
[24] Massey, "Preface", xvi.
[25] Massey, "Preface", xvii.
[26] Massey, "Preface", xvii.
[27] As cited by Massey, "Preface", xvii.

a step forward by suggesting that "Dalits are ready to enter into dialogue with any religio-cultural resources".[28]

Thus, we see that the Dalit biblical commentary has made significant methodological points to enrich the subaltern biblical hermeneutics. Imbued with the inspiration of liberation theology to read the Bible contextually, the *Commentary* integrates the role of social sciences in understanding the context of Dalits. It envisions certain groundedness in the process of interpretation: though integrating the role of exegesis, it expects the interpreters to draw from their own experience of the reality of subalternity so as to interpret the Bible effectively.

Peniel Rajkumar, a Dalit theologian, would suggest that the Dalit approach to the Bible is more sensory and performative rather than textual. As he observes,

> We can talk of trans-textual and sensory dimensions to the emancipatory appropriation of the Bible by ordinary Christian Dalit communities. Given the rampant illiteracy among Dalit communities and their worldview of venerating objects as repositories of divine power, Dalits endorse the power of the Bible to touch and act in a magical way, often placing it on people's heads and shoulders during prayers for healing and deliverance. This magical notion of the Bible testifies to Dalit reception of the performative dimension of the Bible which is crucial to their understanding of the Bible as being emancipatory.[29]

This performative dimension of the Bible, according to him, works effectively also to signify a new identity to Christian Dalits. Against a history of violent denial of access to sacred texts, the Christian Dalits feel empowered to carry the Bible as their sacred texts. This sense of empowerment emerges not so much from textual interpretation as from a sense of ownership. Peniel, thus, argues for a biblical hermeneutical approach that goes beyond textual interpretation, though not excluding it, to the sensory dimension of the Bible. He would apply this approach to read the synoptic healing stories of the New Testament. These biblical narratives of healing, according to him, carry an embodied sense of Jesus's identification with the impure people, like the lepers, woman-with-haemorrhage, and so on. Such a trans-textual approach, therefore, would be fitting for a subaltern hermeneutics, according to Peniel.

Maria Arul Raja too advocates a performative method of biblical hermeneutics, when he says that "the post-modern biblical criticism emphasises the performative axis rather than the informative axis of the modern era,

---

[28] As cited by Massey, "Preface", xvii.
[29] Peniel Rajkumar, *Dalit Theology, Dalit Liberation—Problems, Paradigms and Possibilities* (USA: Ashgate Publishing Company, 2010), 70.

and it is a relevant method for Dalit reading of the Bible".[30] This method, Raja opines, facilitates "a genuine dialogue between the performative dalit consciousness and the performative biblical text".[31] And, such "a method of the Dalit reading of the Bible is oriented towards concrete historical commitment transforming the present reality into a new liberative one".[32]

In interpreting Psalm 22 from the Dalit liberation perspective, K. Jesurathnam presents the biblical lament as an important subaltern interpretative genre. Laments "speak in the language of protest in response to acute suffering... appeal to God for his (sic) intervention".[33] Dalits identify themselves with this genre of lamentation by identifying themselves with the cry contained in the laments: "The lament cry addressed to God seeks to enter into an intense dialogue with God in order to evoke God's response to the cry of the lamenter". Dalit Christians cry out to their God "in anticipation with and in the light of liberative potential that may ultimately come from God".[34] Crying out in the face of suffering and pain is not, according to Jesurathnam, a sign of internalising the marks of oppression, by giving into helplessness and despair. As he continues to reflect: "Dalit Christians do not simply internalise their oppression and suffering. They seek God's intervention against their oppressors in a caste ridden society. They cry in such a way that God's silence may be broken for their cause. The protest cry for Christian Dalits helps to assert their lost identity as they engage in dialogue with their God in this process."[35]

Another important Dalit theologian Devasahayam points out to the gospel of Jesus Christ as the answer to the cry of the oppressed. In his words: "The gospel of Jesus Christ is conceived, as an answer to this unending cry of the oppressed, as the good news of liberation to the oppressed, particularly to the Dalits with a further priority of the liberation of the Dalit woman, who is a victim of complex systems of caste, class, and patriarchy. The concern for humanity should start from the point where it is most disgraced, and disfigured, and that is at the life of Dalit women."[36]

Thus, we see that the subaltern Dalit hermeneuts of the Bible point out to a location from where to begin the reading of the Bible, allow the subaltern and biblical worlds to dialogue with one another, and open oneself up to new meanings of the gospel of Jesus Christ, which become the power to empower the subalterns to continuously seek their freedom. The genres

---

[30] Raja, "Towards a Dalit Reading of the Bible", 31.
[31] Raja, "Towards a Dalit Reading of the Bible", 31.
[32] Raja, "Towards a Dalit Reading of the Bible", 31.
[33] K. Jesurathnam, *Dalit Liberative Hermeneutics—Indian Christian Dalit Interpretation of Psalm 22* (New Delhi: ISPCK, 2010), 262–263.
[34] Jesurathnam, *Dalit Liberative Hermeneutics*, 263.
[35] Jesurathnam, *Dalit Liberative Hermeneutics*, 263.
[36] V. Devasahayam, *Frontiers of Doing Dalit Theology* (Madras: Gurukul/ISPCK, 1996), 5.

which embody these meanings can be varied, as for example, the genre of lamentations could be.

This subaltern reading of the Bible can as well be enriched by methodological insights drawn from the post-colonial approach to the Bible. For example, the insights of Elisabeth Schussler Fiorenza are a case in point: Fiorenza speaks about certain emancipative techniques or conscientising strategies which can meaningfully be incorporated in the subaltern biblical hermeneutics. They are:

- A *hermeneutics of experience* which reflects on socially located experience and lifts into consciousness how much experience is shaped by the inscriptions of dominance and submission.

- A *hermeneutics of domination* deploys a critical analytic of the systemic inscriptions of empire and domination (kyriarchy) in socio-political-religious consciousness and everyday life. It seeks to name the globalisation of inequality and poverty as the context of biblical interpretation.

- A *hermeneutics of suspicion* analyses the mechanism of kyriocentric texts and ideologies that "naturalise" the systems of domination by making the ethos of empire "common sense" and, in the case of sacred scriptures, which sacralises such kyriarchal worldviews and self-understandings.

- A *hermeneutics of evaluation* critically assesses biblical texts and their contemporary inscriptions in terms of the feminist the*logical norm "wo/men's salvation", that is, well-being.

- A *hermeneutics of imagination* creatively envisions a world that is different from the world determined by empire and domination and seeks to identify visions of hope and transformation also inscribed in biblical terms.

- A *hermeneutics of remembrance* engages rhetorical analysis and historical re-construction for rewriting biblical history in terms of wo/men's struggles against empire and for well-being. It thereby reconstructs a different context for biblical texts and interpretations.

- A *hermeneutics of transformation* is at work in the hermeneutical process of de-toxification and has as its goal transformative action for changing the internalised ethos of empire and its structures of domination as well as for empowering wo/men's agency and commitment to alter relations of domination.[37]

---

[37] Elisabeth Schussler Fiorenza, *The Power of the Word—Scripture and the Rhetoric of Empire* (Minneapolis: Fortress Press, 2007), 163–164.

Some Important Themes

While tracing the origin of the concept subaltern in the previous chapter, we saw how Antonio Gramsci spoke of a contradictory consciousness characterising the subaltern consciousness. We saw also that Partha Chatterjee took up the theme of Gramsci, and pointed out the potential of religion, as evident in the counter-religious traditions of India (e.g., *bhakti* movement), to emerge out of the externally imposed consciousness so as to manifest the native emanicipatory consciousness of the subalterns. It would be relevant to continue to reflect along this line and see whether and how the biblical interpretations, as found in subaltern theological explorations, have the potential to emancipate the subaltern person from contradictory consciousness and, in its place, construct a critically emancipatory consciousness. We do see that some of the themes taken up for interpretation by Dalit biblical hermeneuts are quite relevant in this regard.

Interrogating Karma

Belief in fate, leading to fatalism—a sense of resignation to *fait-accompli*, and also at times to certain therapeutic experience while suffering pain—is one of the ubiquitous beliefs found among the people of India. Though it can be explained as a therapeutic belief, its impact upon the agency of an individual or a collective tends to be more limiting than freeing; it tends to constrain the individual or a collective from venturing into new initiatives and tends to inhibit the critical consciousness from emerging.

Belief in fate, however ambiguous it may be, does converge, at least to a certain level, with the doctrine of *karma*, an important theme in the sanskritic Hindu philosophy. Networked closely with the doctrines of transmigration of the soul and of rebirth, *karma* is the philosophy of action that ensures continuity to the journey of *atman* (soul) towards its ultimate liberation; it is present in the life of an individual in terms of the scheme of reward and punishment, depending upon the actions done in the past. When linked to the system of social organisation, it explains the presence of discriminated gradation or hierarchy in the caste-system and lends a ritual legitimation to it. Such a philosophy of action, needless to say, has gone against the subaltern people of India by way of perpetuating a ritual hierarchy on the one hand, and giving a religio-philosophical legitimacy to the ritual inferiority of the subaltern people. It indeed is an important theme to be hermeneutically challenged and negotiated by a subaltern biblical hermeneutics.

Subaltern interpreters of the Bible do acknowledge the relevance of such a task. For example, K. Jesurathnam speaks of a subaltern liberative hermeneutics, which interrogates the Hindu *karma* philosophy with the Christian faith in the vicarious suffering of Jesus Christ. He observes that

"Dalit Christians question the undue imposition of *karma* theory and caste hierarchy based on certain Hindu texts and affirm that in Christ their *karma* is removed and that they are not inferior as labelled by their caste oppressors".[38] It is not only the removal of poverty that is the target of liberative hermeneutics but also the removal of "a sense of guilt and fear" imposed by the belief in *karma*. They oftentimes silently suffer the belief that their previous *karma* has brought about such a socially inferior status to them. It is here that the hermeneut has to help the subaltern people to remove the guilt from their religious consciousness, by believing in the biblical revelation that Jesus Christ, through his cross and resurrection, has suffered on account of the oppressed, and has brought the hope of liberation. As Jesurathnam observes,

> For our sake Jesus Christ suffered on the cross. For the sake of the downtrodden, Christ suffered but through Resurrection, hope and victory is granted to those who believed him. In our Dalit situation, we no longer need to carry the feeling that we suffer because of our fate, rather we have a saviour who changes our fate of suffering into a joy of salvation and we are the free human beings without any guilt of our sins.[39]

He continues:

> Dalit Christians, by accepting the message of the cross and resurrection of Jesus Christ, are freed from their guilt and the *karma* imposed on them. This is why the Indian Christian interpretations of *karma* are helpful to Dalit liberation and emancipation. When such interpretations give a Christian meaning to Hindu *karma*, Dalits are reassured that they are free from their *karma* because of their hope in Jesus Christ.[40]

Negotiating Dharma

Dharma, one of the *four goals (purusarthas)* leading to the ultimate liberation (*moksha*), is a central doctrine of sanskritic Hinduism. Philosophical debates have abounded on this doctrine. On a practical level, *Dharma* stands for an impersonal law, present in the cosmic order, maintained by the sacrifices of the gods and by the ritual sacrifices of the Brahmin priests; and it stands also for an ethical-juridical law which emerges empirically in the operation of the social customs and practices of castes and life-stages of Brahmins. Both as the impersonal law and ethical-juridical law, it operates on its own, without the will of a personal deity, and pre-exists as well as post-exists individual actions (*karma*) of human beings and contributes to the attainment or otherwise of liberation, the *moksha*.

---

[38] Jesurathnam, *Dalit Liberative Hermeneutics*, 263.
[39] Jesurathnam, *Dalit Liberative Hermeneutics*, 161–162.
[40] Jesurathnam, *Dalit Liberative Hermeneutics*, 168.

This doctrine is now being constructed as the core doctrine of popular as well as political Hinduism. This doctrine has had a long life in the Indian sub-continent. We find its abiding presence in popular consciousness, *puranic* literatures, and philosophical texts. Being an all pervasive doctrine, it informs even the day-to-day living of the ordinary folk of this country, and has a sway over their religio-ethical imagination. The orthodox as well as heterodox traditions of India privilege the doctrine, though they may have their own specific understanding of it. In fact the very history of heterodoxy in India can be said to revolve around the hermeneutical engagement with this doctrine. It would therefore be indispensable that the Indian biblical studies too does an inter-textual reading between the Christian biblical inspiration and the doctrine of *dharma* as an exercise in doing public theology. One of the good efforts in this regard has been already made by George Soares-Prabhu, whose insights I discuss in this book in the chapter on Conversation on *Dharma* in the Indian Public.

By way of Concluding

Basing on the clarification of the term subaltern given in the previous chapter, this essay went on to explain the relationship of subaltern studies to post-colonial studies as it obtained in biblical studies. It observed that while the post-colonial biblical studies have contributed significantly to the interrogation of empires, as embedded in the biblical text and as present in today's context, it cannot replace the subaltern approach which has a singular focus upon the interrogation of the Indian caste-hierarchy. It then went on to observe how such a focus has been manifest in the subaltern biblical hermeneutical efforts carried out so far. These endeavours have presented some methodological insights wherein the subaltern biblical hermeneutics is presented as unique in terms of its grounded method of evolving a method from the context of suffering, pain, and the cry against them; they have presented also some central themes: *Interrogating Karma* and *Negotiating Dharma* need to be of continuing engagement for subaltern biblical hermeneutics in India. It is by being involved in this engagement hermeneutically that the subaltern people can emerge with their freedom and dignity.

10

A SUBALTERN PUBLIC THEOLOGY OF THE HOLY SPIRIT

We are witnesses today to a deepening and strengthening of the pneumatological turn in Christian theology. In the context of the Catholic Church's re-awakening to Pneumatology in its post-Vatican II phase,[1] the Western church "reopening the files on the Holy Spirit",[2] and the world-wide growth of Charismatic and Pentecostal movements and theologies, we witness the increasing interest on spirituality and the growth of pneumatological sub-disciplines like spirit christology,[3] mission-theology of the Holy Spirit,[4] pneumatological theology of religions,[5] and so on. Blossoming of these interests and disciplines is indeed the signs of the times which beckon us to reflect further upon the presence and role of the Holy Spirit in our contemporary era.

Pandipeddi Chenchiah, an important theologian of the Rethinking Christianity in India Group, once said, "The Holy Spirit—the doctrine and

---

[1] José Comblin, in 1989, stated succinctly: "Before, there was no pneumatology in the Catholic Church; now it is developing rapidly." José Comblin, *The Holy Spirit and Liberation* (Oregon: Wipf & Stock Publishers, 1989), xii. Yves Congar's three volumes of *I Believe in the Holy Spirit* (New York: The Seabury Press, 1983), originally published in French in1979-80, and *The Word and the Spirit* (London: Geoffrey Chapman, 1986) were notable markers of this development.

[2] Kirsteen Kim points out the context of the reopening as its encounter with the "theology of the Orthodox churches, growing awareness of the theological significance of diverse spiritual traditions, theological reflection on movements of the Spirit for liberation, and especially the recent rise of Pentecostal theology". Kirsteen Kim, *The Holy Spirit in the World—A Global Conversation* (Maryknoll: SPCK & Orbis Books, 2007), 1.

[3] Two good studies on "Spirit Christology" by authors hailing from India are Mohan Doss, SVD, *Christ in the Spirit—Contemporary Spirit Christologies* (New Delhi: ISPCK, 2005) and Christina Manohar, *Spirit Christology—An Indian Christian Perspective* (New Delhi: ISPCK, 2009).

[4] Kirsteen Kim's works, *The Holy Spirit in the World* and *Joining in with the Spirit—Connecting World Church and Local Mission* (London: SCM Press, 2010) are outstanding examples in this regard.

[5] Amos Yong, "The Turn to Pneumatology in Christian Theology of Religion: Conduit or Detour?" *Journal of Ecumenical Studies* 35 (Summer-Fall, 1998): 3-4.

personality—if my instincts are sound, will play a decisive role in Indian theology. They may receive a new interpretation and become the corner-stone of Indian Christian theology".[6] Perhaps it will be a long way to go before Chenchiah's prognosis comes true; however, one can already see signs of its realisation. It is inspiring to see that theologians like Chenchiah, Vengal Chakkarai, A.J. Appasamy, Abhishiktananda, Vandana, Stanley Samartha, Samuel Rayan, and others have already presented significant pneumatological reflections.[7] While appreciating their valuable contributions, we need to note that most of them have made their reflections in relation to the sanskritic philosophical and religious traditions of India. What could be an alternate contribution is reflecting upon it from the subaltern perspective. While attempting to do that, this essay tries to relate it to public theology in the Indian context.

THEOLOGY OF THE HOLY SPIRIT

Experience of the Holy Spirit is perhaps the central concern while doing any theology of the Holy Spirit, leave alone a subaltern public theology. Biblical witnesses to the *experience* dwell upon it as an experience of breath of life, power (*dynamis*) of God to prophesy, presence of God, living water welling up for eternal life, tongues of fire, Spirit of truth, and so on.[8] The patristic tradition, especially from the West, dwelt upon it (situated as it was within the context of apologetics of the Christian faith in triune God surrounded by the Jewish and the Greek religio-philosophical traditions) in metaphysical terms, as an experience to be sacramentally mediated through the unifying hierarchical church. The Eastern Orthodox theology of the Holy Spirit emphasised the process of perfection and deification (*apotheosis*) of the human. The mystical tradition spoke of the flames of the Spirit of God experienced through mysticism.[9] Scholastic theology of the medieval era went back to the metaphysical experience of the Spirit of God, and the Reformation-based evangelical experience treated the Holy

---

[6] As cited in R.H.S. Boyd, *An Introduction to Indian Christian Theology*, 6th ed. (New Delhi: ISPCK, 1994), 156.

[7] For the pneumatological contributions of these theologians, see Kirsteen Kim, *Mission in the Spirit—The Holy Spirit in Indian Christian Theologies* (New Delhi: ISPCK, 2003); Kim, *The Holy Spirit in The World*; P.V. Joseph, *Indian Interpretation of the Holy Spirit—An Appraisal of the Pneumatology of Appasamy, Chenchiah, and Chakkarai* (New Delhi: ISPCK, 2007); Manohar, *Spirit Christology*.

[8] For a detailed account of the Biblical and patristic understanding of the Holy Spirit, Michael Welker, *God the Spirit* (Minneapolis: Fortress Press, 1994); Veli-Matti Kärkkäinen, *Pneumatology* (Michigan: Baker Academic, 2002); Jürgen Moltmann, *The Spirit of Life—A Universal Affirmation* (Minneapolis: Fortress Press, 1992); Gary D. Badcock, *Light of Truth & Fire of Love—A Theology of the Holy Spirit* (Cambridge, UK: William B. Eerdmans Publishing Company, 1997).

[9] Elizabeth A. Dreyer, *Holy Power, Holy Presence—Rediscovering Medieval Metaphors for the Holy Spirit* (NY: Paulist Press, 2007).

Spirit as the illuminator of the meaning of the Scripture and the sanctifier of the believer.[10] The twentieth century witnessed the Pentecostal way of experiencing the Spirit of God in such phenomena as baptism in the Spirit, speaking in tongues, prophecy, verbalised prayers, eloquent preaching, and healing, which give an embodied character to the experience of the Holy Spirit.[11] As a result of these developments, we find today different traditions of the experience of the Holy Spirit existing side by side; and they yield different approaches to the articulations of the theology of the Holy Spirit. The fact of these diverse experiences of the Holy Spirit, not to be confined to one single monolithic experiential mould, is today the very nature of the presence of the Spirit of God, who blows where She wills (John 3:8).

In an edited volume, carrying a sub-title, *Loosing the Spirits*, Veli-Matti Kärkkäinen speaks about two types of pneumatologies today: one, unitive Pneumatology, mostly the traditional one, which dwells upon one Spirit of God, as part of the classical articulation of the doctrine of Trinity; the other, plural Pneumatology, which is mindful of the meaning, role, and effects of other spirits vis-a-vis, along with, and as opposed to the Spirit of God.[12] Kärkkäinen and other contributors to the volume underline the emergence of plural Pneumatology as characteristic of the contemporary era; Kirsteen Kim, in her writings on missiological Pneumatology, opens up a new approach to understanding the spirits of other religions, especially the cosmic popular religions;[13] Sebastian Kim, in his reflections upon Pneumatology from the perspective of public theology, speaks about interacting spirits of the public, considering the spirits of other religions, philosophies, and ideologies as partners with the Spirit of God.[14] Plural pneumatologies appeal to the contemporary post-modern theological mind. However, one needs to clarify the nature of this plurality. First of all, it must be noted that plural pneumatologies do not stand for an indifferent passive pluralism of pneumatologies, which does not wish to engage in a relationship; second, it does not deny the uniqueness of different

---

[10] Kim, *The Holy Spirit in the World*, 5.
[11] For an evangelical theology of the Holy Spirit, see Clark H. Pinnock, *Flame of Love—A Theology of the Holy Spirit* (Illinois: InterVarsity Press, 1996); Frederick Dale Bruner, *A Theology of the Holy Spirit—The Pentecostal Experience and the New Testament Witness* (London: Hodder and Stoughton, 1970).
[12] Veli-Matti Kärkkäinen, "Spirit(s) in Contemporary Christian Theology: An Interim Report of the Unbinding of Pneumatology", in *Interdisciplinary and Religio-Cultural Discourses on a Spirit-Filled World*, eds. Veli-Matti Kärkkäinen, Kirsteen Kim and Amos Yong (Hampshire: Palgrave Macmillan, 2013), 29.
[13] Kim, *Joining in with the Spirit*; Kim, *The Holy Spirit in the World*.
[14] Sebastian C. H. Kim, "Spirits of the Political: Theological Engagement in the Public Sphere'", in *Interdisciplinary and Religio-Cultural Discourses*, eds. Veli-Matti Kärkkäinen, Kirsteen Kim and Amos Yong (New York: Palgrave Mcmillan, 2013), 25-139.

traditions of the spirits; third, it is a dynamic and agonistic plurality, which is ever engaging life and reality contextually. It is a plurality that recognises the different traditions with their uniqueness, does not steamroll the traditions, and is recognised in the way in which it involves in particular contexts, which are agonistically toned, rather than fixed and stable.

Subaltern Theology of the Holy Spirit in India

Looking at it from the subaltern public theological perspective, Pneumatology may be understood as the reflection upon the Christian experience of the Holy Spirit who keeps opening the public from systemic closures and hegemonic universals so as to include the subalterns in those public domains which keep excluding them. Such an opening up involves visions and dynamics, wherein religions, ideologies, and movements, as interactive spirits,[15] can play vital roles. This experience of the Holy Spirit brings power to the subalterns, empowers them in their social existence, awakens their autonomous agency, initiates them into public conversation, helps them interrogate the existing exclusionary hegemonies, enables them to discern and network with the public sites of the presence of God, transforms their identities, and brings them ultimately to the experience of the freedom of the glory of the children of God (Rom 8:21).

This subaltern public theology of the Holy Spirit would, on the one hand, be inspired by the instances of experience of the Holy Spirit as they are occurring in the Indian churches, and, on the other hand, enter into the public sphere *interactively*[16] and *interrogatively* (interrogating the evil spirits of dominance and slavery present in the culture, society, and economic system of the Indian society).

The following are some of the experiences as well as articulations of the Holy Spirit as reported in the Indian subaltern context.

- The outpourings of the Holy Spirit which occurred in the Mukti Mission of Pandita Ramabai, as reported by Ramabai herself in the *Mukti Prayer-Bell, 1907* is one of the early Pentecostal experiences[17]

---

[15] Kim, "Spirits of the Political", 25-139.

[16] "I envisage the public sphere pneumatologically as a realm of interacting spirits, in the sense of ideas, concepts, opinions, ideologies, and philosophies. Christian theology enters this spirit world as one of many spirits negotiating, encountering other spirits in public conversation among equals, and bringing insights from the Holy Spirit into the arena... the Spirit gives the gift of discerning among the 'spirits of the political'. The Spirit also empowers Christians to challenge 'totality' or monopoly in the public realm of life and to people of any religious and socio-political diversity to engage in advocacy, debate, and consensus politics." Kim, "Spirits of the Political", 127.

[17] I am mentioning it as "one of the early ...", because Ramabai writes in the same *Mukti Prayer-Bell*, 1907, that "I had heard of the gift of tongues having been given to God's children in some parts of the country". Ramabai, "Showers of Blessings" in *Pandita Ramabai*, ed. S. M. Adhav (Bangalore: CISRS & Chennai: CLS: 1979), 219. And she

in India. She writes: "Early this year, the Lord began to give us a fresh spiritual uplift, another and greater outpouring of the Holy Spirit... God the Holy Ghost is visiting us in a very special manner."[18] The fruits of this outpouring of the Holy Spirit, as Ramabai mentions, were "deepening spiritual life, continuance in earnest prayer, greater zeal in winning souls for Christ, increasing love, peace, and joy in the Holy Ghost".[19]

In and through her conversion to Christianity and the experience of the outpouring of the Holy Spirit, Ramabai emerged as a singular subaltern self to express its autonomous agency. Going by Ranajit Guha's usage of the term subaltern which stood for the demographic difference between the people of India and the elite, Ramabai can well be taken as a gendered Indian subaltern self. She experienced, on the one hand, subordination on account of being a woman and a widow (being widowed in the Indian Brahminical tradition was an extreme curse), and on the other, subaltern agency in terms of resistance to the dominance of elite ideology, belief, consciousness, and so on. The initiatives taken by her to support the widowed women to reconstruct their lives from the status of being cursed to the status of being blessed stand as proof for her subaltern agency. While the element of resistance to the elite consciousness was readily visible in important stances Ramabai took in respect of the native Brahminic authority and the Anglican hierarchy,[20] it interests us most to find that she resisted the apparent hegemony the English and American view exercised in the domain of authenticating the experiences of the Spirit of God. Against accusations that what the Indians had as experience of the Holy Spirit was the work of the devil, Ramabai raised some sharp questions: "Why should not the Holy Spirit have liberty to work among Indian Christian people, as he has among Christians of other countries? And why should everything that does not reach the high standard of English and American civilisation be taken as coming from the devil?"[21] They are pertinent interrogations where the autonomous agency of the subaltern self, along with its will to resist the hegemonic code of the colonial West, manifested

---

continues: "I am not aware that anything like the present Holy Ghost revival has ever visited India before the year 1905". Ramabai, "Showers of Blessings", 220.

[18] Ramabai, "Showers of Blessings", 218–220.
[19] Ramabai, "Showers of Blessings", 219.
[20] By writing about the condition of women in the tradition-bound Indian context, Ramabai exposed very forcefully the patriarchal element of the Indian Brahminic tradition. Later on, by standing up to the Anglican hierarchy, Ramabai exhibited her spirit of autonomy.
[21] Ramabai, "Showers of Blessings", 223.

in Ramabai. In addition, the initiatives Ramabai took to reconstruct the selves of widowed women, who began to experience "deepening of spiritual life ... increasing love, peace, and joy in the Holy Ghost" added to the subaltern agency in her.

- Indian Christian theology of the Holy Spirit came to be articulated by the members of the Rethinking Group in India during the early twentieth century. Different from the then existing practice of integrating the *advaitic* tradition with Indian Christian theology, Pandipeddi Chenchiah, an important theologian in the Rethinking Group, took inspiration from the evolutionary vision of Sri Aurobindo and spoke of the Yoga of the Spirit. He proposed this Yoga as a transformative process which changed a person to be a new creation in Christ, a "new mutation or a new phase in evolution effected by the Holy Spirit"[22]—the *mahasakti*, the great cosmic power. The new creation in Christ liberated a person from the *karmic* cycle and made her a new creation, with full potential for salvation, without any need of further rebirth.

  This transformation envisioned by Chenchiah, though a "transformation of interior life" as Christina Manohar would interpret it,[23] goes beyond an individual's personal inner life to impact upon the societal life of a subaltern person. The Yoga of the Spirit which has the potential to free a person from the cycles of *karmic* causation empowers a hitherto excluded subaltern self in a religious way. The *karmic* law of causation has, in the perception of subaltern people and scholars, seriously paralysed the subaltern self from emerging as autonomous agents. That the fact of a person born as a Dalit, a tribal, a woman, a transgender, and so on, has to do with the causation of one's past *karma* freezes a person's agency irreversibly and perpetuates a subordinate position. Therefore, freedom from this *karmic* causation, due to the Yoga of the Spirit, becomes meaningful for a subaltern theology of the Holy Spirit.

- One can draw much inspiration from Samuel Rayan's poetic-pneumatological reflections for a subaltern theology of the Holy Spirit. Rayan visualised the theology of the Holy Spirit as an activity, as a matter of doing rather than an idea or a conceptual scheme. It was an activity flowing out of a state of being spiritual, which meant "to be carried by the Spirit, and be profoundly transformed by her"[24] on

---

[22] Manohar, *Spirit Christology*, 291.
[23] Manohar, *Spirit Christology*, 292.
[24] Kurien Kunnumpuram, S.J., ed., *In Spirit and Truth—Indian Christian Reflections on Spirituality and Worship*, in Selected Writings of Samuel Rayan, (Mumbai: The Bombay St. Paul's Society, 2012), 21.

the one hand, and be "open and responsive" to the movement of the Spirit in history, on the other. Rayan would say, "The Holy Spirit is the centre and the horizon of our life and openness and response to her in terms of justice, mercy, and solidarity constitute spirituality".[25]

As Kirsteen Kim observes, "Rayan identified the Spirit at work in historical revolutions that liberate the poor, whatever the cultural or religious milieu in which they take place. He debunked the idea that Asian peasants were passive, and drew attention to repeated revolts over the centuries, as examples of movements of the Spirit of liberation".[26] Rayan writes:

> One rarely, if ever, speaks about the spirituality of peasants, still less about the spirituality of peasant revolts. We must nevertheless pay attention to the perception of the peasants and tribals concerning reality, their sensitivity and openness to historical situations, and their readiness to act in response to the call of freedom and justice... There is in these struggles a sense of dignity and a search, even a passion, for justice which is understood not only as individual but mainly as collective and corporate... Here is an outgoing and a risk-taking struggle in defence of life which is God's precious gift and in defence of dignity and freedom of the community in which God's Reign comes.[27]

Rayan's understanding of the spirituality of the peasants synchronises well with aspects of subaltern agency which a subaltern studies scholar would readily recognise. What Ranajit Guha attributed to a peasant in a secular language as qualities of a subaltern, that is, risk-taking, sensitive and open, defending dignity and freedom at all costs, and so on, get reflected appropriately in Rayan's theological language related to the Spirit of God. Rayan's reflections inspire us for a subaltern Pneumatology.

- Arvind Nirmal, one of the pioneers of Dalit theology, has reflected briefly about the Holy Spirit from the Dalit perspective.[28] His use of the biblical imagery of the dry bones (Ezra 37) to stand for the lifeless condition of the Dalits, and the power of the Spirit to bestow life upon these dry bones is inspiring. He thinks of the Holy Spirit also as the comforter who groans with the Dalits in their sufferings, and as the healer who heals the oppressed. There are several other Dalit theologians who have incorporated reflections about the Holy Spirit

---

[25] Kunnumpuram, *In Spirit and Truth*, 27.
[26] Kim, *The Holy Spirit in the Third World*, 90.
[27] Kurien Kunnumpuram, *In Spirit and Truth*, 60.
[28] Arvind P. Nirmal, "Towards a Christian Dalit Theology", in *A Reader in Dalit Theology*, ed. Arvind P. Nirmal (Madras: Gurukul Lutheran Theological College & Research Institute, n.d.), 69.

in their theological writings. An important contribution to Dalit Pneumatology emerges from the Dalit Bible Commentary that has been published.[29] This valuable work sheds a subaltern light on the nature, function, and role of the Holy Spirit in the Bible.

- Peter Arockiadoss (1946–2008) perhaps has put forward the most direct reflections on a Dalit subaltern Pneumatology. In an article titled as, "The Spirit of New Creation—An Exploration into Dalit Pneumatology", written in 1997, Arockiadoss identifies two arenas where the Spirit of God is manifest: one, the outbursts of Charismatic and Pentecostal experience, and the other the people's movements, especially the Dalit movements. The Charismatic and Pentecostal experience, according to him, "transports us to the times of the early church", when the church was "truly a movement of the Holy Spirit, a subaltern movement for fuller humanity",[30] totally dependent on the gifts of the Holy Spirit for its existence and growth. Unfortunately, he says, the subsequent institutionalisation of the church, with the support of the State, "buried" the Spirit under its "wealth, political power, dogmas, canon laws, sacraments, liturgical rubrics, etc".[31] Only recently, he opines, "has the long spell of the famine of the Spirit has begun to change", and "there is a revival of interest in the Holy Spirit".[32] While welcoming this change, Arockiadoss counsels us with the words of St. Paul not to "quench the Spirit" (1Thess 5:19), but, however, "test everything" (1Thess 5:21). As regards testing, Arockiadoss points out pertinently that the "perspective of the Dalits, the tribals, and the oppressed women have the epistemological priority over other groups to perform this testing ministry".[33]

The second arena of the activity of the Holy Spirit, according to Arockiadoss, was the then emerging people's movements, especially the subaltern movements of the Dalits, tribals, and women. He recognises the role of the Holy Spirit in these movements as subverting the status quo, and "forging a new humanity built on new values like love, freedom, fellowship, justice, equality, and so on".[34] Without the "finger of God, that is by the might of the Holy Spirit",[35] he says, these

---

[29] James Massey, gen. ed. *Dalit Bible Commentary—New Testament* (New Delhi: Centre for Dalit/Subaltern Studies, 2010).
[30] P. Arockiadoss, "The Spirit of New Creation—An Exploration into Dalit Pneumatology", in *Frontiers of Dalit Theology*, ed. V. Devasahayam (ISPCK & Gurukul Summer Institute, 1997), 433.
[31] Arockiadoss, "The Spirit of New Creation", 433–34.
[32] Arockiadoss, "The Spirit of New Creation", 434.
[33] Arockiadoss, "The Spirit of New Creation", 434.
[34] Arockiadoss, "The Spirit of New Creation", 435.
[35] Arockiadoss, "The Spirit of New Creation", 435.

subaltern movements, the tiny Davids, could not confront the might of the Goliaths or Pharaohs, or the "cunning of the Brahmins".[36]

Going by these two arenas of the manifestation of the Holy Spirit, Arockiadoss reflects about the characteristic actions and the fruits of the Holy Spirit. The first and foremost characteristic action of the Holy Spirit, according to him, is recreation and resurrection. At the creation, "like a mother hen lovingly brooding over her eggs",[37] the Holy Spirit hovered over the chaos and created the cosmos. Similarly, the same Spirit broods over our gloomy world, characterised by the reality of darkness, lifeless and formless void, and recreates it "to make it a just world fit".[38] As Arvind Nirmal had already used the passage of dry bones from Ezekiel, Arockiadoss too gives it a lively interpretation: "The condition of the Dalits had been exactly similar to the valley of dry bones—lifeless and hopeless. But the breath of God has been blowing into this valley. Prophets like Dr. Ambedkar have been prophesying: O dry bones, hear the word of God... Behold, I will cause breath (Spirit) to enter you, and you shall live".[39] As a result, "The bones are now coming together... sinews appear and unite them... flesh grows upon them... they stand up and become a great multitude of powerful people".[40] Arockiadoss asserts that it is because of the power of the Holy Spirit that the lives of the Dalits are recreated and resurrected, and it is because of the empowerment of the Spirit that the Dalit movements are able to exist dynamically in an unjust socio-political situation.[41]

The second characteristic action of the Holy Spirit, according to Arockiadoss, is revolution and liberation. In order to recreate a just world, the "Spirit of God has been master-minding historical revolutions", which do not stop with the transformation of individual hearts, but effect "the structural transformation in all areas of human society".[42] That the Spirit is symbolised by fire, wind, and water might stand for soothing, comforting, and consoling, but as raging fire, whirling wind or roaring waters, can symbolise revolt and rebellion. Arockiadoss continues: "It was by the anointing of the Spirit, the Dalit Jesus embarked upon the mission to announce the good news to the poor, to break the imposed culture of silence and inaction, to open the prisons and set the captives free, and announce the advent

---

[36] Arockiadoss, "The Spirit of New Creation", 435.
[37] Arockiadoss, "The Spirit of New Creation", 437.
[38] Arockiadoss, "The Spirit of New Creation", 437.
[39] Arockiadoss, "The Spirit of New Creation", 437–438.
[40] Arockiadoss, "The Spirit of New Creation", 438.
[41] Arockiadoss, "The Spirit of New Creation", 438.
[42] Arockiadoss, "The Spirit of New Creation", 439.

of the liberating jubilee year to the oppressed."[43] These actions of Jesus were "subversive and revolutionary".[44]

The third characteristic action of the Holy Spirit, according to Arockiadoss, is maternal care and concern. The Holy Spirit, which performed the motherly function of brooding over the creation, has been gradually made into a male Spirit by the patriarchal church. The Dalit culture and consciousness, which according to Arockiadoss, are maternal, life-giving, and nourishing, are now "challenging the church to rectify the one-sided male orientation".[45] Arockiadoss opines that we can see the "Holy Spirit as the Magna Mater, the matrix of all life and fertility".[46]

The fourth characteristic action of the Holy Spirit is being the advocate of the poor and the powerless. Jesus promised to "his feeble disciples another advocate, who would defend them and lead them to the fullness of truth".[47] When this promise was fulfilled, the disciples faced all the difficulties and persecutions very bravely. Similarly, the "Holy Spirit defends the poor and makes them present in history".[48] Arockiadoss points out that, "It is by the Spirit-empowered actions, the caste system is being rattled today, patriarchy is being dismantled, violations of human rights are being exposed and condemned, and environmental concerns have become international agenda".[49] It is by the power of the Holy Spirit, Arockiadoss asserts, that the poor, the Dalits, the tribals, the women, and other marginalised people are "becoming the new political agents with their own just agenda".[50]

Arockiadoss goes on to reflect upon the fruits of the Holy Spirit from the Dalit perspective.[51] As a giver of the gift of life, Holy Spirit is bestowing life upon the Dalits, who have hitherto been deprived of life due to the unjust caste system.[52] As a giver of the gift of new vision, the Holy Spirit helps us see the Dalits as made in the image and likeness of God, and fight against the Brahminism which hides

---

[43] Arockiadoss, "The Spirit of New Creation", 439.
[44] Arockiadoss, "The Spirit of New Creation", 439.
[45] Arockiadoss, "The Spirit of New Creation", 442.
[46] Arockiadoss, "The Spirit of New Creation", 443.
[47] Arockiadoss, "The Spirit of New Creation", 442.
[48] Arockiadoss, "The Spirit of New Creation", 443.
[49] Arockiadoss, "The Spirit of New Creation", 443.
[50] Arockiadoss, "The Spirit of New Creation", 443.
[51] Arockiadoss, "The Spirit of New Creation", 444–454. Due to paucity of space, I mention them only briefly here.
[52] In this regard, Arockiadoss instructs that it is time that the church examined itself on the workings of caste within its own body, and conscientised the non-Dalits about their "caste arrogance and ignorance of their Christian faith and its radical social demands", Peter Arockiadoss, *Equal and Free* (Dindigul: Vaigarai Publications, 2010), 25–26.

the oppression that the Dalits are undergoing. As a giver of the gift of freedom, the Holy Spirit grants both the freedom of choice to live in a responsible way as well as the freedom from enslaving forces, both internal and external. As a giver of new speech, the Holy Spirit grants the Dalits, who were victims of the culture of silence, the power and authority of speech, which is manifest in religious and secular spheres. As a giver of the gift of new action, the Holy Spirit enables the people to build up Dalit, tribal, women, and ecological movements for freedom and empowerment. And, as a giver of the gift of community living, the Holy Spirit "acts in order to give" the Dalits "their due or rightful place ... in the human community"[53] wherefrom they have been kept excluded due to the workings of the varna system.

Arockiadoss's Dalit pneumatological reflections are incisive, energetic, and prophetic. They dwell upon the agency of the Dalits and other marginalised communities, the historical hurdles which prevent their agency from emerging, and the divine power of the Holy Spirit which works to empower them to emerge as active political actors in history. The Holy Spirit cares for the feeble Dalit victims of caste oppression, plays the role of advocacy for their liberation, causes a revolution against the forces of oppression, and resurrects them out of the lifeless chaotic situation. The divine agency of the Holy Spirit makes the Dalits the agents of their history.

- The contemporary Pentecostal movement in India has contributed significantly to the emergence of the subaltern self. A study done from the subaltern perspective by V.V. Thomas on the emergence of Dalit Pentecostal churches in Kerala, published under the title, *Dalit Pentecostalism–Spirituality of the Empowered Poor*, argues that Pentecostalism provides the site for Dalit subjectivity to emerge and develop, and form a Dalit Christian to be the "maker of his or her own destiny".[54] Based on a case study of the *Church of God*, V.V. Thomas arrives at the conclusion that the Dalits within this church emerged out of their "subservient" role to the missionaries and the Syrian Christians by breaking away and establishing the Dalit Pentecostal Church. In this, Thomas sees "the beginning of a stir among the Dalits to develop an identity of their own on the basis of their subjectivity",[55] and an effort to "give full expression to their own

---

[53] Arockiadoss, "The Spirit of New Creation—An Exploration into Dalit Pneumatology", 451.
[54] V.V. Thomas, *Dalit Pentecostalism—Spirituality of the Empowered Poor* (Bangalore: Asian Trading Corporation, 2008), 384.
[55] Thomas, *Dalit Pentecostalism*, 387.

understanding of Pentecostalism".[56] Thomas argues that the Holy Spirit enkindled the aspirations of the Dalits for equality, dignity, and freedom and moved them towards the Pentecostal movement, and it was the same Spirit who propelled them to initiate their own Dalit Pentecostal churches. In this process, they exercised their agency, refused to lie low and take everything as God's will,[57] and become an assertive people.

SUBALTERN PUBLIC THEOLOGY OF THE HOLY SPIRIT IN INDIA

Pneumatological insights, emerging from the Indian theologians and movements, help us to propose some rudiments of a subaltern public theology of the Holy Spirit. The Yoga of the Spirit, the outpouring of the Spirit, the spirituality of the peasants to respond to the call of freedom and justice, the characteristic actions and fruits of the Spirit, and the empowering experience of the Holy Spirit in Charismatic and Pentecostal churches—all of them can be considered to have made significant contribution to the emergence of the subaltern agency. Enabling subaltern agency in and through such theological reflections and experiences of the Holy Spirit and relating them to the concerns of the public sphere give birth to a subaltern *public* theology of the Holy Spirit. As argued earlier, the primary concerns of a subaltern public theology in India are: (1) re-envisioning secularism as emancipatory secularity; and, (2) engaging the plurality of religions so as to construct the subaltern agency on the one hand, and interrogate the oppressive hegemony of dominant traditions on the other, in the public sphere. Working on the realisation of these concerns becomes the process of doing a subaltern public theology.

Subaltern vision of secularity as *emancipatory secularity* becomes the means for opening the public for every citizen of this country. It is not an anti-religious secularity, but a religiously enriched secularity, practised through the modern instruments of the State, judiciary, legislature, and civil society. One of the central agenda for this secularity is to initiate and nurture a fundamental inclusive process, whereby every form of exclusion—economic, political, social, cultural, religious, and so on—is eliminated. Doing away with the discriminatory system of caste and working for the enjoyment of civil liberties, ensuring every citizen's right to livelihood, education, sanitation, dignity, religious freedom, and so on, are part of this process of opening the public to everyone.

Second, the question of plurality of religions too acquires new implications from a subaltern perspective. Promoting *conversations* between religions in the civil sphere, besides being a channel of promoting

---

[56] Thomas, *Dalit Pentecostalism*, 388.
[57] Thomas, *Dalit Pentecostalism*, 395.

understanding and harmony, becomes also a way of nurturing public ethics, which works towards the emancipation of the subaltern people. Conversation between religions, therefore, will bring together not merely the dominant world religions, but also the subaltern religious traditions, which exist symbiotically with the history, culture, and social identity of the subaltern people. In this context, the hegemonic agenda of majoritarianism, which is being pursued with the support of the political power in India, becomes the Goliath which the subaltern religious traditions have to confront in the public sphere.

One could adopt various methods to go about actualising these goals: pursue legal means to protect the principles of secularism and religious freedom, and so on; or, involve in political negotiations through political representatives; or, approach it through the organs of civil society. The latter seems to have great potential with enduring results. It provides the platform to bring together religious traditions, ideologies, and movements around emancipatory goals. Creating enduring structures of cross-cutting networks between persons of various identities in this civil sphere can become the concrete step to be followed. Herein, religious mutuality can be meaningfully nurtured, civil liberties can be effectively protected, hegemonies can be confronted and weakened, and projects of freedom for the subalterns can be publicly pursued. It is in creating such sites of empowering civil society that the Yoga of the Spirit, the transforming and creative power of the Spirit of God can be meaningfully encountered.

COMMUNICATING EMPOWERMENT IN THE PUBLIC SPHERE

An important concern at this juncture is, how can conversations be made possible between different religions and belief-systems in cross-cutting civil groups? One possibility could be going about it in one's own way, unmindful of others. The now-salient cultural-linguistic approach perhaps would support such a stance, because, according to this, one can communicate only within one's own linguistic world. Another way of going about it would be the opposite, that is, proscribing religion from the public, because it could be a conversation stopper. It is in such a context that we experience the promptings of the Spirit of God to take up the challenge of proposing a religious language which can liberate the subalterns, even while being intelligible to multiple others in the public.

The Spirit of God invites us to take up the challenge of communicating empowerment to the subalterns through the public sphere. With the power of the Spirit of God, we need to walk the tightrope of intelligibility on the one hand, and the bountiful meaning of the symbolic language of religions on the other. While the former goes with our commitment in a historical context, the latter situates our commitment within a transcendental referent, God. Paul sets a good example in this regard. On the question of speaking in tongues, Paul welcomed it, but to the extent that it was intelligible to others. He posed a pointed question (1 Cor 14:16), "If you bless with the spirit, how can anyone in the position of an *outsider* say the "Amen" to your thanksgiving when he does not know what you are saying?" This shows his sensitivity to the need for communicating to the outsider, the other. It shows the great regard Paul had for the intelligibility of revelatory communication, bringing in the need of interpretation. He advises the Christian community: "If any speaks in a tongue, let there be only two or at the most three, and each in turn, and let one interpret. But if there is no one to interpret, let each of them keep silence in church, and speak to himself and to God" (1 Cor 14:27–28). It is this interpretative communicative ability, continuously bestowed upon us by the Spirit of God, which becomes the anchor of the public sphere, and of the public theology of the Holy Spirit.

By Way of Concluding

Doing a subaltern theology of the Holy Spirit from the Indian context is relevant in our era when the pneumatological turn in Christian theology is deepening. A subaltern public theology of the Holy Spirit would premise itself primarily upon the possibility of constructing and nurturing the subaltern agency in the context of divine-human encounter in situations of subordination. While the recognition and nurturance of the autonomous subaltern agency has been the main aim of the *Subaltern Studies Project*, it did not pay sufficient attention to the role of religion. A subaltern theology would base itself on the recognition of the positive role of religion.

Indian Christian theology has continued to put forth significant insights on the theology of the Holy Spirit. Members of the Rethinking Group which emerged during the first part of the twentieth century have intoned the Indian theology of the Holy Spirit. Among them, the insights of Pandipeddi Chenchiah on the Yoga of the Spirit and the Christian made a new creation by the *mahasakti* of the Holy Spirit are relevant to the subaltern Pneumatology in that they free a subaltern from the cycles of *karmic* causation and create the subaltern as a new free being. One finds such a freedom experienced in the person of Pandita Ramabai, whose testimony to the outpourings of the Holy Spirit in her Mukti Mission, bear witness, among others, to her autonomous subaltern agency. Following up on such subaltern pneumatological beginnings, reflections of persons like Samuel Rayan and P. Arockiadoss are significant to construct a subaltern theology of the Holy Spirit. Among them, the reflections of Arockiadoss on the characteristic actions and the gifts of the Holy Spirit from Dalit perspective can enflesh a subaltern Pneumatology from the Indian context.

Subaltern Pneumatology, inchoate though, would do well to relate itself to public theology, which is an acute need of the hour. The primary concerns of public theology—re-envisioning of secularity and responding to plurality of religion—need to be approached from the perspective of the subaltern theology of the Holy Spirit. Opening the public for the subalterns and resisting the hegemony of majoritarianism in the civil sphere so as to promote the agency of the subalterns, in and through the experiences and reflections on the Holy Spirit, are important concerns of this theology. Creating cross-cutting networks of different identities for enduring conversations between religions, ideologies, and movements, and drawing inspirations from divine-human encounters as they occur in conditions of subordination, will be the meaningful ways in which the subaltern public theology of the Holy Spirit can be pursued.

11

ENCOUNTER OF END-TIME BELIEFS AS IT OCCURRED IN PANDITA RAMABAI

End-Time Beliefs as Sites of Conversations

Contemporary Indian scenario requires of us to explore the sites of conversations between different religious traditions. As religious nationalism seeks to build itself up by homogenising the religious universes, it would do well to unearth the meaningful differences that exist in the realm of beliefs and practices of different religious others. One of the salient beliefs, often relegated to the backyard of a religious universe, but very much consequential to the here and now, is that which relates to end-times. Speaking *about* the end is a way of speaking *in* and *into* the present,[1] with its potentials of effective engagement with the present, even while situating the present within the existential triad of the past, the present, and the future. This essay is a very modest attempt to reflect about Hindu end-time *karmic* belief and Christian eschatology, as they encountered each other in Pandita Ramabai, a well-known personality of the nineteenth century India.

I am aware of the pitfalls of approaching the Hindu belief with a Christian theme of eschatology; I could be faulted for approaching it as an effort to overlay it with a Christian category, as part of the continuing Orientalist temptation. Also, the content of the belief diverges so much that it becomes problematic to treat it under the same horizon of understanding: while eschatology is a doctrine on last things or end times, most of the Hindu religious traditions apparently consider time as endless. And therefore the real challenge! What can be attempted here is only a heuristic

---

[1] It is in place here to recall the study of Murray Milner who suggests that there is an inverse co-relation between the central tenets of Hindu eschatology and the Indian caste-system. Murray Milner, Jr. "Hindu Eschatology and the Indian Caste System: An Example of Structural Reversal", *The Journal of Asian Studies* 52, no. 2 (May, 1993): 298–319.

exploration, focusing on the broad theme of the religious imagination of the future.

Hindu belief, as found in the philosophically and religiously articulated dominant traditions like Vedic, *advaitic*, theistic (Vaishnava and Saiva traditions), and other philosophical systems, mediates a vision of time primarily in terms of its beginningless-ness and endlessness (*sanatana*). However, they do not deny an account of time. Bror Tiliander who published a useful volume of "Christian and Hindu Terminology", identifies the Hindu account of time as below:

> Hindu eschatology counts (time) with four yugas: 1. *Krta-yuga*, consisting of 4,000 god-years and in addition, 400 years of dawn and 400 years of twilight. One god-year is equal to 360 solar years. Thus, *Krta-yuga* consists of 1,728,000 solar years. 2. *Treta-yuga*, consisting of 3,000 plus 300 plus 300 god-years=1,296,000 solar years, 3. *Dvapara-yuga*, consisting of 2,000 plus 200 plus 200 god-years=864,000 solar years, 4. *Kali-yuga*, consisting of 1,000 plus 100 plus 100 god-years=432,000 solar years. Four yugas form one *Maha-yuga*. 1,000 *Mahayugas* make one *Kalpa*. At the end of the same, the universe is dissolved. A *Kalpa* is called a *Brahma* day. After a *Brahma* day follows a *Brahma* night. 360 *Brahma* days and *Brahma* nights make one *Brahma* year=3,110,400,000,000 solar years. 100 *Brahma* years make one *Brahma* life time. At the end of the same, everything is dissolved except *Prakriti*, the primeval matter which is eternal and will be the cause of a new creation and so *in infinitum*.[2]

This expansive sense of time as *sanatana* does not occupy a Hindu mind with an arithmetic progression; it informs their religious sensibility in terms of such doctrines as *samsara*, *karma*, *dharma*, and *moksha*. The last of these doctrines, that is, *moksha* deals with the ultimate goal or the ultimate liberation. This liberation is believed to occur as the final release from the cycles of rebirths a life-form undergoes in its journey. The *advaitic* monistic vision considers this liberation as the moment of *atman* (soul/spirit) attaining the eternal bliss of realising itself as the *Brahman*; the theistic traditions (Vaishnava, Saiva) consider it as the point of the *atman* reaching the abode of *Iswara*. This journey is that which constitutes life as *samsara*, a perenniality of births and rebirths.

Rebirths are occasioned by the workings of *karma*, a belief embraced by almost all the major Hindu traditions, including the heterodox Jainism and Buddhism with their own interpretations. As Surendranath Dasgupta, a well-known Indian philosopher, observes:

> All the Indian systems agree in believing that whatever actions is done by an individual leaves behind it some sort of potency which has the power to ordain for him joy or sorrow in the future according as it is good or

---

[2] Bror Tiliander, *Christian and Hindu Terminology—A Study in their Mutual Relations with Special Reference to the Tamil Area* (Uppsala: Almqvist & Wiksell, 1974), 255.

bad. When the fruits of the actions are such that they cannot be enjoyed in the present life or in a human life, the individual has to take another birth as a man or any other being in order to suffer them.[3]

Thus, the doctrine of *karma* holds that every action produces its effect, and the effect continues to impact upon the agent (of the action) beyond her single birth. It is the bad *karma*, that is, the accumulated effects of human selfishness, which takes an individual through multiple births. As the *Chandokya Upanisad* states, "Those whose conduct has been good, will quickly attain some good birth, the birth of a brahmana, or a ksatriya, or a vaisya. But those whose conduct has been evil, will quickly attain an evil birth, the birth of a dog, or a hog, or a candala".[4] Thus, the operation of *karma* merits the achievement or otherwise of birth in particular social groups too.

The category of good conduct brings us to the next important doctrine of Hinduism, *Dharma* (which is discussed in detail in Chapter 12). This polymorphic doctrine, astutely philosophical as well as popular, stands for order in cosmological, ritual, religious, moral, and social realms. It means simultaneously the regularity of the cosmic seasonal order with smooth transitioning (*rta*), the perfect execution of the ritual order of sacrifice by the Brahmin priests, the effective appeasement of gods through ritual sacrifices which would in turn ensure the cosmic order, the righteous moral order, and finally the perfect social order, based on the performance of duties appropriate to one's birth in a social group. Though spoken much of in universal philosophical terms, *Dharma* is fundamentally an empirically-bound discourse grounded in the *practice* of it in life-worlds. As Paul Hacker, an Indologist, would say, "Historical Hinduism never attempted to derive the *dharma*-ness of *dharma* from a universal philosophical or religious principle... *dharma* is radically empirical".[5] The practice of this *dharma* with "its contents on the castes and life-stages, encompassing the entire realm of what is moral, ritual, legal, and customary, and effecting through its observance an otherworldly salvation...",[6] provides the power to break away from the cycles of rebirth to attain the *moksha*. And the *moksha* is eternity, permanence, and liberation, and it is ensured the maximum, as per the workings of *karma*, only to the Brahmin, whose birth as a Brahmin male has put him in the penultimate stage nearing *moksha*.

Hindu belief in last things, then, understood through the categories of *samsara, karma,* and *dharma,* envisioning time in its endless-ness and

---

[3] Surendranath Dasgupta, *A History of Indian Philosophy—Philosophy of Buddhist, Jaina and Six Systems of Indian Thought*, vol. 1, 7th ed. (New Delhi: Motilal Banarsidas Publishers, 2012), 71.
[4] *Chandogya Upanisad*, v. 10.7.
[5] Dasgupta, *A History of Indian Philosophy*, 71.
[6] Dasgupta, *A History of Indian Philosophy*, 483.

even beginningless-ness, situating an individual within it in terms of the cycles of rebirths, provides the opportunity to attain *moksha* (liberation) through the practice of *dharma*, as it pertains to one's duties in a caste. In actual historical terms, it is an eschatology premised on the life-itinerary and religious endeavours of a Brahmin as the agent of history.

The Hindu belief encountered Christianity as the latter reached the Indian soil. The core of Christian eschatology is that a person, constituted by body and soul, created by God, redeemed from sin by the death and resurrection of Jesus Christ, journeys through death, and at the second coming of Jesus Christ presents herself for the last judgement, which will either damn or transform her into a new creation to eternally experience the direct vision of God. In this, there is a linear progression towards eternity, unimpeded by cycles of rebirth, and this linearity has also been historicized and collectivised in terms of "secular utopias". Rudolf Bultmann, a well-known biblical theologian, would tell us that Christian eschatology, starting with the early Christian expectation of imminent *Parousia*, which almost swallowed up history, has undergone a gradual but steady process of historicisation in the Western Christian context, giving birth to secular utopias on the one hand, and even to nihilism on the other.[7] Indian experience of Christian eschatology, as found in sites of encounters (individuals, initiatives of inculturation like *ashrams*, and people's movements for conversion to Christianity) is the historical intimation of the Christian eschatological linearity. One can find the resonances of Christian eschatologies even beyond the borders of Indian Christianity in the modern socio-religious movements and subaltern religious saints from whom alternate religious traditions emerged. Beyond these religious realms, one can find the Christian eschatological resonances also in secular movements/ideologies, developmental projects, political institutions, dimensions of civil society, and so on. While it would be greatly enriching to explore all these sites, I would like to present here, as an indicative sample, just one Indian Christian personality, Pandita Ramabai, in whose writings aspects of the encounter of Christian eschatology with the Hindu belief are found.

Pandita Ramabai Encountering the Christian Eschatological Belief

The life and religious commitment of Pandita Ramabai (1858-1922) is educative and inspiring especially in view of its challenging itinerary. Born as the sixth child to a Brahmin couple, she embarked upon a journey from her native region of southern Karnataka when she was a three-month old baby, carried in a basket by her family members. Anand Shastri Dongre,

---

[7] Rudolf Bultmann, *The Presence of Eternity—History and Eschatology* (New York: Harper & Brothers, 1957).

the father of the child, was a learned person in Hindu Shastras, and earned a livelihood as an itinerant reciter in temples. Later when a severe famine struck the region, the parents as well as other siblings of Ramabai succumbed to it one by one, leaving Ramabai with her younger brother to fend for themselves. They wandered along the breadth and width of the subcontinent as young reciters of shastraic *slokas* in temples—a skill they had picked up from their parents. The children grew up as itinerant reciters. When Ramabai arrived in Kolkata at the age of 20, she had matured in her learning of Hindu scriptures so well as to earn the title of *Pandita* (learned) bestowed upon her by the club of learned persons there. She was indeed a brilliant scholar, gifted with the skill for vast learning. When her sole close relationship, her brother too died of sickness, and finding herself all alone, she married a friend of her brother, who gave her a good companionship, but only for two years, when death snatched him too. Now left with a girl-baby, Ramabai travelled back to her native region, the western India, and came into contact with Anglican sisters who became her friends and facilitated her journey to England, where, she got converted to Christianity, and lived the rest of her life as a Christian, though in and out of denominational Christianities, until the end of her life.

The literatures that she has left on her perceptions of Indian religions, Indian womanhood, experience of her conversion, her travels in England and America, and finally her Marathi translation of the New Testament of the Bible are an inspiring and scholarly oeuvre. Among them can be found her insightful narratives related to her encounter with Christian eschatology in the Hindu milieu.

In one of her writings, Ramabai narrates the shock she had when she saw for the first time some Indian Brahmins partaking of meals with the English: "They ate bread and biscuits and drank tea with the English people and shocked us by asking us to partake of the refreshments. We thought the last age, *Kali Yuga* that is, the age of quarrels, darkness, and irreligion had fully established its reign in Calcutta since some of the Brahmins were so irreligious as to eat food with the English."[8] The shock she had was a pointer to the hostile religious attitude the Hindu Brahmins had towards the English on account of their being a cause for the dawn of the evil age, the *Kali Yuga*. From this point of antipathy, Ramabai gradually turned herself into someone who resides with the English, got converted to Christianity and lived a life of a resided Christian. The change that occurred in her had not the least to do with her discontent with the Hindu Shastras, as she narrates:

---

[8] Pandita Ramabai, "A Testimony of Our Inexhaustible Treasure", in *Pandita Ramabai Through Her Own Works*, comp. & ed. Meera Kosambi (New Delhi: Oxford University Press, 2000), 301.

> While reading the *Dharma Shastras*, I came to know many things which I never knew before. There were contradictory statements about almost everything. What one book said was most righteous, the other book declared as being unrighteous... but there were two things on which all those books, the *Dharma Shastras*, the sacred epics, the *Puranas* and modern poets, the popular preachers of the present day and orthodox high-caste men, were agreed, that women of high—and low-caste, as a class were bad, worse than demons, unholy as untruth; and that they could not get *Moksha* as men [did]. The only hope of their getting this much-desired liberation from *karma* and its results, that is, countless millions of births and deaths and untold suffering, was the worship of their husbands. The husband is said to be the woman's god; there is no other god for her... She can have no hope of admission into *Svarga*, the abode of the gods without his pleasure, and if she pleases him in all things, she will have the privilege of going to *Svarga* as his slave, there to serve him and be one of his wives among the thousands of the *Svarga* harlots who are presented to him by the gods in exchange for his wife's merit... As for the low-caste people, the poor things have no hope of any sort. They are looked upon as being very like the lower species of animals, such as pigs; their very shadow and the sound of their voices are defiling.[9]

While being suffocated (speaks about being shut up in a dark room)[10] of this systemic inability for the women and the low-caste to reach the *Svarga*, Ramabai is exhilarated about her encounter with Christianity: "How good, how indescribably good! What good news for me, a woman, a woman born in India among Brahmans, who hold out no hope for me and the likes of me! The Bible declares that Christ did not reserve this great salvation for a particular caste or sex."[11] Availability of salvation to all, that too in an *unmerited* manner, contrary to the availability of *moksha* on the basis of one's merit (*karma*), comes as a great religious achievement for her. Again, the way Christianity speaks about the reality of sin in this life, and the possibility for all of redemption from it, unlike the impossibility of escaping from *karma*, draws her closer to Christianity. She writes:

---

[9] Ramabai, "A Testimony", 302–303.

[10] "I do not know if anyone of my readers has ever had the experience of being shut up in a room where there was nothing but thick darkness and then groping in it to find something of which he or she was in dire need. I can think of no one but the blind man, whose story is given in St. John, chapter nine. He was born blind and remained so for forty years of his life; and then suddenly he found the Mighty One, Who could give him eyesight. Who could have described his joy at seeing the daylight, when there had not been a particle of hope of his ever seeing it? Even the inspired evangelist has not attempted to do it. I can give only a faint idea of what I felt when my mental eyes were opened, and when I, who was 'sitting in darkness saw Great Light,' and when I felt sure that to me, who but a few moments ago 'sat in the region and shadow of death, Light *had* sprung up.'" Ramabai, "A Testimony", 311.

[11] Ramabai, "A Testimony", 312–313.

The Bible says that God does not wait for me to merit his love, but heaps it upon me without my deserving it. It says also that there is neither male nor female in Christ: The righteousness of God which is by faith of Jesus Christ, unto all and upon all of them that believe: for there is no difference; for all have sinned, and come short of the glory of God; being justified by his grace through the redemption that is in Christ Jesus (Rom 3: 22–24).[12]

That this redemption is granted *to this life itself* strikes her boldly. She says with gladness that, "I had not to wait till after undergoing births and deaths for countless millions of times, when I should become a Brahman man, in order to get to know the Brahma".[13] Relative immediacy of the Christian eschatology strikes Ramabai boldly in terms of its experience in the present. She continues to write: "The Holy Spirit made it clear to me from the word of God, that the salvation which God gives through Christ is present, and not something future. I believed it, I received it, and I was filled with joy."[14] This is perhaps one of the rare moments of Ramabai's testimony wherein the presencing of the future finds expression. As attested to in the earlier statements, the experience of presencing of the future breaks forth as a real possibility for someone who otherwise would not stand to get it at all. This presencing of salvation is to be understood not as a denial of future,[15] but a future embedded in the overwhelming of the present, an overwhelming that does not foreclose the future, but that which provides the strength of belief to continue to look towards the eternal life. This overwhelming of the present comes as a gift, a rupture, an unmerited gift, and an enormous opening of the present from out of its being bondaged to the past. The Christian eschatological belief that there is a new life to be hoped for comes as a relief to her against the context of the Hindu belief that dwelt upon merging into the Brahma, or the Buddhist eschatology of ending with a *Sunya*.[16]

Ramabai was taken hold of by the Christian eschatological promise: the relative immediacy of salvation; the relief of freedom from the state of incapacity on account of being a woman to attain *moksha*; the belief that salvation can come as a gift, without any merit (a requirement deeply engrained in the doctrine of *karma*); the belief that sin is *universal*, corrupts everyone regardless of one's social status; the belief that redemption from

---

[12] Ramabai, "A Testimony", 311.
[13] Ramabai, "A Testimony", 313.
[14] Ramabai, "A Testimony", 313.
[15] Because, she always spoke of the "eternal life" in a very emphatic manner. In the section where she writes about the eternal life, the way she gives emphasis to it, even with typographical techniques like italics, and capital letters point to the important place the future eternal life had in her vision.
[16] She expresses her desperation, "And then, was there any joy and happiness to be hoped for? No, there is nothing but to be amalgamated into Nothingness Shunya, Brahma". Ramabai, "A Testimony", 313.

sin is available through faith in Christ; the belief that there is a new life to be hoped for in the future; and that all these aspects of Christian eschatology overwhelms the present moment of life with joy and happiness.

The encounter that occurred in Ramabai helps us become aware of certain aspects of convergences and divergences of Hindu and Christian end-time beliefs:

1. The Hindu belief is premised upon a sense of time, in terms of its beginningless-ness, endless-ness and eternity. This expansive sense of time is mediated through the belief in *samsara*, which makes it cyclical through the workings of *karma*, which, in turn, is either accumulated or expended on account of one's *dharma*, which is the gateway to *moksha*, the ultimate liberation from the cycles of *karmic* rebirths.

2. However, due to the doctrines of *karma* and *dharma*, premised on merit and demerit, these eschatological categories work in history to deprive certain sections of people of the possibility of progressing towards the ultimate liberation.

3. Christian eschatology presents time in a measure, situated within a historically embedded future, achieved through a religious vocation that passes through sin-forgiveness-redemption-salvation, which is available to all irrespective of merit/demerit, difference in birth, and so on. This manner of conceiving time in a religious idiom seems to help the individuality of a person to emerge with her agency. The life of Ramabai is a telling example.

4. Ramabai's is a life characterised by a suffocation of being incapacitated to progress towards *moksha* on the one hand, and by a deeply-felt yearning for it on the other. The historical debility to attain *moksha* felt by her womanhood is responded to by a sin-salvation scheme of Christian eschatology. It fills her heart with the hope of becoming a new creation. Ramabai's hope is substantive in that it is premised upon her conversion to acknowledge her sinfulness, repent for it, and become a new creation. The unmerited grace in Christianity and the merit-based *karmic* cycles of rebirths come into play in the life of Ramabai.

5. It is educative to note the convergence and divergence in transcendence at work in both end-time beliefs: the Hindu eschatology is premised upon the immortality of *atman*. It is an eternal continuity of the *atman*, the soul, which has no beginning and no end. When the *atman*, with its strenuous efforts, sheds its layers of ignorance accrued due to *karma*, it realises that it is identical with the Brahman, the ultimate eternal reality. The transcendence implied in

this endeavour of *atman* is towards the inner self, going beyond the *karmic* cycles of rebirths. It could be addressed as a horizontal transcendence. Christian eschatology, on the other hand, presents a different experience of transcendence in its doctrine of resurrection of the dead, which distinguished it even at its very early stage from the Jewish and Greco-Roman eschatological beliefs. Resurrection of the dead is characteristically different from the immortality of the soul in that it implies a vertical transcendence, in believing that it is God, the totally transcendental other, who can transform a person or resurrect the dead.

6. The two important categories which come into play in the encounter are self-realisation, and transformation into a new creation. The Hindu belief speaks of the final release of *atman* from cycles of rebirths to realise itself as Brahman, while the Christian eschatology speaks about the resurrection of the dead, implying a radical transformation that makes a person a new creation. While Hindu eschatology presents the eschatological moment as coming into one's own, Christian eschatology presents the moment as transforming to be a new reality. While the former situates the future within an aeonic present, the latter situates the present within an irruptive future. Both can fecundate each other, but only in an ambience of freedom and mutuality.

Futuring the Present and Presencing the Future

Hindu religious eschatologies, emerging from the sanskritic Hindu monistic as well as theistic traditions, though diverging on the ideal of *moksha* as the ultimate point of self-realisation or reaching the abode of the Divine, converge on the modus operandi (practice of eschatology) of continuous transmigration of *atman, jivatman*, and so on, until the final eschatological goal is achieved. In this modus operandi, time becomes perennial, cyclic, continuous, and so on, leading into eternity. The perennial time sustains the present as its core, and continues with the past repetitively and engages affirmatively with the present, moving along a successive line to eternity. What happens in this process is a futuring of the present, in the sense that the present, as it obtains in history, is carried into the future. It is as if the present is moving towards a future.

On the other hand, the Christian eschatology, along the same criterion of the practice of eschatology, comes from the future to the present. With its *irruption* of the eschatological reign, inaugurated by a messianic prophet, Christianity *presences* a future, and gives a pull towards the future. Presencing is a radical opening of the present, something like the clearing of the sky at the occurrence of lightning. Or, in social anthropological terms, it is the height of liminality that occurs between and betwixt. Based on its call for repentance and conversion, the modus operandi of Christianity makes a lightning rupture in time, makes it discontinuous with the past, engages transformatively with the present, and moves along a relatively vertical line to eternity.

These two eschatologies, if postulated as ends of a continuum, bring forth multiple points of convergence and divergence. The radicality of the end-points are reconciled or compromised at multiple points, as can be seen in their expressions in social relationships. The subaltern religious traditions of India are a case in point. They have a significant cross-fertilisation, which move towards a point of clearing, and therefore opening up of the present, brought forth by the encounter of subaltern consciousness with the Christian messianic eschatology, combined with the enlightenment secular utopias. That being one strand of the conversation between the Hindu and Christian eschatologies, many more are on the anvil today. And the encounter continues, at deeper recesses of the Indian collective consciousness as well as in the practical world. The encounter, in all reckoning, is far from over!

12

CONVERSATION ON *DHARMA*

Dharma has become a public discourse in India today. The political Right attempts to present a doctrine known as *sanatana dharma*, collating oftentimes with *Hindu dharma*, to be the religio-cultural and ethical common ground for all Indians, regardless of their different religious and ethical systems or communitarian identities. It is being suggested accordingly to accept newer identities like *Hindu Christianity, Hindu Islam, Hindu Buddhism*, and so on. Such an effort has been prevalent for a long time, but is reinvigorated in the contemporary political climate, when a political dispensation drawing support from the rightist Hindutva ideology is in power. This dispensation, with its political party and its religio-cultural organisations, seeks to construct a political ontology of *dharma* to undergird its political practice.

This revival of the doctrine of *dharma* has deeper implications for the cultural, religious, and social life of the people of India, especially its *different religious others*. It has serious consequences also for the kind of democracy that is evolving through this revival. In this context, this essay attempts to trace the contours of the nature, dynamics, and social implications of the doctrine of *dharma* from the perspective of public theology, whose dynamics consists of bringing about conversations between different comprehensive doctrines for common good. The present essay goes analytically into the semantics of this doctrine, explores its historical variants, and attempts to highlight its convergences and divergences with other religious visions so as to contribute to the practice of public theological conversation in India.

Contemporary Discourse of *Dharma* in the Indian Public

As mentioned earlier, discourse on *dharma* has become publicly consequential in India today. We find cultural, religious, ethical, social, and political agencies involved in the discourse, promoting it to the status of a religio-ethical and civilisational common ground for India. In a book titled, *Hindu Dharma—The Universal Way of Life*, Chandrasekarendra

Saraswathi Swami, a well-known *Acharya* (religious teacher) of sanskritic Hinduism, makes a case for the universality of Hindu *dharma*. He makes a claim that the Vedic religion, the core of Hindu *dharma*, has been present all over the planet even before any other religion developed.[1] As a typical votary of sanskritic Hinduism, he thinks that this *dharma*, rooted in the Vedic religion, is the universal law that is present in the world and that human beings have derived their law (*dharma*) from this cosmic law; that as nature experiences harmony when the physical laws go in order, so will human beings experience order when they submit themselves to this age-old *dharma*.[2] Swami divides this *dharma* into two: one *saamaanya dharma* and the other as *visesha dharma*[3]—while the former is the common law that pertains to everyone, the latter is what is special to each category of people. Both the versions of *dharma* must be practised without any let-up so that we can experience order and harmony within the individual self as well as in the wider society. Further on, Swami identifies this *dharma* as the *varnsasrama dharma*,[4] whose practice is part and parcel of the universal *dharma* he speaks of as the Hindu *dharma*, a universal way of life. Swami evokes high respect within sanskritic Hinduism and his writings are valued greatly within this tradition. Such versions of Hindu *dharma* abound today, and they go into the making of a universality for the Hindu religion, a dream project of the Hindu Right in the Indian political arena today. This project, supported with the doctrine of *dharma*—an attempt at interfacing "faith and political", becomes a concern of public theology for us today. It requires of us to make an enquiry into the doctrine of *dharma* and enable an inter-religious conversation in the public sphere.

DHARMA AS A CIVILISATIONAL COMMON GROUND

Chaturvedi Badrinath, a Sahitya Academy Awardee, makes a claim that *dharma* is "not religious or anti-religious; it is secular".[5] He explains

---

[1] Chandrasekarendra Saraswathi Swami, *Hindu Dharma—The Universal Way of Life* (Chennai: Bharathiya Vidya Bhavan, 1995), 70.

[2] Swami, *Hindu Dharma*, 31.

[3] In his words: "The duties common to all Hindus, the universal code of conduct, have the name of 'samanya *dharma*.' Non-violence, truthfulness, cleanliness, control of the senses, non-acquisitiveness (one must not possess material goods in excess of what is needed for one's bare requirements, not even a straw must one own in excess), devotion to Isvara, trust in one's parents, love for all creatures—these form part of the samanya *dharma*. Then each varna has its own special code of conduct or 'visesa *dharma*' determined by its hereditary vocation." Swami, *Hindu Dharma*, 85.

[4] In his words: "Hinduism alone has a sturdy sociological foundation, and its special feature, '*varnasramadharma*', is an expression of it ... Critics of Varna *dharma* brand it as 'a blot on our religion' as 'a vicious system which divides people into high and low.' But, if you look at it impartially, you will realize that it is a unique instrument to bring about orderly and harmonious social life." Swami, *Hindu Dharma*, 71.

[5] Chaturvedi Badrinath, *Dharma, India and World Order—Twenty One Essays* (Edinburgh: Saint Andrews Press, 1993), 11.

further: "The true identity of Indian civilisation has been *dharmic* and not Hindu. The word Hindu itself is not to be found in any of the ancient or medieval Indian texts. Nor was there ever any such thing as Hinduism. The one concern from which everything in Indian thought flowed, and on which every movement of life ultimately depended, is *dharma*, order."[6] Religion, according to him, divides, while, *dharma* as a civilisational concept, unites. The divisive religion should be separated from politics, but, the latter must always go with *dharma*, as a civilisational virtue. In his words, "Religion *must* be separated from politics, as it has been in the modern West for a sane world: every shade of political thought and practice that is sane must necessarily have its basis in *dharma*".[7]

Badrinath presents this civilisational *dharma* as an alternative to the Western religious or secular ethos: "Dharmic thought is independent of any alleged divine revelation or any ancient tradition embodied in sacred scriptures. It takes as its only data the facts of human experience in all its vast and varied range."[8] It has a different secular vision, devoid of the ills Western secularism is supposed to have been infected with. It is "rational, but not rationalistic, empirical but not empiricist".[9] It does not distance oneself from the other, but treats them as a whole, bound in a relationship of universal responsibility.[10]

Finally, this civilisational virtue, according to Badrinath, can also provide an alternative framework to solve the issues of social injustice in India. "The problem of injustice, and of the revolt against it, cannot be solved by a constitution alone. *Dharma*, as a unified view of the relation of one being with another, provides a different framework."[11] It "is the way of achieving balance between the inner space of the individual and the outer space of society. It leads to a common ethical ground of one man's relationship with another; the abiding elements of it are *maitri*, friendship, and *karuna*, compassion. It does not matter whether you reach it from the side of Vedanta, or from the side of Buddhism, or from any other side".[12] Thus, Badrinath argues for this civilisational *dharma* to be treated as a common ethical ground for everyone regardless of their particular religio-ethical traditions. It then behoves us to understand the doctrine of *dharma* in depth.

---

[6] Badrinath, *Dharma*, 32.
[7] Badrinath, *Dharma*, 34.
[8] Badrinath, *Dharma*, 11.
[9] Badrinath, *Dharma*, 124.
[10] Badrinath, *Dharma*, 29.
[11] Badrinath, *Dharma*, 29.
[12] Badrinath, *Dharma*, 40.

DHARMA IN SANSKRITIC HINDUISM

Patrick Olivelle, a well-known Indologist, says: "*Dharma* is undoubtedly the most central and ubiquitous concept in the whole of Indian civilisation. It is central not only in the Brahmanical/Hindu traditions but also in the Buddhist and Jain. This very centrality, however, also made it possible for the concept to be given new twists and meanings at different times and by different groups, creating a dauntingly broad semantic range."[13]

Etymologically, *dharma* comes from the Sanskrit root *dhr*, which means to hold, or to support.[14] The earliest usage of the word occurs in the creation narratives of *Rgveda*, wherein it refers to the action of the gods,[15] in relation to the creation and maintenance of the cosmic order, that is, holding the sky and earth apart, taking care of the smooth transitioning of seasons, protecting the creatures, and so on. RV 8.41.10 says: "He (*Varuna*) measured out the first creation, who (held) apart both worlds with a pillar and like the billy-goat supported the sky."[16] Here, measuring out, holding apart, and supporting were the *dharma* of the god *Varuna*. These and other cosmic actions of the gods were understood as the primordial sacrificial actions, which were the very foundations of the cosmic order.

These foundational *dharmic* actions of the gods were transferred to the priests' (Brahmin) ritual sacrificial actions[17] which were said to "imitate" the cosmic sacrificial actions of the gods. "The sacrifice was a means to achievement of worldly or otherworldly goals that was effective in and of itself. And this sacrifice was a prominent part of *dharma*."[18] The sacrificial actions of the priests, or the *dharma* of the priests, became indispensable to the stability, regularity, and permanence of the cosmic order.

In a further semantic nuance, the meaning of *dharma* flowed into yet another vital connotation of the term, that is, the ethical-juridical. The cosmic and ritual order became the normative order to which human beings were required to submit themselves so as to ensure the regularity and permanence of the cosmic order. In the words of Paul Horsch, it became "the foundation of order and regularity...a general law, to which

---

[13] Patrick Olivelle, trans. and ed. *Dharmasutras—The Law of Codes of Apastamba, Gautama, Baudhayana, and Vasistha* (Oxford: Oxford University Press, 1999), xxxvii.

[14] For a detailed understanding of the etymological origin of this word, Patrick Olivelle, *Dharma—Studies in its Semantic, Religious and Cultural History* (New Delhi: Motilal Banarsidas Publishers, 2009).

[15] Paul Horsch, "From Creation Myth to World Law: The Early History of *Dharma*", in *Dharma—Studies in its Semantic, Religious and Cultural History*, ed. Patrick Olivelle (New Delhi: Motilal Banarsidas Publishers, 2009), 2.

[16] Horsch, "From Creation Myth to World Law", 2.

[17] Horsch, "From Creation Myth to World Law", 6.

[18] Horsch, "From Creation Myth to World Law", 483.

human beings must conform".[19] It became an essential ethical-juridical concern of human beings not to allow the order to collapse, and to that effect, they were required to observe the *dharma*, the law—the law of order and regularity.

Eventually, the cosmic, ritual, and ethical-juridical senses came to locate themselves upon a social order, whose maintenance became the most important concerns of humanity. This social order was the one spoken of in the *dharmasutras* and the *dharmasastras*. While the Vedas dwelt mostly upon the cosmic and ritual senses of *dharma*, these *dharmasutras* and *dharmasastras*, which emerged towards the end of the Vedic era, dwelt primarily upon its social semantic which emerged through the operation of the system of castes and life-stages. As Paul Hacker would say, "The system of castes and life-stages, itself belonging to the system of *dharma*, is the framework in which all the contents of *dharma* are enmeshed".[20] It was, as we know it, the *varnasrama dharma* which provided the framework for the idea of *dharma* as enunciated in *dharmasutras*.

The empirical sense of this *dharma* obtained to the extent it actualised the potentialities of its subjects, the Brahmins. It was they who interpreted the doctrine of *dharma*, taking recourse to the authority of the Vedas, while in the process establishing the authority of the Vedas themselves. As Albrecht Wezler would put it, "The realm of tradition and practice from which a valid *dharma* may be derived is limited to those who know the Veda, that is, to those Brahmins who really follow their class obligation of studying the Veda. This restriction clearly goes beyond attempts, testified to elsewhere, to determine the group authoritative for *dharma*".[21] Similarly, the *dharmasutras*, whose main subject was again *dharma*, too considered the Brahmins as its subjects. As Olivelle would say, "The principal audience of these texts was undoubtedly Brahmin males, who were also the principal creators and consumers of all the literature produced in the vedic branches. The Brahmin is the *implied* subject of most rules in the *dharmasutras*".[22]

This social sense of the *dharma*, as Hacker and others would hold,[23] was highly empirical in nature, and its meaning emerged in the way it operated in particular social settings of customs related to castes. As Wezler would opine, "The whole of the *dharma* corpus can be viewed as a record

---

[19] Horsch, "From Creation Myth to World Law", 8.
[20] Paul Hacker, "*Dharma* in Hinduism", in *Dharma—Studies in its Semantic, Cultural and Religious History*, ed. Patrick Olivelle (Delhi: Motilal Banarsidas, 2009 (2004)), 478.
[21] Albrecht Wezler, "Dharma in the Veda and the Dharmasastras", in *Dharma—Studies in its Semantic, Cultural and Religious History*, ed. Patrick Olivelle (Delhi: Motilal Banarsidas, 2009), 221.
[22] Olivelle, *Dharmasutras*, xxxiv.
[23] Hacker, "*Dharma* in Hinduism", 478.

of custom".²⁴ In the words of Hacker, "There is no superordinate principle from which *dharma* and *adharma* may be derivable"²⁵ and "Historical Hinduism never attempted to derive the *dharma*-ness of *dharma* from a universal philosophical or religious principle... the Hindu concept of *dharma* is radically empirical".²⁶ As he continues, "*Dharma*, based in its contents on the castes and life-stages, encompassing the entire realm of what is moral, ritual, legal, and customary, and effecting through its observance an otherworldly salvation, is not derivable from a philosophical principle or from a religious source, but rather only empirically ascertainable, whether from the Veda or from the consensus of the good with regard to geographical place".²⁷

This *dharma*, which evolved through the social practices of castes, which carried within it the cosmic, ritual and ethical-juridical senses, had also a "religious" sense, showing the path of liberation or salvation to humanity. It is mentioned in the *Dharmasastras* as one of the components of the *purusarthas* leading to *moksha*, the ultimate liberation. In this sense, it came to be known as the Hindu *dharma* or Hindu religion (as being presented today), which stood for the eternity or timelessness of the cosmic-ritual, ethical-juridical and social order as explained in the *Dharmasastras*.

This *dharma* is impersonal, and not derived from the will of a deity. As Hacker would put it: "*Dharmasutra* text explicitly denies that gods declare or expound *dharma*...Hinduism is innately impersonal... Dharma is not the will of a personal god or gods."²⁸ Though emerging during a transitional time when polytheism was giving way to monotheistic traditions in India,²⁹ *dharmasutras* did not associate *dharma* with gods or personal deities. What emerged from the *dharmasutras* was then an impersonal *dharma* and this is embodied in the sanskritic Hindu religion.

The impersonal character of *dharma*, since it does not operate as per the will of a deity, obtains a substance of its own or a reality of its own, which pre-exists as well as post-exists an action. Since the *dharmic* order is eternal, when one submits oneself to it, one realises the *dharma* which is already there. Similarly, the *dharmic* substance extends even beyond a course of actions (a life-time's action) in terms of an individual's liberation. As Hacker would observe, "*Dharma* is rather a concrete model of behaviour with positive significance for salvation that somehow exists already before its performance and waits for realisation, or rather is a collection of such models. *Dharma in performance* then is conduct that corresponds to this

---

[24] Wezler, "*Dharma* in the Vedas", 211.
[25] Hacker, "*Dharma* in Hinduism", 482.
[26] Hacker, "*Dharma* in Hinduism", 482.
[27] Hacker, "*Dharma* in Hinduism", 483.
[28] Hacker, "*Dharma* in Hinduism", 482–483.
[29] Hacker, "*Dharma* in Hinduism", 482.

model, *adharma* conduct that deviates from it. Finally, the *dharma*-substance exists also after performance as the realised model of behaviour".[30] Thus, *dharma* gets intimately linked to *karma*, that is, actions which carry their consequences through various births over centuries and millennia.

From the foregoing exploration, *dharma* may be understood as an impersonal law, present in the cosmic order, maintained by the sacrifices of the gods and by the ritual sacrifices of the Brahmin priests, and as an ethical-juridical law which emerges empirically in the operation of the social customs and practices of castes and life-stages of Brahmin individuals. Both as the impersonal law and the ethical-juridical law, it operates on its own, without the will of a personal deity, and pre-exists as well as post-exists individual actions (*karma*) of individuals and contributes to the attainment or otherwise of liberation, *moksha*. This *dharma* is projected today as the Hindu *dharma*.

It must be noted that apart from this sanskritic Hindu version of *dharma*, the *sramanic* traditions like Jainism and Buddhism have their own variants of it. They add very important dimensions to the discourse on *dharma*. It would do well to explore them as an exercise in public theology; however I leave the enquiry to another occasion.

DHARMA IN INDIC SUBALTERN RELIGIOUS TRADITIONS

The Indian subcontinent has witnessed, right from very ancient times, alternate traditions emerging out of or by the side of mainline traditions—whether theistic or non-theistic. The many internal variations within the mainline theistic traditions like Saivism and Vaishnavism are proof enough for the heterogeneous religio-philosophical experiences of the people. Among them, what emerged during the modern era, especially from the nineteenth century onwards, as socio-religious movements from among the subaltern or marginalised section of the people are significant in the context of reflecting upon the doctrine of *dharma*. Many subaltern religio-philosophical movements have discoursed upon the doctrine of *dharma*, and have contributed to a healthy practice of contextual interpretation, appropriation, and interrogation of the doctrine.

As a sample, I would like to briefly mention the way *Ayya Vazhi*,[31] a subaltern religious phenomenon, emergent in the erstwhile Travancore kingdom located at the southernmost tip of the Indian sub-continent, discoursed upon this doctrine. *Ayya Vazhi* arose during the first part of the nineteenth century, at the intersection of tradition and modernity in India. The life, activities, and teachings of a mystic, Vaikundasamy by name,

---

[30] Hacker, "*Dharma* in Hinduism", 486.
[31] For a detailed study of this phenomenon, see G. Patrick, *Religion and Subaltern Agency* (Chennai: Department of Christian Studies, 2003).

became the fountainhead of this religious phenomenon, which progressively constituted itself with the participation of his followers. What interests us more here is the way this phenomenon interpreted the *dharmic* doctrine. Through its mythography, oracles, and symbolic ritual activities, it proclaimed a new understanding of *dharma* as, "Uplift of the lowly is *dharma*"—a radical reversal of the *varnasrama dharma*. Its prime narrative dwelt upon the story of the God Vishnu incarnating in the person of Vaikundasamy,[32] for the purpose of destroying the *kali yugam* (age of unrighteousness) and establishing the *dharma yugam* (age of righteousness). *Kali yugam*, the age of evil as per the classical sanskritic Hindu mythology, was contextualised by this religious phenomenon to stand for the evil empire of the king of Travancore who exploited the subaltern people of their labour by imposing unmeaning taxes upon them and of their dignity by maintaining an inhumanly rigid system of social discrimination. Ironically though, this reign was eulogised by the court historians as *dharma yugam* (age of righteousness); the king had acquired the title of *dharmaraja* (king of righteousness), primarily because he followed the *dharmasastras*, adopted the rules and regulations of *varnasrama dharma*, and pampered the Brahmins through a number of charitable institutions and actions. It was against this context, Vaikundasamy, the mystic, came with the oracular statement of uplift of the lowly as *dharma*; and the religious phenomenon came to institute several symbolic activities whereby the subaltern people began to feel empowered and dignified. These proclamations and symbolic activities mobilised the people, which became a cause of concern both for the native kingdom and for the British. The mystic was arrested and tortured in an attempt to disperse the people away from him. However, the religious phenomenon steadily grew, and it played a vital role in the emancipatory history of a subaltern people of this area.

What we see in the history of this phenomenon is a radical re-interpretation of the doctrine of *dharma* from the perspective of the subalterns for their emancipatory project. Very meaningfully, this re-interpretation took place within a context wherein the subaltern people's religious sense was creatively provoked by their traditional theistic religion on the one hand, and the emerging Christian religion on the other. The followers of this phenomenon did not want to be part of the Christian religion, because it would mean going away from their own religio-cultural roots, however, they had to face up to the challenges thrown up by Christianity, which spoke of equality and dignity for all; neither did they want to remain within the ruler's religion—the classical Vaishnavism, because it was used by the king and other caste people to oppress them. It was in this context, a re-interpretation of *dharma* from the subaltern perspective emerged and

---

[32] It is to be kept in mind that the sanskritic Hindu tradition does not accept this incarnation among its classical list of *avatars*.

operated effectively. Similar is the story with many other subaltern religious traditions of the modern era.

DHARMA OF JESUS

The doctrine of *dharma* has been approached also by some Indian Christian theologians, who have tried to interpret Christianity as a new *dharma*. A well-known biblical theologian George Soares-Prabhu reflected upon this in his essay on "*Dharma* of Jesus". He spoke of the *dharma* of Jesus as Jesus's foundational experience of God's love—Love of God and Love of neighbour. In his words: "The basic religious experience that shapes his (Jesus's) life and gives form to the movement he founds is the experience of God's unconditional love which empowers us (to the extent we experience it) to love our fellow human beings as unconditionally as God does (Luke 6: 32-36). The fully realised follower of Jesus will be the person who fully loves."[33] Soares-Prabhu distinguishes this *dharma* from that of sanskritic Hinduism by saying that for Jesus, the supreme goal of life is the unconditional love of God, while for the latter, it is the absolute freedom of the individual self from earthly ties. "The supreme goal of life (of Indian traditions)", as he says, "is the absolute and unconditional freedom which results from the experiential realisation of the ultimate relativity of the empirical self and of the world it inhabits.... For Jesus on the other hand, the supreme goal of life is not unconditional freedom but *conditional* love".[34] It is conditioned by one's response (in terms of repentance) to God's unconditional love. Thus, the *dharma* of Jesus is centred on the great command of love of God and neighbour.

This *dharma* of Jesus is prophetic in nature. Jesus was a great prophet to emerge in the biblical history. A prophet in the biblical tradition was one who encountered the God of history through a call-experience and received a mandate to lead the people towards an alternative community, where there would be no poor, no bondage, and so on. This prophet was involved in a politics of justice, and spoke for the powerless, the poor, the needy, and the oppressed with "a consistency and a passion" which was "unrivalled in the religious history of humankind".[35] This passionate concern for justice was not a peripheral aspect of prophecy, but the most essential one, an "integral part of their prophetic calling, deriving from the God-experience which constitutes it".[36] A prophet's experience of God

---

[33] George Soares-Prabhu, "The *Dharma* of the Biblical Prophet", in *Biblical Spirituality of Liberative Action—Collected Writings of George M. Soares-Prabhu, S.J.* ed. Scaria Kuthiralkkattel S.V.D. (Pune: JDV, 2003), 142.
[34] Soares-Prabhu, "The *Dharma*", 142. It becomes conditional *to the extent* it experiences the unconditional love of God.
[35] Soares-Prabhu, "The *Dharma*", 113–114.
[36] Soares-Prabhu, "The *Dharma*", 115.

as love integrally remained together with experience of God as justice. A prophet, thus, was essentially of a communitarian personality, receiving a call in view of a community, and passionately gripped with the life-concerns of the people. In the tradition of the biblical prophet, Jesus's *dharma* was a prophetic *dharma* par excellence, and Jesus's followers were enjoined to observe this *dharma*.

Soares-Prabhu undertakes a reflection upon the relationship between the discipleship of Jesus and the *purusarthas* of the sanskritic Hinduism, with an implied question of whether the discipleship of Jesus as a special vocation could find any point of convergence with the *purusarthas*. *Purusarthas*, the *dharma-artha-kama-moksha* progression, though oriented to the final *moksha*, dwell very much upon one's duties here and now by fulfilling the dictates of *dharma, artha,* and *kama*. These three stages are substantively this-worldly and material, and one cannot by-pass these stages to reach *moksha*. Similarly, the *dharma* of Jesus, as a doctrine of love of God and love of neighbour lays stress upon the this-worldly well-being of humanity. While this common interest seems to be embodied in both traditions, the points of divergence emerge in the philosophical underpinnings as well as the *sadhana* to reach the goals of human existence. In terms of philosophy, the *purusarthas* rest upon the pilgrimage of the individual self, the *atman*, leaving one by one the earthly attachments so as to attain the final liberation. Its supreme goal, in the words of Soares-Prabhu, "Has always been the complete freedom which comes from immunity to the pressures and pulls of desire for objects of various kinds and for approval of others, and in which the social goal is (creating)... a few 'free' individuals living on the margins of a rigid and highly stratified social structure".[37] On the other hand, the Christian special virtues—the evangelicals, which are kind of counterparts of the *purusarthas*—obedience, poverty, chastity, "cannot be taken as merely negative affirmations of a person's freedom from the bondage of attachment to persons and things. They are primarily conditions of availability, making it possible for a person to dedicate himself to the compelling task of creating a more human world".[38] And, in terms of the *sadhana*, the subjects of *purusarthas* are determined in terms of castes and duties as enunciated in the *dharmasutras* and *shastras* which imply a fundamental exclusion of social groups. *Dharma* is basically the "*kula* or *jati-dharma*", keeping the Brahmin at the centre. On the contrary, the Christian discipleship keeps the excluded, the poor, the marginalised, and the oppressed at the very centre of their experience of God. Thus, there are clear divergences between the *purusarthas* and Christian discipleship, though both the traditions seem to embody a common interest in this-worldly well-being.

---

[37] Soares-Prabhu, "The *Dharma*", 262.
[38] Soares-Prabhu, "The *Dharma*", 271.

Transformative Transcendence, Transitory Transcendence

Exploring the doctrine of *dharma* inter-textually, bringing into play insights from the sanskritic Hindu, the subaltern Indic, and the Christian traditions awakens us to some meaningful possibilities of interplay of the different aspects of the experience of the Divine in human life and history. The sanskritic Hindu ideal of *dharma*, whether treated as the impersonal eternal law (cosmic, ritual sacrificial, human-social) or as the ethical code, becomes a stage or a part of the *yatra* (pilgrimage) of life, as pointed out in the *purusharthas*. "A stage" in the *yatra* does not mean fleetingly renouncing, but, substantial, temporal, and material. This stage pertains to the householder, the *grahasta* (perhaps the only stage majority of the people have lived out for centuries together) who involves substantively in the *vyavaharika* (this-worldly concerns) of life, which has, paradoxically though, been structurally situated in terms of the *varnasrama dharma*. This stage, for an ideal Hindu as depicted in the sanskritic literature, is a transitory phase—a *thirtha* (an abode) so to say, in the aeonic pilgrimage of the *atman*. What an individual, as the temporal identity of the *atman*, experiences in this pilgrimage can be said to be an experience of freedom from various life-stages by way of a transitory transcendence. It is transitory in the sense that it transits from one stage to another.

The *dharma* of Jesus takes one along a different journey. It begins with the foundational experience of the unconditional love of God, the divine power of a personal God, here and now, as an event of encounter, but with a condition of acceptance of the divine love, which is heeding to the call of repentance as proclaimed by Jesus. This encounter of the unconditionality of the Divine and the conditionality of the human response provides the condition of possibility for the *dharma* of Jesus. This encounter is approached through the medium of a prophet who is utterly free for the Divine, who radically holds on to the absolute sovereignty of God by experiencing the relativity of temporal powers or historical structures. The kind of encounter of the Divine approached through the prophetic medium engages with the present tranformatively. The here and now irrupts into the life of human beings as an opportunity for experiencing the love of God. It is a radical opportunity for transformation, which will free the individual and the society from all forms of unfreedom.

These two variants of *dharma* have points of convergences and divergences. In the first place, both of them offer experiences of transcendence. Whether as a law or as an experience of unconditional love, they take us on a path of transcendence. What comes as a divergence is the way both the traditions engage with the present—the contemporary temporal present. While the sanskritic Hindu tradition engages with the present in a substantively transitory sense poised towards eternity, the Christian *dharma* involves with the present transformatively. Both these dimensions need to complement one another, and even interrogate one another, so that we can continue to experience the traces of the Divine in our inter-subjective existence on this planet.

Conversation and Interrogation

Conversation is the *sadhana* proposed by public theologians today. Its aim is to promote a mutual enrichment between religio-ethical traditions which occur in any public so as to re-generate humanity with a revitalised ethical vision and to make the plurality of traditions a vital source for religious nourishment of humanity. Mutuality is the desideratum of this conversation. Mutuality can emerge only on the basis of a healthy recognition of multiple others present in a public, and of a whole-hearted involvement in a give-and-take interactive relationship. The Indian public needs to recognise the presence of multiple others in its religious public, as evidenced in the very *dharmic* terrain itself. Each one's interpretation is unique and irreplaceable, and this uniqueness can become a source of learning and wisdom only when there is a possibility to converse as well as interrogate one another.

By Way of Concluding

The doctrine of *dharma* has existed for long in philosophical and *puranic* literatures as well as in ritual performative traditions, incorporated into the caste practices of the Indian society. It has now become a public discourse carrying political connotations as well. It is the opportune time to do a public discourse on the doctrine. The classical sanskritic Hindu philosophical insights, the themes of heterodox traditions, the emancipatory interpretations given by subaltern traditions, and the adaptations by other religions like Christianity on this important doctrine need be brought together in conversation so as to enlighten the wider public of this country.

GLOSSARY

Ad Dharm	– original ethical religion
Advaita	– "non-dualism"—one of the central doctrines of classical Indian philosophical systems; *advaitic* is the adjective.
Akandas	– devotional poetry
Artha	– means of life
Atman	– soul, self, the eternally immutable inner reality
Bhakti	– devotion, piety; *bhakta*–devotee
Bhakti Marga	– path of devotion
Buddha thanmam	– Buddhist ethics
Chandalas	– a "lower caste" that deals with removal of corpses
Dalit	– literally the word "Dalit" means "the broken"; in Indian society, it stands for a conglomerate of a number of communities, which have suffered "caste" oppression in the historical past and continue to suffer, in subtler forms, until this day.
Dhamma	– the Buddhist rendering of the sanskritic word Dharma; *Thanmam* is a Tamil rendering of the same word; *meyaram*, a Tamil word to mean "true ethics".
Dharma	– universal ethical religion
Dharmayugam	– aeon of righteousness
Grahasta	– house-holder
Hari	– Hindu god Vishnu
Jati-dharma	– ethics of caste
Jnana marga	– path of knowledge/wisdom
Kali Yuga	– aeon of evil
Kama	– pleasure
Karma	– an Indic belief which holds that actions of a previous birth accrue to a person in the succeeding birth in the form of "karma";

	its implied beliefs are "rebirth", or "cycles of rebirth", and "transmigration of souls".
Karuna	– compassion
Mlecchas	– a derogatory term for foreigners
Mahasakti	– great power
Moksha	– liberation
Purana	– literally "ancient tradition"; however, it stands for major epics of the Ramayana and the Mahabharatha; *puranic* is the adjective.
Purusarthas	– goals of life according to sanskritic Hinduism
Sangamam	– confluence
Sadhana	– method
Saamaanya Dharma	– law pertaining to commoners
Samsara	– pereniality of this worldly life
Sanatana	– eternal
Sastras	– sacred teaching
Satnami	– true name
Sramanic	– heterodox
Thirta	– an abode
Thuvayal Thavasu	– It means literally "washing penance"; it was a ritual requiring the adherents to wash themselves, their clothes, etc., in a ritual ambience as a form of penance.
Thavasu	– penance
Tilak	– a vermillion mark at the centre of the forehead.
Varna	– literally means "colour"; stands for the archetypal division of caste
Vaishnavism	– one of the two major theistic religious traditions of India; worships Vishnu as the supreme deity.
Vittobha/Vitthala	– Hindu god, considered as a manifestation of *Krishna*, an avatar (incarnation) of Vishnu.
Visesha Dharma	– law pertaining to special category of people
Vyavaharika	– pertaining to practicality of life

BIBLIOGRAPHY

Adhav, S.M. *Pandita Ramabai*. Bangalore: The Christian Institute for the Study of Religion and Society, & Madras: The Christian Literature Society, 1979.

Adler, Gary J., Jr. ed. *Secularism, Catholicism and the Future of Public Life—A Dialogue with Ambassador Douglas W. Kmiec*. Oxford: Oxford University Press, 2015.

Ahmad, Aijaz. "The Making of India". *Social Scientist* 33 (2005): 11–12.

Alam, Javeed. "Ethically Speaking, What Should be the Meaning of Separation for Secularism in India". *Social Scientist* 35 (2007): 3–18.

Aloysius. G. *Religion as Emancipatory Identity—A Buddhist Movement among the Tamils under Colonialism*. Mumbai: New Age International Publishers, 1998.

———. G. *Ambedkar on Nation & Nationalism*. New Delhi: Critical Quest, 2009.

Amaladoss, M. T.K. John, and G. Gispert-Sauchm, eds. *Theologising in India*. Bangalore: Theological Publications in India, 1981.

Ambedkar, B.R. *The Philosophy of Hinduism*. e-copy

———. *Buddha and His Dhamma*. e-copy.

Arockiadoss, P. "The Spirit of New Creation an Exploration into Dalit Pneumatology". In *Frontiers of Dalit Theology*, edited by V. Devasahayam, 433 – 456. New Delhi: ISPCK/Gurukul, 1997.

———. *Equal and Free*. Dindigul: Vaigarai Publications, 2010.

Atherton, John. *Public Theology for Changing Times*. London: SPCK, 2000.

Bardia, Meera. "Dr. B. R. Ambedkar. His Ideas about Religion and Conversion to Buddhism". In *The Indian Journal of Political Science* 70, 3 (2009): 737–749.

Barua, Ankur, "Ideas of Tolerance – Religious Exclusivism and Violence in Hindu-Christian Encounters". *International Journal of Public Theology* 7 (2013): 65–90.

Bautista, Julius and Francis Khet Gee Lim, eds. *Christianity and the State in Asia: Complicity and Conflict*. Abingdon: Routledge, 2009.

Begbie, Jeremy. "Christ and Cultures: Christianity and the Arts". In *The Cambridge Companion to Christian Doctrine*, edited by Colin E. Gunton, 101–121. Cambridge: Cambridge University Press, 1997.

Bell, Daniel M. Jr. "State and Civil Society". In *The Blackwell Companion to Political Theology*, edited by Peter Scott and William T. Cavanaugh, 241–255. New York: Blackwell, 2004.

Béteille, André. *Democracy and Its Institutions*. New Delhi: Oxford University Press, 2012.

Bhadrinath, Chaturvedi. *Dharma, India and the World Order: Twenty One Essays*. Scotland: Saint Andrew Press, 1993.

Bhagavan, Manu and Anne Deldhaus, eds. *Claiming Power from Below—Dalits and the Subaltern Question in India*. New Delhi: Oxford University Press, 2008.

Bhargava, Rajeev. *Secularism and its Critics—Themes in Politics*. New Delhi: Oxford University Press, 1998.

———. *The Promise of India's Secular Democracy*. New Delhi: Oxford University Press, 2010.

Bockmuehl, Markus, ed. *The Cambridge Companion to Jesus*. Cambridge: Cambridge University Press, 2001.

Borg, Marcus J. *Spirit, Culture, and the Life of Discipleship*. HarperCollins e-books.

Bowles, Adam. *Dharma, Disorder and the Political in Ancient India—The Aappadharmaparvan of the Mahabharatha*. Leiden: BRILL. 2007.

Boyd, Robin. *Introduction to Indian Christian Theology*. Delhi: ISPCK, 1994.

———. "The Use of the Bible in Indian Christian Theology". *Indian Journal of Theology* 22/4 (1974): 141–162.

Brown, Delwin, Sheila Greeve Davaney and Kathryn Tanner, eds. *Converging on Culture—Theologians in Dialogue and Criticism*. Oxford: Oxford University Press, 2001.

Bultmann, Rudolf. *The Presence of Eternity—History and Eschatology*. New York: Harper & Brothers, 1957.

Calvert-Koyzis, Nancy and Heather Weir, eds. *Breaking Boundaries—Female Biblical Interpreters who Challenged the Status Quo*. New York: T & T Clark, 2010.

Caputo, John D. *What Would Jesus Deconstruct: The Good News of Postmodernity for the Church*. Michigan: Baker Academic, 2007.

Carter, Warren. *Mathew and the Margins—A Sociopolitical and Religious Reading*. New Delhi: Theological Publications in India, 2007.

Caygill, Howard. *Levinas and the Political*. London: Routledge, 2002.

Chakravarti, Uma. *Rewriting History: The Life and Times of Pandita Ramabai*. New Delhi: Kali for Women, 1998.

Chandra, Satish. "Religion and State in India and Search for Rationality". *Social Scientist* 30, 3/4 (2002): 78–84.

Chatterjee, Partha. "Secularism and Tolerance". In *Secularism and Its Critics*, edited by Rajeev Bhargava, 345–379. New Delhi: Oxford University Press, 1999.

———. "The Nation and Its Outcasts". In *The Nation and Its Fragments*, Partha Chatterjee. New Delhi: Oxford University Press, 1999.

———. "Caste and Subaltern Consciousness". In *Subaltern Studies VI—Writings on South Asian History and Society*, edited by Ranajit Guha, 169–209. New Delhi: Oxford University Press, 1989.

Chhibber, Pradeep K. *Religious Practice and Democracy in India*. Cambridge: Cambridge University Press, 2014.

Ciotti, Mauela. *Retro-modern India—Forging the Low-caste Self*. London: Routledge, 2009.

Clarke, Sathianathan. *Dalits and Christianity—Subaltern Religion and Liberation Theology in India*. New Delhi: Oxford University Press, 1999.

Clarke, Sathianathan, Deenabandhu Manchala, and Philip Vinod Peacock, eds. *Dalit Theology in the Twenty-first Century—Discordant Voices, Discerning Pathways*. New Delhi: Oikumene & Oxford University Press, 2010.

Crockett, Clayton. *Radical Political Theology*. New York: Columbia University Press, 2011.

Crossan, John Dominic. *God and Empire—Jesus against Rome Then and Now*. New York: HarperCollins, 2007.

Das, Veena, Dipankar Gupta, and Patricia Uberoi, eds. *Tradition, Pluralism and Identity*. New Delhi: SAGE, 1999.

Dayam, Joseph Prabhakar and P. Mohan Larbeer, eds. *Margins in Conversation—Methodological Discourses in Theological Disciplines*. Bangalore: BTESSC, 2012.

Devasahayam, V. *Doing Dalit Theology in Biblical Key*. Chennai: ISPCK/Gurukul, 1997.

Dienberg, Thomas. "Mysticism and 'Public' Theology—Theoretical Background and Some Theological Reflections". In *Mysticism, Spirituality and Secularism—An Indepth Search for Meaning and Authenticity in a Pluralistic World*, ed. Varghese Manimala, 93–111. New Delhi: ISPCK & HMI, 2015.

———. "Mystical Experience—Tradition and the Aspect of Resistance and Public Theology". In *Mysticism, Spirituality and Secularism—An Indepth Search for Meaning and Authenticity in a Pluralistic World*, edited by Varghese Manimala, 112 - 129. New Delhi: ISPCK & HMI, 2015.

Dongre, Rajas Krishnarao and Josephine F. Patterson. *Pandita Ramabai—A Life of Faith and Prayer*. Madras: The Christian Literature Society, 1963.

Doniger, Wendy and Matha C. Nussbaum, eds. *Pluralism and Democracy in India—Debating the Hindu Right*. New York: Oxford University Press, 2015.

Dreyer, Elizabeth A. *Holy Power, Holy Presence—Rediscovering Medieval Metaphors for the Holy Spirit.* NY: Paulist Press, 2007.

Dube, Saurabh. *Untouchable Pasts—Religion, Identity and Power among a Central Indian Community, 1780-1890.* Albany: State University of New York Press, 1998.

Dumont, Louis. *Homo Hierarchicus—The Caste System and Its Implications.* Chicago: University of Chicago Press, 1980.

During, Simon. *Cultural Studies—A Critical Introduction.* London and New York: Routledge, 2005.

Eck, Diana L. "The Imagined Landscape: Patterns in the Construction of Hindu Sacred Geography". In *Tradition, Pluralism and identity,* edited by Veena Das, Dipankar Gupta, and Patricia Uberoi. 23-46. New Delhi: SAGE, 1999.

Elliot, Carolyn M., ed. *Civil Society and Democracy—A Reader.* New Delhi: Oxford University Press, 2003.

Fiorenza, Elisabeth Schussler. *The Power of the Word—Scripture and the Rhetoric of Empire.* Minneapolis: Fortress Press, 2007.

Forrester, Duncan B. "Lesslie Newbigin as Public Theologian". In *A Scandalous Prophet—The Way of Mission after Newbigin,* edited by Thomas F. Foust et al. 3-12. Michigan: William B. Eerdmans, 2002.

FFoust, Thomas F., George R. Hunsberger, J. Andrew Kirk, and Werner Ustorf, eds. *A Scandalous Prophet—The Way of Mission after Newbigin.* Michigan: William B. Eerdmans, 2002.

Franco, Fernando, Jyotsna Macwan and Suguna Ramanathan. *Journeys to Freedom: Dalit Narratives.* Kolkata: Samya, 2004.

Freeman, Curtis W. *Undomesticated Dissent—Democracy and the Public Virtue of Religious Nonconformity.* Texas: Baylor University Press, 2017.

Friesen, Duane K. *Artists, Citizens, and Philosophers—Seeking the Peace of the City—An Anabaptist Theology of Culture.* Ontorio: Herald Press, 2000.

Fuchs, Stephen. *Against Essentialism—A Theory of Culture and Society.* Cambridge: Harvard University Press, 2001.

———. *Godmen on the Warpath—A Study of Messianic Movements in India.* New Delhi: Munshiram Manoharlal, 1992.

Gamaliel, James Cajanam. *Dharma in the Hindu Scriptures and in the Bible.* New Delhi: ISPCK, 1999.

Gameson, Richard and Henrietta Leyser, eds. *Belief & Culture in the Middle Ages.* Oxford: Oxford University Press, 2001.

Ganeri, Jonardon. *The Concealed Art of the Soul: Theories of Self and Practice of Truth in Indian Ethics and Epistemology.* Oxford: Oxford University Press, 2007.

Ganguly, Debjani. *Caste, Colonialism and Counter-Modernity—Notes on a Postcolonial Hermeneutics of Caste*. London: Routledge, 2005.

———. "History's Implosions—A Benjaminian Reading of Ambedkar". In *Journal of Narrative Theory* 32, no. 3 (2002): 326–347.

Gascoigne, Robert. *The Church and Secularity: Two Stories of Liberal Society*. Washington, DC: Georgetown University Press, 2009.

Geetha, V. and Nalini Rajan. *Religious Faith, Ideology, Citizenship*. London: Routledge, 2011.

Gnanavaram, M. "Hermeneutical Issues in Dalit Theology". *AJTR* 11, no. 1, 2 (1998): 118–9.

Gottschalk, Peter. *Beyond Hindu and Muslim—Multiple Identity in Narratives from Village India*. New Delhi: Oxford University Press, 2001.

Gottwald, Norman K and R A Horsely, eds. *The Bible and Liberation: Political and Social Hermeneutics*. New York: Orbis Books, 1993.

Guha, Ranajit. "The Prose of Counter-Insurgency." In *Subaltern Studies II—Writings on South Asian History and Society*, edited by Ranajit Guha, 1–42. New Delhi: Oxford University Press, 1986.

———. ed., *Subaltern Studies I—Writings on South Asian History and Society*. New Delhi: Oxford University Press, 1982.

Hacker, Paul. *"Dharma* in Hinduism". In *Dharma—Studies in its Semantic, Cultural and Religious History*, edited by Patrick Olivelle, 475–492. Delhi: Motilal Banarsidas, 2009 (2004).

Heinsworth, Deidre King and Scott R. Paeth, eds. *Public Theology for a Global Society* [Essays in Honour of Max L. Stackhouse]. Cambridge, UK: William B Eerdmans. 2010.

Hogan, Linda, Solange Lefebvre, Norbert Hintersteiner, and Felix Wilfred, eds. *From World Mission to Inter-Religious Witness*. Concilium, no. 1. UK: SCM Press, 2011.

Hogg, A. G. *Karma and Redemption*. Madras: CLS, 1909.

Horsley, Richard A. ed. *Oral Performance, Popular Tradition and Hidden Script in Q*. Leiden: BRILL, 2006.

Horsley, Richard A. *Hidden Transcripts and the Arts of Resistance—Applying the Work of James C. Scott to Jesus and Paul*. Leiden: BRILL, 2004.

Ingleby, J. C. *Missionaries, Education and India—Issues in Protestant Missionary Education in the Long Nineteenth Century*. New Delhi: ISPCK, 2000.

Jaffrelot, Christophe. *Religion, Caste & Politics in India*. Delhi: Primus Books, 2010.

Jeyakumar, Samuel. *Dalit Consciousness and Christian Conversion: Historical Resources for a Contemporary Debate*. New Delhi: ISPCK, 1999.

Jeyanth, Mathew, S.J., ed. *Indian Theologies—In Search of Methods and Models of Theologizing*. New Delhi: Christian World Imprints & Jnana-Deepa Vidyapeeth, 2017.

Jesurathnam, Kondasingu. *Dalit Liberative Hermeneutics—Indian Christian Dalit Interpretation of Psalm 22*. New Delhi: ISPCK, 2010.

Jogdand, P.G., ed. *New Economic Policy and Dalits*. New Delhi: Rawat Publications, 2000.

John. T.K. S.J., ed. *One Volume Dalit Bible Commentary—New Testament*. New Delhi: Centre for Dalit/Subaltern Studies, 2010.

John, Mathew. "Decoding Secularism: Comparative Study of Legal Decisions in India and US". *Economic and Political Weekly* 40/18 (2005): 1901–1906.

Johnson, Kristen Deede. *Theology, Political Theory and Pluralism—Beyond Tolerance and Difference*. Cambridge: Cambridge University Press, 2007.

Jondhale, Surendra and Johannes Beltz, eds. *Reconstructing the World—B. R. Ambedkar and Buddhism in India*. New Delhi: Oxford University Press, 2004.

Joseph, George M. *Critique of Modern Culture – Marx and Gandhi*. Pune: Jnanam, 2005.

Joshi, Sanjay. *Fractured Modernity—Making of a Middle Class in Colonial North India*. New Delhi: Oxford University Press, 2001.

Joy, C. I. David. *Mark and its Subalterns: A Hermeneutical Paradigm for a Postcolonial Context*. London: Equinox, 2008.

Juergensmeyer, Mark, ed. *Religion in Global Civil Society*. Oxford: Oxford University Press, 2005.

Kakar, Sudhir. *Culture & Psyche—Selected Essays*. New Delhi: Oxford University Press, 1997.

Kalapati, Joshua. *Dr. Radhakrishnan and Christianity—An Introduction to Hindu-Christian Apologetics*. Delhi: ISPCK, 2002.

Kamitsuka, David G. *Theology and Contemporary Culture—Liberation, Postliberal and Revisionary Perspectives*. Cambridge: Cambridge University Press, 1999.

Kanjamala, Augustine, S.V.D. *The Future of Christian Mission in India—Toward a New Paradigm for the Third Millenium*. Bangalore: Theological Publications in India, 2016.

Kappen, S. *Jesus and Cultural Revolution—An Asian Perspective*. Mumbai: BUILD, 1983.

–––. *Tradition, Modernity, Counterculture—An Asian Perspective*. Bangalore: Visthar, 1994.

Kärkkäinen, Veli-Matti, Kirsteen Kim and Amos Yong, eds. *Interdisciplinary and Religio-Cultural Discourses on a Spirit-filled World—Loosing the Spirits*. New York: Palgrave Macmillan, 2013.

Kärkkäinen, Veli-Matti. *Pneumatology—The Holy Spirit in Ecumenical, International, and Contextual Perspective*. USA: Baker Academic, 2002.

Katju, Manjari. *Hinduising Democracy—The Vishva Hindu Parishad in Contemporary India*. New Delhi: New Text, 2017.

Kim, Kirsteen. "The Holy Spirit in a Spirit-filled World: Broadening the Dialogue Partners of Christian Theology." In *Interdisciplinary and Religio-Cultural Discourses on a Spirit-filled World—Loosing the Spirits*, edited by Veli-Matti Kärkkäinen, Kirsteen Kim & Amos Yong, 243–257. New York: Palgrave Macmillan, 2013.

———. *Joining in with the Spirit—Connecting World Church and Local Mission*. London: SCM Press, 2012 (2010).

———. "Mission in the Spirit: Dialogue, Inculturation, Liberation: Indian Christian Theologies of the Holy Spirit." In *The Holy Spirit in the World – A Global Conversation*, Kirsteen Kim, 67–102. Maryknoll, NY: Orbis/SPCK, 2007.

———. *Mission in the Spirit—The Holy Spirit in Indian Christian Theologies*. New Delhi: ISPCK, 2003.

Kim, Sebastian, C.H. and Pauline Kollontai, eds. *Community Identity—Dynamics of Religion in Context*. London: T & T Clark, 2007.

Kim, Sebastian and Kirsteen Kim. *Christianity as a World Religion*. London: Bloomsbury, 2008.

Kim, Sebastian, C.H., et al., eds. *Peace and Reconciliation—In Search of Shared Identity*. London: Routledge, 2016.

Kim, Sebastian, C.H., *In Search of Identity—Debates on Religious Conversion in India*. New Delhi: Oxford University Press, 2003.

———. *Christian Theology in Asia*. Cambridge: Cambridge Press, 2008.

———. *Theology in the Public Sphere—Public Theology as a Catalyst for Open Debate*. UK: SCM Press, 2011.

———. "Spirits of the Political: Theological Engagement in the Public Sphere". In *Interdisciplinary and Religio-Cultural Discourses on a Spirit-filled World—Loosing the Spirits*, edited by Veli-Matti Kärkkäinen, Kirsteen Kim and Amos Yong, 126–138. New York: Palgrave Macmillan, 2013.

Kosambi, Meera, comp., ed., and trans. *Pandita Ramabai Through Her Own Words: Selected Works*. New Delhi: Oxford University Press, 2000.

Kunnumpuram, Kurien ed. *In Spirit and Truth—Indian Christian Reflections on Spirituality and Worship* (Selected Writings of Samuel Rayan, S.J. Vol. II). Mumbai: The Bombay Saint Paul Society, 2012.

Laborde, Cecile. *Liberalism's Religion*. Cambridge: Harvard University Press, 2017.

Ladd, George Eldon. *Jesus and the Kingdom—The Eschatology of Biblical Realism*. London: SPCK, 1966.

Lalrinthanga, H. *Church and State—Relationship in the Mizo Socio-Political Life 1952-2006*. New Delhi: ISPCK, 2013.

Lannoy, Richard. *The Speaking Tree—A Study of Indian Culture and Society*. New Delhi: Oxford University Press, 2006 (1971).

Loomba, Ania. *Colonialism/Post-colonialism*. 2nd ed. New York: Routledge, 2005.

Lourdusamy, Stan. *People's Liberation—Characteristics of Parties, Movements and People's Struggle in India*. Bangalore: Indian Social Institute, 1985.

Ludden, David ed. *Reading Subaltern Studies—Critical History, Contested Meaning, and the Globalisation of South Asia*. Delhi: Permanent Black, 2001.

Lumsdaine, David Halloran, ed. *Evangelical Christianity and Democracy in Asia*. New York: Oxford University Press, 2009.

Luzbetak, Louis J. svd. *The Church and Cultures—New Perspectives in Missiological Anthropology*. New York: Orbis Books, 1989.

Lynch, Gordon. *Understanding Theology and Popular Culture*. USA: Blackwell, 2005.

Mahajan, Gurpreet and Helmut Reifeld, eds. *The Public & The Private—Issues of Democratic Citizenship*. New Delhi: SAGE, 2003.

Mahajan, Gurpreet and Surinder S. Jodhka, eds. *Religion, Community and Development*. London: Routledge, 2010.

Malik-Goure, Archana. *Jyotiba Phule—A Modern Indian Philosopher*. New Delhi: Suryodaya Books, 2013.

Malhotra, Rajiv. *Indra's Net—Defending Hinduism's Philosophical Unity*. Noida: HarperCollins India, 2014.

Manohar, Moses, P. *A New Political Paradigm for India—A Christian Perspective*. New Delhi: Promilla & Co., Publishers in association with Bibliophile South Asia and ICSA Books, 2009.

Marshall, Bruce, D. "Christ and Cultures: The Jewish People and Christian Theology". In *The Cambridge Companion to Christian Doctrine*, edited by Colin E. Gunton, 81–101. UK: Cambridge University Press, 1997.

Massey, James and T. K. John S.J., eds. *Rethinking Theology in India—Christianity in the Twenty-first Century*. New Delhi: Centre for Dalit/Subaltern Studies & Manohar, 2013.

Massey, James. *Towards Dalit Hermeneutics: Re-Reading the Text, the History and the Literature*. New Delhi: Centre for Dalit Studies, 2001.

Mathew, Philip and Ajit Muricken, eds. *Religion, Ideology and Counter-Culture—Essays in Honour of S. Kappen*. Bangalore: Horizon Books, 1987.

Mauffe, Chantel. "Religion, Liberal Democracy and Citizenship". In *Political Theologies—Public Religions in a Post-secular World*, edited by Vries, Hent de and Lawrence E. Sullivan, 318–326. New Delhi: Social Science Press and Orient Longman, 2007.

Melanchthon, Monica Jyotsna. "A Dalit Reading of Genesis 10-11:9". In *Scripture, Community, and Mission*, edited by Philip L. Wickeri, 161–176. Hong Kong: Christian Conference of Asia, 2002.

———. "Liberation Hermeneutics and India's Dalits". In *The Bible and the Hermeneutics of Liberation*, edited by Alejandra Fr. Botta and Pablo R. Andinach 199–213. Atlanta: Society of Biblical Literature, 2009.

Mendieta, Eduardo, ed. *The Frankfurt School on Religion—Key Writings by Major Thinkers*. New York: Routledge, 2005.

Menon, Dilip. *Blindness of Insight—Why Communalism in India is about Caste*. New Delhi: Navayana, 2004.

Metz, Johann Baptist. *Theology of the World*, Translated by William Glen-Doepel. New York: Herder and Herder, 1969.

———. *Faith in History and Society—Toward a Practical Fundamental Theology*, Translated by David Smith. New York: The Seabury Press, 1980.

———. *The Emergent Church—The Future of Christianity in a Postbourgeois World*, translated by Peter Mann. New York: The Crossroad, 1981.

———. *A Passion for God—The Mystical-Political Dimension of Christianity*, translated by J. Matthew Ashley. New York: Paulist Press, 1998.

Milbank, John. *Theology and Social Theory—Beyond Secular Reason*. New York: Blackwell. 1990.

Milner, Murray Jr. "Hindu Eschatology and the Indian Caste System: An Example of Structural Reversal". In *The Journal of Asian Studies* 52 no. 2 (1993): 298–319.

Moltmann, Jürgen. *The Trinity and the Kingdom—The Doctrine of God*. Minneapolis: Fortress Press, 1993 [1981].

———. *God for a Secular Society—The Public Relevance of Theology*, Translated by Margaret Kohl. London: SCM, 1999.

———. *The Living God and the Fullness of Life*. Louisville, KY: Westminster/John Knox Press, 2015.

Nandy, Ashis. "The Politics of Secularism and the Recovery of Religious Tolerance". In *Secularism and its Critics*, edited by Rajeev Bhargava, 321–344. New Delhi: Oxford University Press, 1999.

Niebuhr, Richard H. *Christ & Culture*. New York: Harper & Row, 1951.

Nilsen, Alf Gunvald and Srila Roy, eds. *New Subaltern Politics—Reconceptualizing Hegemony and Resistance in Contemporary India*. New Delhi: Oxford University Press, 2015.

Nirmal, Arvind. *A Reader in Dalit Theology*. Madras: Gurukul Lutheran Theological College and Research Institute.

Nelavala, Prasuna Gnana. "Dalit Feminist Pneumatology: Towards Life of Fullness". In *Towards Theology of Justice for Life in Peace (Minjung— Dalit Theological Dialogue)*, edited by Kwon Jinkwan and P. Mohan Larbeer, 73–88. Bangalore: BTESSC, 2012.

Olivelle, Patrick, ed. *Dharma—Studies in its Semantic, Cultural and Religious History*. Delhi: Motilal Banarsidas, 2009 (2004).

———. ed. and trans. *Dharmasutras—The Law of Codes of Apastamba, Gautama, Baudhayana, and Vasistha.* Oxford: Oxford University Press, 1999.

Omvedt, Gail. *Seeking Begumpura.* New Delhi: Navayana, 2008.

Omvedt, Gail. *Understanding Caste—From Buddha to Ambedkar and Beyond.* Delhi: Orient Longman, 2011.

Pandithar, Iyotheethasar. *Buddha's Ativedam.* Chennai: Tamilkudi Arasu Pathipagam, 2010.

———. *Iyotheethasarin Aaivukal 1 & 2.* Tamilkudi Arasu Pathipagam, 2010.

Parekh, Bhikhu. "Minority Practices and Principles of Toleration". *The International Migration Review* 30 no. 1 (1996): 251–284.

Patmury, Joseph, ed. *Doing Theology with the Poetic Traditions of India—Focus on Dalit and Tribal Poems.* Bangalore: PTCA/SATHRI, 1996.

Peetush, Ashwani Kumar. "Diversity, Secularism and Religious Toleration". *India International Centre Quarterly* 40 no. 3/4 (2014): 158–173.

Pettergree, Andrew. *Reformation and the Culture of Persuasion.* Cambridge: Cambridge University Press, 2005.

Phan, Peter C., ed. *Christianities in Asia.* Oxford: Blackwell, 2011.

Pieris, Aloysius. "Political Theologies in Asia". In *The Blackwell Companion to Political Theology*, edited by Peter Scott and William T. Cavanaugh, 256–270. New York: Blackwell, 2004.

Pinto, Simon. "Political Pneumatology: The Spirit in Governance." *Indian Theological Studies* LIV (2017): 37–52.

Plant, Raymond. *Politics, Theology and History.* Cambridge: Cambridge University Press, 2001.

Priest, Alice. "The Catholic Church's Theological Approach to Other Religions— From Conversion to Conversation". *Australian eJournal of Theology,* 9 (March 2007). http://aejt.com.au/__data/assets/pdf_file/0009/378612/ AEJT_9.23_Priest_To_Conversation.pdf, accessed October 29, 2017.

Puniyani, Ram, ed. *Ghar Wapsi, Conversions and Freedom of Religion.* Delhi: Media House, 2015.

Raja, Maria Arul, A. "Breaking Hegemonic Boundaries: An Intertextual Reading of the Madurai Veeran Legend and Mark's Story of Jesus". In *Scripture, Community, and Mission,* edited by Philip L. Wickeri, 251–260. Hong Kong: Christian Conference of Asia, 2002.

———. "Towards a Dalit Reading of the Bible: Some Hermeneutical Reflection". *Jeevadhara* 25 no. 151 (1996): 29–34.

Ram, Ronki. "Untouchability in India with a Difference—Ad Dharm, Dalit Assertion and Caste Conflicts in India". *Asian Survey* XLIV (2004): 6.

Rajkumar, Peniel Jesudason Rufus. "The Diversity and Dialectics of Dalit Dissent and Implications for a Dalit Theology of Liberation". In *Dalit Theology in the Twenty-first Century—Discordant Voices, Discerning Pathways*, edited by Sathianathan Clarke et al., 55–77. New Delhi: Oxford University Press, 2010.

Rovisco, Maria and Sebastian C. H. Kim, eds. *Cosmopolitanism, Religion and Public Sphere*. London: Routledge, 2014.

Rayan, Samuel. "New Efforts in Pneumatology." In *God's Hope Becoming Visible—Indian Christian Reflections on Some Relevant Issues of our Times* (Collected Writings of Samuel Rayan S.J.), edited by Kurien Kunnumpuram, SJ, 77 – 112. New Delhi: ISPCK, 2013.

———. *The Holy Spirit—Heart of the Gospel and Christian Hope*. Maryknoll, NY: Orbis Books, 1978.

Rhee, Helen. *Early Christian Literature: Christ and Culture in the Early Second and Third Centuries*. London: Routledge, 2005.

Robinson, Rowena and Marianus Joseph Kujur, eds. *Margins of Faith: Dalit and Tribal Christianity in India*. New Delhi: SAGE, 2010.

Rodrigues, Valerian. *The Essential Writings of B.R. Ambedkar*. New Delhi: Oxford University Press, 2002.

Roover, Jakob de, Sarah Claerhout and S. N. Balagangadhara. "Liberal Political Theory and the Cultural Migration of Ideas: The Case of Secularism in India". *Political Theory* 39 no. 5 (2011): 571–599.

Rowland, Christopher, "Scripture: New Testament". In *The Blackwell Companion to Political Theology*, edited by Peter Scott and William T. Cavanaugh, 21 – 34. USA: Blackwell, 2004.

Runessan, Anna. *Exegesis in the Making—Postcolonialism and New Testament Studies*. Leiden: BRILL, 2011.

Samartha, S. J. "The Holy Spirit and the People of Various Faiths, Cultures and Ideologies". In *Courage for Dialogue—Ecumenical Issues in Inter-Religious Relationships*, edited by S. J. Samartha, 63–77. Geneva: World Council of Churches, 1981.

Sanna, Gouthama. *C. Iyotheethasa Pandithar*. New Delhi: Sakithya Academy, 2005.

Sarkar, Tanika. "Hindutva's Hinduism". In *Public Hinduisms*, edited by John Zavos, et al., 264–282. New Delhi: SAGE, 2012.

Sawyer, John F. A., ed. *The Bible and Culture*. New York: Blackwell, 2006.

Schilder, Klaas. *Christ and Culture*. Indiana: Premier, 1977.

Scott, Peter and William T. Cavanaugh, eds. *The Blackwell Companion to Political Theology*. New York: Blackwell, 2004.

Sen, Amartya. *The Argumentative Indian—Writings on Indian Culture, History and Identity*. London: Penguin Books, 2005.

Sengupta, Padmini. *Pandita Ramabai Saraswati—Her Life and Work*. Bombay: Asia Publishing House, 1770.

Shah, Timothy Samuel, Alfred Stepan and Monica Duffy Toft, eds. *Rethinking Religion and World Affairs*. New York: Oxford University Press, 2012.

Shahan, Michael ed. *A Report from the Front Lines—Conversations on Public Theology*. (A Festschrift in honour of Robert Benne). Cambridge: William B. Eerdmans, 2009.

Smith, Mark J. *Culture—Reinventing the Social Sciences*. New Delhi: Viva Books, 2002.

Soares-Prabhu, George M. "The *Dharma* of Jesus". In *Biblical Spirituality of Liberative Action—Collected Writings of George M. Soares-Prabhu, SJ*, edited by Scaria Kuthiralkkattel S.V.D., 3–12. Pune: JDV, 2003.

———. "The *Dharma* of the Biblical Prophet". In *Biblical Spirituality of Liberative Action—Collected Writings of George M. Soares-Prabhu, SJ*, edited by Scaria Kuthiralkkattel svd, 105–125. Pune: JDV, 2003.

———. "The Christian *Purusarthas*—Meaning and Goals of Life in Jesus' Teachings". In *Biblical Spirituality of Liberative Action - Collected Writings of George M. Soares-Prabhu, SJ*, edited by Scaria Kuthiralkkattel svd, 260 -275. Pune: JDV, 2003.

Spinner-Halev, Jeff. "Hinduism, Christianity and Liberal Religious Toleration". *Political Theory* 33 no. 1 (2005): 28–57.

Stackhouse, Max L. "How and Why We Go Public?" In *Transforming Praxis, God, Community and Church*, edited by C.I. David Joy, 36–46. New Delhi: ISPCK, 2008.

———. *God and Globalization—Globalization and Grace*, Vol. 4. New York: Continuum, 2007.

———. *Public Theology and Political Economy*. Grand Rapids, MI: Wm. B. Eerdmans, 1987.

Stackhouse, Max L. with Don S. Browning. eds. *The Spirit and the Modern Authorities*. Pennsylvania: Trinity Press International, 2001.

Stackhouse, Max L with Peter J. Paris, eds. *God and Globalization—Religion and the Powers of the Common Life*. Pennsylvania: Trinity Press International, 2000.

Staub, Dick. *The Culturally Savvy Christian—A Manifesto for Deepening Faith and Enriching Popular Culture in an Age of Christianity—Lite*. San Francisco: John Wiley & Sons, 2007.

Storrar, William F. and Andrew R. Morton, eds. *Public Theology for the 21st Century* [Essays in Honour of Duncan B. Forrester]. London: T & T Clark, 2004.

Sugirtharaja, R.S. ed. *The Postcolonial Biblical Reader*. USA: Blackwell, 2006.

———. *The Bible and the Third World—Precolonial, Colonial and Postcolonial Encounters*. Cambridge: Cambridge University Press, 2004.

———. "Reading Back: Resistance as a Discursive Practice". *The Bible and the Third World—Precolonial, Colonial and Postcolonial Encounters*, edited by R.S. Sugirtharaja, 74–109. Cambridge: Cambridge University Press, 2004.

Susaimanickam, J. "Dalit Hermeneutics—A Proposal for Reading the Bible". *Vaiharai* 5/3, no. 4 (2000): 3–24.

Swami, Chandrashekarendra Saraswathi. *Hindu Dharma—The Universal Way of Life*. Mumbai: Bharathiya Vidya Bhavan, 1995.

Thankavelu, K. *Forerunner of Tamil Nationalism—Iyotheethasap Pandithar*. Chennai: Tamilkudi Arasu Pathipagam, 2010.

Thapar, Romila. *Historical Interpretations and the Secularising of Indian Society*. Bangalore: Visthar, 1999.

———. *The Past as Present—Forging Contemporary Identities through History*. New Delhi: ALEPH, 2014.

———. *The Public Intellectual in India*. New Delhi: Aleph Book Company, 2015.

Thiemann, Ronald, F. *Constructing a Public Theology—The Church in a Pluralistic Culture*. Louisville, KY: Westminster/John Knox Press, 1991.

Tillich, Paul. *Writings in the Philosophy of Culture*. Berlin: De Gruyter, 1990.

———. *Theology of Culture*. London: Oxford University Press, 1959.

Thumma, Anthonyraj. *Dalit Liberation Theology—Ambedkarian Perspective*. New Delhi: ISPCK, 2000.

Tracy, David. *The Analogical Imagination—Christian Theology and the Culture of Pluralism*. London: SCM Press, 1981.

Vahanian, Gabriel. *The Death of God—The Culture of the Our Post-Christian Era*. New York: George Braziller, 1961.

Vandana. *Waters of Fire*. Madras: The Christian Literature Society, 1981.

Ward, Graham. *Cultural Transformation and Religious Practice*. Cambridge: Cambridge University Press, 2005.

———. *Challenges in Contemporary Theology: Christ and Culture*. Malden, MA: Blackwell, 2005.

Wakankar, Milind. *Subalternity and Religion: The Prehistory of Dalit Empowerment in South Asia*. London: Routledge, 2010.

———. ed. *The Thoughts of Iyothee Thasar I (Religion and Literature)*. Palayamkottai: FRRC, 1999.

Webster, John C. B. *Religion and Dalit Liberation—An Examination of Perspectives*. New Delhi: Manohar, 1999.

Wilfred, Felix. "Towards a Subaltern Hermeneutics: Beyond the Contemporary Polarities in the Interpretation of Religious Traditions". *Jeevadhara* 25/151 (1996): 46–62.

———. *On the Banks of Ganges—Doing Contextual Theology*. New Delhi: ISPCK, 2002.

―――. "Empowering Culture". In *Dalit Empowerment*, Felix Wilfred, 78–96. New Delhi: ISPCK, 2007.

―――. *Asian Public Theology—Critical Concerns for a Challenging Time*. New Delhi: ISPCK, 2010.

―――. ed. *Theology to Go Public*. New Delhi: ISPCK, 2013.

―――. "Asian Christianity and Public Life—The Interplay". In The Oxford Handbook of Christianity in Asia, edited by Felix Wilfred, 558-574. New York: Oxford University Press, 2014.

―――. *Christians for a Better India*. New Delhi: ISPCK, 2014.

Zachariah, George. "The Parable of the not so Prodigal Daughters: A Postcolonial Dalit Womanist Reading". *Exegesis in the Making—Postcolonialism and New Testament Studies*, edited by Anna Runessan, 225–235. Leiden: BRILL, 2011.

Zavos, John, Pralay Kanungo, Deepa S. Reddy, Maya Warrier, and R.B. Williams, eds. *Public Hinduisms*. New Delhi: SAGE, 2012.

Ziebertz, Hans-Georg. "Dispute about the Public Significance of Religion: An Opening Reflection". In *The Public Significance of Religion*, edited by Leslie J. Francis and Hans-Georg Ziebertz, 1–18. Leiden: BRILL, 2011.

INDEX

A

Abhishiktananda 150
Ad Dharm 115, 187, 198
advaitic 111, 119, 154, 166, 187
aesthetics 35, 42, 55, 62, 64, 119
affirmative action 10, 24, 50
aggiornamento 6
agonistic 151
agonistically 13, 152
akhandas 115
Alan Rice 86
Alasdair McIntyre 95
Albrecht Wezler 179
Aloysius Pieris 7, 8, 23, 24
altruism 19
Ambedkar ix, xiv, 12, 24, 25, 65, 98, 104, 117, 118, 120, 121, 122, 123, 124, 125, 126, 127, 128, 129, 130, 131, 132, 133, 134, 157, 189, 192, 193, 197, 198
ameliorative secularism 98
analytical mediation 7
Anand Shastri Dongre 168
Anglican hierarchy 153
Anne Feldaus 107
anthropocentric 26
Antonio Gramsci 73, 103, 105, 145
Aparna Sundar 107
apocalyptism 57
Appasamy, A.J. 140, 150
arbitrariness of significations 58
archetypal 121, 188
Arendt 19, 20, 21
aristocratic elite 59
Ashis Nandy 99
Augustinian 12
automatons 42, 61, 69
Ayya Vazhi vii, 181

B

baptism in the Spirit 151
bhakta 120, 187
bhakti 187
bhakti marga 140
bourgeois Christianity 3
bourgeois theology 22
Buddha thanmam 112, 187
Buddhist *bhikku* 112

C

Catherine Pickstock 11
Cecile Laborde 94
Chamar 111, 116, 118
Chandokya Upanisad 167
Charles Taylor 16, 18, 64, 93, 94
Chaturvedi Badrinath 176
Christian Left 9
Christian *poiesis* xiii, 63, 64, 65, 68
Christopher Eisgruber 94
church-centric political theology 1
Clayton Crockett 191
Compendium 71, 79, 83
comprehensive doctrines 11, 22, 66, 76, 95, 100, 175
contextual secularism 98
contextual theology 10, 22, 39
conversation stopper 11, 76, 91, 161
cosmopolitan 54
covert rebellion 139
cultural capital 53
cultural hegemonies 82

D

Dalit self 110, 111, 117, 118, 119, 120
Dalit theology 9, 10, 21, 39, 136, 141, 155

Daniel Bell xiii, 10, 70
David Lumsdaine 46
David Tracy 2, 80
Debjani Ganguly 117, 124
decolonisation 138
deification 150
Devasahayam 9, 136, 144, 156, 189, 191
dharma xiv, 106, 148, 166, 167, 168, 172, 175, 176, 177, 178, 179, 180, 181, 182, 183, 184, 185, 186, 187
dharmasutras 179
discursive public 23, 24, 41
disenchanted ethos 69
Donald E. Smith 25, 26, 99
Dorothee Solle 2
Duncan Forrester 11, 21
dynamics of the empire 138

E

Edmund Husserl 89
Elisabeth Schussler Fiorenza 138, 144, 145
epistemologies 59
eschatological future heaven 42
ethnocentrism 44, 70, 94

F

fallenness of modernity 43
Ferdinand de Saussure 58
Fetishism 121
fideism 38
folkloristics 59, 97
foundational theology 7
fractured modernity 43
Francis Fukuyama 94
Francois Lyotard 35

G

Gail Omvedt 107
Gayatri Spivak 108, 109
George Lindbeck 3, 63
George Soares-Prabhu 148, 183
Ghasi Das 116

Gianny Vattimo 16
Gordon Kaufman 63
Grace Davie 16
Graham Ward 11, 62, 64
Gustavo Guttierrez 2

H

Hans Frei 3, 63
Harichandra 112
Herbert Marcuse 76
hermeneutics of domination 145
hermeneutics of evaluation 145
hermeneutics of experience 145
hermeneutics of imagination 145
hermeneutics of remembrance 145
hermeneutics of suspicion 145
hermeneutics of transformation 145
hidden transcript 139
Hindu Buddhism 175
Hindu Christianity 175
Hindu Islam 175
Homi Baba 108
Homo Hierarchicus 105, 106, 132, 191
Hugo Assmann 2, 6
Huntington 56

I

ideal scheme 118, 126, 127, 131, 133
Immanentism 60
Immanuel Kant 60
imminent *Parousia* 168
incommensurable 11, 95
Interrogating *Karma* 146, 148
intra-textual 10, 63, 66, 125

J

James Massey 136, 141, 156
James Scott 138, 139
Jeffrey Stout 95
Jesurathnam 140, 144, 146, 147, 193
jivatman 173
jnana-marga 119
Joachim of Fiore 32
Johann Baptist Metz 2, 3, 4, 5

Johannes Beltz 123, 193
John Courtney Murray 2
John de Gruchy 21
John Derosche 8
John Dewey 124
John Hick 86
John Locke 60, 73, 92
John Milbank 2, 11, 93
John Rawls 11, 16, 22, 94, 95
Jonathan Quong 94
Jose Casanova 17, 18
Joseph Cardijn 4
Jürgen Habermas 11, 16, 18, 42, 61, 72, 74, 76
Jürgen Moltmann 2, 4, 11, 33, 150

K

Kali Yuga 169, 187
karmic 154, 162, 165, 172, 173
karmic cycle 154
karuna 177
koinoniapolitike 73
Korkaivendan 113
Kosuke Koyama 8
Krishna Mohan Banerjea 140
ksatriya 167
kyrios 138

L

laicite 26, 92, 98
Lawrence Sager 94
Leonardo Boff 2, 6
Levi-Strauss 58
liberal democracy 12, 89, 93, 94, 96, 98, 99, 100
liberal egalitarian 94
Liberalism's Religion 94, 195
Liberation Theology 7, 9, 136, 191, 200
liberative praxis 6, 56
linguistic self-referentiality 58
Louis Dumont 105, 106, 132
Lucien Legrand 57

M

mahasakti 154, 162
Mahatma Phule 65, 104, 115
Mangoo Ram 115
Manimekalai 113
Manu Bhagavan 107
manusmriti 127
Marathi Bible 141
Maria Arul Raja 141, 142, 143
Martin E. Marty 2
Max Horkheimer 76
Max Muller 127
Max Stackhouse 2, 38
messianic prophet 173
Michel Wieviorka 55, 69
Milind Wakankar 108
minimal secularism 95
moksha 147, 166, 167, 168, 170, 171, 172, 173, 180, 181, 184
Mukkuvars 107
Mukti Mission 152, 162
Mukti Prayer-Bell 152
Murray Milner 165
Muthurai 113
mythography 182
mythos 11, 133

N

Namkirtan 110
Negotiating *Dharma* 147, 148
Nehemiah Goreh 140
New Subaltern Studies 107

O

Oliver O'Donnovan 2

P

Pandipeddi Chenchiah 149, 154, 162
Pandita Ramabai ix, 141, 152, 162, 165, 168, 169, 189, 190, 191, 195, 199
Partha Chatterjee 105, 106, 119, 145, 190
Patrick Olivelle 178, 179, 193
Paul Hacker 167, 179

Paul Horsch 178
Paulo Freire 9
Paul Tillich 42, 61, 69
Peniel Rajkumar 136, 143
Peter L. Berger 16, 18
phenomenology 58, 59, 88, 89, 124
Pierre Bourdieu 55, 63, 70
Pinkalai Nikandu 113
Pippa Norris 16
Plato 125
pneumatological 149, 150, 154, 159, 162
Political Theology ix, 1, 2, 4, 24, 123, 132, 189, 191, 197, 198, 199
polytheism 180
positivity of religion 16, 72, 120
practical theology 35
Prajapathi 140
pseudo-secularism 25
public transcript 139
Pundit C. Iyothee Doss 111
purusarthas 147, 180, 184

R

Radical Orthodoxy 11, 12, 63
Raja Ram Mohan Roy 65, 140
Rajeev Bhargava 26, 76, 96, 98, 190, 197
Rajiv Malhotra 99
Ranajit Guha 103, 104, 105, 106, 153, 155, 190, 192
religious resurgence 17
religious revitalisation 17
Richard Horsely 138
Richard John Neuhaus 2, 11
Richard Niebuhr 60
Richard Rorty 11, 76, 91
Romila Thapar 25, 97, 99
Ronald Dworkin 94
Ronald Inglehart 16
Ronald Thiemann 2, 11
Rowan Williams 32
Rudolf Bultmann 168

S

saamaanya dharma 176
Saba Mahmood 94
sadhana 184, 186
Samuel Rayan 8, 150, 154, 162, 195, 198
Sarvajanik Satyadharma Pustak 115
Sastras 188
Sathianathan Clarke 136, 198
Satnami 116, 188
Saurabh Dube 107, 116, 117
Savariappa Naidu 113
Sebastian Kappen 7, 12, 56, 67
Sebastian Kim 24, 36, 47, 80, 151
Seevakasinthamani 113
Shankar Deva 110, 111
Sharada Sadan 141
Sheila Greeve Davaney 59, 60, 190
Silapathikaram 113
Social Gospel 4
Sri Aurobindo 154
Stanley Fish 94
Stanley Hauerwas 2, 11
Stanley Samartha 150
structural sins 9
Sudamani 113
Surendranath Dasgupta 166, 167
Syndicated Hinduism 97
systemic intransigence 110

T

Talal Asad 94
Tirukural 113
Tissa Balasuriya 8

U

upanishadic 96

V

Vaikuntasamy 111
Valerian Rodrigues 123, 131, 132
Vandana 150, 200
varnashramadharma 121
Vedanta 99, 177
Veerasoliam 113

Veli-Matti Kärkkäinen 150, 151, 194, 195
Vengal Chakkarai 150
vertical transcendence 173
vyavaharika 185

W

Walter Fernandes 8
Walter Rauschenbusch 4
Warren Carter 140
William Cavanaugh 94
William Storrar 21, 200
Winnifred Sullivan 94

www.ingramcontent.com/pod-product-compliance
Lightning Source LLC
Chambersburg PA
CBHW030317080526
44584CB00012B/598